Women's History as Scientists

Controversies in Science

Women's History as Scientists

A Guide to the Debates

Leigh Ann Whaley

A B C • C L I O

Santa Barbara, California • Denver, Colorado • Oxford, England

Library of Congress Cataloging-in-Publication Data

Whaley, Leigh Ann.
    Women's history as scientists : a guide to the debates / Leigh Ann Whaley.
        p. cm.
Includes bibliographical references and index.
    ISBN 1-57607-230-4 (hardcover : alk. paper) ISBN 1-57607-742-X (e-book)
    1. Women scientists—History. 2. Women intellectuals—History. I. Title.

    Q130.W46 2003
    305.43'5'09—dc21

                                                            2003011314

07 06 05 04 03   10 9 8 7 6 5 4 3 2 1

This book is also available on the World Wide Web as an e-book.
Visit abc-clio.com for details.

ABC-CLIO, Inc.
130 Cremona Drive, P.O. Box 1911
Santa Barbara, California 93116-1911

This book is printed on acid-free paper ∞.
Manufactured in the United States of America

Contents

Preface

This book focuses on the debates surrounding women and science. Rather than providing a biographical compendium of great women scientists and their contributions to this field, the book is centered on the pivotal question: Are women capable of doing science?

The first task is to define what is meant by science. When most people think about science, they think of physics, chemistry, biology, mathematics, zoology, the medical sciences, engineering, and the like. A modern definition of science reads, "Science is a system of procedures for gathering, verifying, and systematizing information about reality. The knowledge that has been developed in fields such as physics, astronomy, biology, through scientific procedures is fascinating and awe inspiring, a tribute to human creativity and perseverance" (Bleier 1986, 19).

The older definitions of science, dating from the Middle Ages, are the most relevant to the debates under consideration here because they tend to be much broader in scope than our modern understanding of the word. The English word "science" is derived from the Latin *scientia*, knowledge, from *scire*, to know. One older way of understanding science was to refer to the state of knowing; but more commonly, science meant a systematic body of knowledge. Instead of being limited to knowledge of the material world as the term is generally understood today, a science could be any systematic body of knowledge. An example of the older definition of science may be found in *Chambers Cyclopaedia*, dating from the early 1700s. Here science means "knowledge, vision . . . the distinction to be drawn between theoretical perception of truth and moral conviction." The *Oxford English Dictionary* defines science as "a branch of study which is concerned either with a connected body of demonstrated truths or with observed facts. . . ." Science, even in its broadest sense, requires a capacity for abstract thought, the type of thought needed to classify facts and derive (or perceive) general laws, and a willingness to carefully follow established methods for discovering new truths, without being distracted by emotional considerations. The *Oxford English Dictionary* provides a useful definition for making clear the distinction between older definitions and the dominant meaning of the term "science" today: "In modern use, often treated as synonymous with 'Natural and Physical science' and thus restricted to those branches of study that relate to the phenomena or the material universe and their laws, and sometimes with the implied exclusion of mathematics" (*OED* 1989, 649).

One of the first published uses of the term "scientist" in the English language in the modern, limited sense was in William Whewell's 1834 review of Mary Somerville's "On the Connexion of the Physical Sciences," in the *Quarterly Review*. His definition described "scientist" as "a name by which we can designate the students of knowledge of the material world collectively . . . a general term by which these gentlemen [of the British Association for the Advancement of Science] could describe themselves with reference to their pursuits" (Whewell 1834, 54).

In the latter part of the nineteenth century, science came to be associated with positivism, a philosophical position that held that theology and metaphysics could give no real knowledge, that their quest for ultimate reality should be abandoned, and that only the sciences focusing on the material world could give real knowledge. Thus, scientists and philosophers focused on the experimental, progressive, and cumulative aspects of knowledge, as opposed to the more metaphysical. French scientist Henri Poincaré wrote that science, by the early 1900s, no longer included the disciplines of philosophy and theology. Science had become the "systematization of everyday and technical language, which helped men organize information gathered from the experience of natural phenomena" (cited in Corsi and Wiendling 1983, 5). The Austrian scientist and philosopher Ernest Mach wrote in a similar vein when he claimed that science developed in opposition to human philosophical or theological constructions (cited in Corsi and Wiendling 1983, 5). Physicist Pierre Duhem went further by claiming that science systematized and expressed in mathematical terms the human experience of natural phenomena (cited in Corsi and Wiendling 1983, 5).

Our modern and rather narrowly defined understanding of science is thus very different from the way premodern scientists and philosophers conceived of the term. *Scientia,* or science, understood as a field of activity that produced reliable knowledge, included theology and the physical sciences.

Philosopher Sandra Harding has argued that "women have been more systematically excluded from doing serious science than from performing any other social activity, except perhaps frontline warfare" (Harding 1986, 10). What are the reasons for this? The question of whether that exclusion is justified has repeatedly been hotly debated by both the major thinkers of the day and less famous historical actors. At the heart of this issue is the very nature of woman as compared with that of man. The dominant view, which persisted well into the twentieth century, was that women were incapable of rigorous intellectual activity because of their "weak" nature, which involved the biological function of reproduction. This meant that the systematic pursuit of knowledge involved in science was barred to them, even though not everyone was in agreement with the dominant ideology. Related to this particular view of woman's inferior nature was the question of education. Education is the key to any sort of intellectual achievement, especially scientific. The problem of education was also hotly debated into the twentieth century; the question of to what extent women could and should be educated was debated in the Western world.

In Western civilization, the "woman question" was first discussed in depth during classical times by the Greek philosophers Plato and Aristotle. Their views, articulated over two thousand years ago, became institutionalized and continue to be influential even in our own day. Thus, this book will begin at the time of Plato and Aristotle and follow the debate right into the twentieth century.

Chapter 1, "The Classical Debate: Can Women Do Science?", provides a detailed analysis of the debate that took place in the ancient world about the nature of woman. Concepts such as woman's innate physical inferiority and man's superiority were central to the debate. On one side of the debate was the philosopher Aristotle, who wrote: "It is advantageous for animals to be governed by men . . . between the sexes, the male is by nature superior and the female inferior, the male ruler and the female subject" (Aristotle *Politics* 1254b, 13–15). The influential Hippocratic corpus (consisting of medical treatises written by authors during the fourth and fifth centuries B.C.) provided a basis for Aristotle's opinion, presenting women as a deviation from the male norm. The medical men based their belief in women's inferiority upon the authority of the science of the day, arguing that because of woman's biological function of reproduction, women were incapable of reason. This side of the classical debate has played a central role, because it is here that notions of female inferiority were first given a supposedly rational and empirical basis.

The most famous opponent of this ideology was Plato, who said "that men and women with the same natural ability should receive the same education and training . . ." (Plato *Republic* V 452a). On the same side were the earlier philosopher and mathematician Pythagoras and two pioneering women who were actually practicing scientists, Theano (Pythagoras's wife) and Hypatia, the first female scientist about whom we have substantial information.

Chapter 2, "The Medieval Woman in Science: Contradictions within the Church and the University," describes the contradictory behavior of the Christian church in its treatment of women during the medieval era and the impact of this behavior on women of science. The church of Rome was the most important institution in Western civilization during the Middle Ages. It controlled knowledge and education. The church's treatment of women reflected the ambiguous role that Christianity assigned to women, based upon the very different roles played by Eve and Mary according to the Bible. During the early Middle Ages, from the seventh to the tenth centuries, women were able to assume power within the context of the convent. For a brief time, male church leaders encouraged a limited degree of learning for women. Some prominent thinkers at the time, such as Saint Columban, put forth the view that women could become more like men through education. In other words, women could be masculinized and therefore have the potential to think. As long as women accepted the ultimate authority of the church and did everything to glorify it, they were given an amazing amount of freedom. In this environment some women, most notably Hildegard of Bingen and Herrad of Lansberg, made significant contributions to science. During the eleventh and twelfth centuries, all of this changed—women lost any authority they had held in the monasteries, and polemics condemning women because of their nature began filling the sermons. It was at this time that the codification of the laws of the church, known as canon law, took place under John Gratian. Gratian himself held the typical misogynist view of women among Christian theologians of his time. Women were inferior to men and must be completely servile to them.

Important scholastic philosophers such as Thomas Aquinas (best known for his *Summa Theologica*) underscored these views of women. Aquinas wrote that the very fact of being a woman meant inferiority and subordination. He pointed to the female body and its dangers and the fear of Eve. Aquinas based his thinking on St. Augustine, an early Church Father, and Aristotle. The pope endorsed this attitude.

Chapter 3, "The *Querelle des Femmes:* The Debate about Women," investigates the debate that raged during the period of the late Middle Ages and the so-called Renaissance over the nature and value of woman, traditionally called the *querelle des femmes,* the quarrel about women. This debate was initiated by the fifteenth-century French humanist Christine de Pizan, who argued with male writers of the time, a time when misogynist views of woman dominated European court literature. During this period, there was a flood of tracts, treatises, and pamphlets over the nature of woman. Women like de Pizan took a conscious stand in opposition to male defamation and mistreatment of women. Although not a scientist herself, de Pizan wrote about scientific subjects and argued on behalf of woman's reason and woman's capacity to be a scientist.

The *querelle* was essentially a debate over the role and value of women in European society in the form of thousands of tracts, treatises, and pamphlets on the nature of woman, how she treated men, and whether she could be educated. The *querelle* was connected to the whole idea of controlling women. Initially, the debate centered on the themes of love and marriage. Defenders and detractors of women tried to demonstrate the goodness or evilness of women, rather than debating their intellectual capacity. The *querelle des femmes* was dominated by French writers. For this reason, the chapter will focus primarily on the French contributors to the debate.

Chapter 4, "The Debate about Education and the Inferiority of Women," considers the intense debate that raged throughout Europe during the seventeenth century over the question of women's education. The chapter begins with an overview of educational changes during the Protestant Reformation of the sixteenth century and continues with a focus on the period of the Scientific Revolution. New discoveries in science provoked women into rethinking their position in society. They discovered that they did not need to have a classical education to learn the physical sciences.

The debate about education considered more than the question of whether women should be educated. It involved several questions, such as the capacity of females for learning, the type and amount of education girls should receive, and so on. Even those who argued in favor of some form of education were not in complete agreement. This chapter presents the various arguments put forth by the major contributors to the debate. On the one hand were the men and women who promoted the education of girls, particularly science education. The principal exponents of the proeducation group were Marie de le Jars Gournay, Anna Maria van Schurman, Bathsua Makin, Mary Astell, Johann Amos Comenius, and Poulain de la Barre, and to a lesser extent, the poet and feminist Lady Mary Chudleigh, and Madeleine de Scudéry. Comenius and the women he inspired were at odds with the prevailing opinion articulated by most theorists of the day, including writers such as Molière, Malebranche, Fénelon, the Abbé Fleury, and Madame de Maintenon. This group put forth the argument that women were naturally unfit to do science, but they were not entirely against some form of education. Underlying the various arguments for or against education and the nature of education to be received were the views these theorists held of the role of women.

Chapter 5, "The Cartesian Debate," discusses the renewal of the *querelle des femmes* by the followers of French philosopher and scientist René Descartes. Although most thinkers still contended that women were incapable of abstract thought and any form of scientific reasoning, one can find arguments on both sides of the question. Some of the major players who took part in the quarrel were Nicolas de Malebranche and Nicolas Boileau-Despreaux, on the one hand, and Jacques Du Bosc and Poulain de la Barre, on the other. Poulain used the Cartesian method to argue that all conventional wisdom or received thought should be removed to arrive at the truth. The inferiority of women, he asserted, was an opinion rather than a fact. He drafted a curriculum for women that included the physical sciences, medicine, and mathematics in addition to other academic subjects. Bernard le Bovier de Fontenelle, a French scientist and man of letters, also appreciated women's potential to undertake academic pursuits. In 1686 he published a work of science, *Considerations on the Plurality of Worlds,* that was designed for women. Some contemporaries, such as playwright Aphra Behn, who translated the work into English, criticized Fontenelle for his condescension toward intellectual women. During the seventeenth century, one finds a growing interest among women of the upper classes in the sciences from Christina, queen of Sweden, to Marie Meurdrac, author of a textbook in chemistry.

This chapter also considers the rise of the salons in France during the seventeenth century and their importance, if any, for women and science. The type of woman who frequented this institution, known as the "précieuse," was ridiculed by contemporaries for her interest in learning. This sort of female set off a further debate amongst many men on the question of whether women could and should pursue knowledge in a systematic way, including knowledge of the physical sciences.

Chapter 6, "The Professionalization of Science: The Exclusion of Women," examines the impact that the professionalization of science had on women. Between the twelfth and fifteenth centuries, universities were founded in Europe, and with the exception of Italy, women were barred from attending these institutions. During the seventeenth century new institutions devoted specifically to the pursuit of science were founded. These were the Royal Society of London and similar academies on the Continent. For the most part, women did not seem to challenge the professionalization of science. However, not everyone was willing to accept the latest blow to women in science. One woman who caused considerable debate and controversy was Margaret Cavendish, the duchess of Newcastle, called Mad Madge by her contemporaries. In addition to producing fourteen books on science in subjects ranging from natural history to atomic physics, she attacked eminent scientists of her day, such as Robert Hooke, curator of experiments at the Royal Society, and she sparked a great debate at the society itself when she expected to be invited to speak to its members.

Chapter 7, "The Age of the Enlightenment: Science as an Unsuitable Subject for a Lady," concentrates on the debates that occurred during the intellectual revolution of the eighteenth century, the Enlightenment. The debate over the different natures of male and female intensified during this so-called age of reason. During the period of the High Enlightenment in the mid-eighteenth century a new corpus of literature was produced in England, France, and Germany, demanding finer discriminations about the differences between the sexes than had been articulated in the past.

The late eighteenth century produced three views about women's nature and abilities: (1) Women were mentally and socially inferior to men (Rousseau), (2) women were equal but different, and (3) women were potentially equal in both mental ability and contribution to society (Condorcet and Helvétius). Leading the debate was the French philosophe, Jean-Jacques Rousseau, whose antifeminist writings were highly influential. According to Rousseau, woman's role was to devote herself to motherhood and to the service of her male partner. Women were passive, weak, sensuous, and accommodating, while men were strong and rational. Other philosophes, including those who put together the *Encyclopédie,* the great eighteenth-century compendium of knowledge edited primarily by Diderot, echoed Rousseau's sentiments. In Germany, Immanuel Kant took up Rousseau's views. Women, he argued, had a different kind of mind than men, a mind in which abstract thinking was impossible.

One of the few voices on the other side of the debate was the French astronomer and director of the Paris observatory, Joseph-Jérôme de Lalande. He produced *Astronomie des dames,* the first short history of women astronomers, which was dedicated to a woman astronomer, Madame du Pierry. The French mathematician, philosophe, and revolutionary the Marquis de Condorcet was a prominent feminist. Condorcet, secretary of the French Academy of Sciences many years before the French Revolution, promoted female education and participation outside the private sphere.

Chapter 8, "The 'New Science' and the Debate about Women," is concerned with the debate that raged over women in science, now for the most part understood as the physical sciences, as well as over women in any public roles throughout the nineteenth century, a debate shaped first by the new theories of evolution and the ideas put forth by the craniologists and phrenologists, second by romanticism and utopian socialism, and third by positivism. There appeared to be a new enthusiasm for justifying female intellectual inferiority among the leading thinkers of the day. Many of these thinkers were themselves scientists of some type and were keen to justify their views with "hard" scientific evidence.

In the English-speaking world, the major players in the debate were evolutionists like Charles Darwin, who asserted in his book *The Descent of Man* (1871) that "man is more courageous, pugnacious and energetic than woman and has more inventive genius" (Darwin 1981, 316). He predicted that the present inequality between the sexes would continue. Other significant contributors were the English social scientist Herbert Spencer, who wrote that women's bodies stopped evolving with the onset of menstruation and thus women fell short in emotional and intellectual faculties. The Scottish biologist, sociologist, and town planner Patrick Geddes, known as Scotland's Renaissance man, was also a significant contributor to the debate, as was the evolutionist, physiologist, and comparative psychologist George John Romanes. Even a practicing woman scientist, Mary Somerville, who set an example for many, had a low opinion of female intelligence.

In France, several divergent views emerged. The Romantic writer, historian, and revolutionary Jules Michelet put forth one of the most significant perspectives. Michelet, although not a trained physician, was heavily influenced by scientific writings, and his works on women, *La Femme* (Woman, 1858) and *L'Amour* (Love, 1860), clearly demonstrate this influence. He analyzed women's physiology and then their role in society. The modern father of sociology, the positivist thinker Auguste Comte, eventually came to believe that woman's nature was hostile to scientific abstraction and concentration. Interestingly, earlier in his life, Comte had been somewhat of a feminist, influenced by the thought of Mary Wollstonecraft and John Stuart Mill.

Related to these theories were those propounded by various European craniologists (usually medical men or serious scientists of one sort or another) who asserted that the male brain was more powerful because it weighed more. The head, brain weight, facial angle, and cranial capacity were the focus of nineteenth-century scientific studies to prove female inferiority and male superiority. Scientists took craniology and its counterparts very seriously during the latter years of the nineteenth century throughout Europe. One of the thinkers upon which Darwin relied when writing his *Descent of Man* was Carl Vogt, professor of natural history and craniologist at the University of Geneva. Elizabeth Fee has called the years 1870–1890 the "baroque" age of craniology, meaning that the movement was at its height (Fee 1979, 427). The British Anthropological Society used arguments put forth by craniologists to prohibit female membership. The French surgeon and founder of the discipline of anthropology, Paul Broca, was one of the leading lights of this movement.

Chapter 9, "'Doctoring Only for Men': Women and Medicine," traces the intense debates that raged from medieval times to the late nineteenth century over the question of women physicians, both as practitioners of medicine and as writers. The debate began with the writings and work of Trotula and the Ladies of Salerno, who established the first secular hospital in history. Trotula wrote medical treatises, both with her husband and on her own. Her book *The Diseases of Women* was the standard medical handbook until Louise Bourgeois began writing in the seventeenth century. The controversy surrounding women and medicine dates from the sixteenth century, when the German surgeon and physiologist Kaspar Wolff of Basle denied that a woman like Trotula was capable of producing a medical treatise. He attributed her work to a man. The German medical historian Karl Sudhoff argued that Trotula and the Ladies of Salerno were not physicians but midwives. The controversy continued throughout the seventeenth century and focused on midwives and the attempt by men to exclude them from the practice of medicine. This chapter concludes with an examination of the nineteenth-century arguments for and against women attending medical school.

Chapter 10, "The Feminist Critique of Science," elucidates the most recent debate concerning women and science, the feminist debate. It emerged in the 1960s out of a more general debate surrounding the methodology of science. Before this era, it was widely accepted that science was value-free, that scientific knowledge was acquired through logical reasoning applied to experiments conducted in a laboratory and was not influenced by the values of the wider society. A number of philosophers and historians of science, such as Thomas S. Kuhn, Paul Feyerabend, and Norwood Russell Hanson, contested the neutrality of science. Feminists are in agreement with Kuhn and his colleagues that science is neither objective nor value-free.

Feminist scientists, including women from several disciplines—philosophy, sociology, history of science, and the physical sciences—focus on questions such as why there are so few women in science when they are no longer barred from institutions such as universities. They scrutinize the intrinsic relationship between gender and science and the discrimination women face within the scientific community in spite of the gains they have made. They are concerned with many long-standing societal attitudes that still reflect entrenched assumptions about the incompatibility between women and education and women and knowledge. Some of the leading lights in this debate are Margaret Rossiter, who analyzed women scientists in the United States; Evelyn Fox Keller, a physicist turned historian and philosopher of science at the Massachusetts Institute of Technology, arguably the most influential of these women; sociologist Helen E. Longino; and historian of science Londa Schiebinger. Although the feminist debate is international in scope, it has been strongest in the United States, and it continues to this day.

The idea of writing a book on the history of women in science evolved from topics covered in the European women's history courses I teach at Acadia University, a small undergraduate university in rural Nova Scotia. I would like to acknowledge the financial support I have received from Acadia University, which allowed me to conduct research in various European libraries. In addition, I am grateful for the help I have received from the many people at ABC-CLIO who were involved with the making of this book at its various stages, most significantly, Kristi Ward and Carol Smith. Both worked very hard in their own fields of expertise: Kristi with the commissioning and development of the book and Carol with the editing and production. Thanks also to Art Stickney and Scott Horst (illustrations). Finally, I thank the loved ones in my life for their support and encouragement. This book is dedicated to them.

1

The Classical Debate: Can Women Do Science?

Before the Greek physicians and philosophers of the Classical Age took up the question of the nature of women, the Greeks of course had attitudes toward women, attitudes that are revealed in their literature. The earliest Greek writings, traditionally ascribed to Homer, date from the eighth century B.C. The images of women in the *Iliad* and the *Odyssey* and other Homeric poetry are generally negative. Women were to be kept down, or some kind of disaster would occur. However, in Homer's pantheon of gods and goddesses, we do find a number of powerful female figures. These include Hera (Zeus's wife), Aphrodite (goddess of love), Hestia (goddess of the hearth and home), Athena (goddess of war, wisdom, and agriculture), and Artemis (goddess of the hunt). But all of these women were limited in their traits compared to their male counterparts. Artemis, the huntress, is less powerful than her twin brother Apollo (Anderson and Zinsser 2000, 1:15–17).

Ancient Greek society was fundamentally patriarchal in nature. Women were always under the control of a male, either a father or a husband, and they were not in charge of their own lives (Martin 1996). Women were viewed as essentially evil creatures. This perception can be traced back to the writings of the eighth-century poet Hesiod, who provided us with the story of Pandora and her box. In his poem *Works and Days* he described human misfortunes as beginning from a woman's curiosity: Pandora opens the box she has been told not to open and lets out "pains and evil" (cited in Anderson and Zinsser 2000, 1: 49). Zeus made Pandora beautiful, but he did so in order to take revenge on human beings for the theft of fire by Prometheus; thus Pandora, generally seen as the first and prototypical woman, is "an evil thing, in which all men may rejoice in their hearts as they welcome their own destruction" (cited in Peradotto and Sullivan 1984, 24).

Pandora opening the box (Bettmann / Corbis)

This story is repeated many times in Greek myths. The general consensus among Greek writers of all genres is that woman is evil, unclean, and lacking in rational self-control and soundness of mind. (With respect to uncleanliness Hesiod wrote, "Let a man not clean his skin in water that a woman has washed in" (cited in Carson 1990, 135).

The reason for this belief in female uncleanliness is that women are "wet" rather than "dry" in their physical makeup. There are references to female wetness in all of the major Greek writers, and it is quite possible that Aristotle, writing as a scientist, picked up this view from them. (Anne Carson provides numerous examples of wetness from Homer, Aristophanes, Alkaios, and others [1990, 137–142].) Female wetness is closely connected to female sexuality, which was considered uncontrollable and beastlike.

The great Athenian lawmaker Solon institutionalized the subordinate role of women in a series of laws passed around 594 B.C. These laws, which dealt primarily with the family and property, affirmed the male's control over the female. The primary role of woman was to "perpetuate her father's or husband's *oikos* (household)" (Anderson and Zinsser 2000, 32).

In general, the ancient Greeks tended to view the female as passive and weak. However, there were differences in viewpoints and the extent to which they took this belief. These differences will be explored later in this chapter.

Aristotle and His Predecessors

The preeminent Greek philosopher Aristotle, who lived from 384 to 322 B.C., had much to say about the nature of women and the nature of women in relation to men. The question of whether or not women are capable of doing science is intrinsically related to the very nature of the female, and thus Aristotle is of primary importance, for it is his views on the nature of women that have dominated Western civilization. He thought he had provided a scientific basis for the traditional Greek belief in female inferiority. "Aristotle was the first to take over the western mind by a single theory of the concept of woman" (Allen 1997, 1). Aristotle began a revolution, in the sense that he provided a new definition of what it meant to be male or female. His views on women superseded those of earlier thinkers and persisted well into the early modern era.

Philosophers do not write in a vacuum. They are influenced by their society and by those philosophers who came before them, and this is just as true for Aristotle as for anyone else. Before Aristotle, there were philosophers who wrote on the subject of women and the female contribution to the reproductive process. Thus, in order to understand what Aristotle had to say about female nature, it is crucial that we consider what the thinkers before Aristotle wrote, for in many ways Aristotle was influenced by and responded to their theories. Aristotle's debate with his predecessors focused on the role of male and female in the reproductive process. The pluralists held that both sexes were responsible for reproduction, a view that was the basis of their belief in some form of equality between the sexes (Allen 1997, 84).

Pythagoras and Women

The ancient Greek philosopher and mathematician Pythagoras (ca. 580–ca. 500 B.C.) was an early contributor to the debate about women. The accuracy of what is known about Pythagoras and his followers is difficult to determine. Because Pythagoras did not leave any records, we must rely on what was written about him a few hundred years after his death. There are references to Pythagoras in various ancient sources, including the writings of Xenophanes, Heraclitus, Empedocles, Plato, Aristotle, and some of Aristotle's students. Porphyry, Iamblichus, and Diogenes Laertius all wrote accounts of his life that included explanations of his teaching. These authors relied on earlier sources for their material.

The basis of Pythagoras's thought was that everything was composed of numbers. Pythagoras invented ten principles of opposites—limited-unlimited, odd-even, one-many, right-left, male-female, rest-motion, light-darkness, good-bad, square-oblong, and straight-curved—and applied them to the universe. The female principle may be located on the left, with darkness, bad, curved, and so on. Aristotle's views on women were influenced by the Pythagorean set of opposites, although his interpretation of female nature was far more negative than that of the Pythagoreans.

The importance of harmony, balance, and reason was a crucial aspect of Pythagorean philosophy, and the nature of the human soul was a central concern. According to Pythagoras, the soul had three parts: intelligence, reason, and passion. Diogenes Laertius, writing in the third century A.D., informs us that Pythagoras stated: "Reason is immortal, all else is mortal" (Diogenes Laertius 1941, 2: 347). Because reason lacked gender, the Pythagoreans maintained that women could think and be educated. Indeed not only were women educated among the Pythagoreans, some made a contribution to science.

Pythagoras established a community, composed primarily of family and friends, and a school at Croton. Although he often lectured in public, it was only with the smaller group, the community, which included women, that Pythagoras shared his most complex ideas. According to Iamblichus, there were also over one hundred women in the school. He wrote of seventeen women, who were "the most illustrious of those who counted among the happy number of disciples of the wise man Pythagoras." Iamblichus provided a list of the names of these 17 women and of 218 men (Iamblichus 1989, 112–113).

Women, just like men, could be students of philosophy, which of course included mathematics and the natural sciences, although separate schools were constructed for the two sexes (Allen 1997, 21). Aristoxenus, a disciple of Aristotle, recorded that the Pythagoreans believed that "boys and girls alike must be reared in hard work, exercise and endurance of the right kind" (cited in Freeman 1946, 258).

Not only did the Pythagorean sect allow women to receive an education, some contemporary sources indicate that women had a role in the formation of some of the Pythagorean theories. Diogenes Laertius wrote: "Aristoxenus asserts that Pythagoras derived the greater part of his ethical doctrines from Themistoclea, the Delphic priestess" (Laertius 1941, 2: 339).

Theano, who was apparently Pythagoras's wife, wrote a document entitled "On Piety," which clarified his thoughts on the metaphysical role of numbers: "But he did not say that all things come to be from number; rather in accordance with number" (cited in Waithe 1987, 12). Iamblichus referred to a woman named Aesara who wrote about "human nature" and asserted that the writings of two Pythagorean women, Theano and Aesara, formed "important manifestations of the harmony of the cosmos" (cited in Waithe 1987, 12). Apparently Theano not only worked in the areas of physics, medicine, and child psychology but was a mathematician in her own right. Her work on the principle of the Golden Mean and the corresponding Golden Rectangle are considered to be among her most significant contributions (McLemore 1979).

It seems that women philosophers (including those who were mathematicians) must have been to some degree recognized and accepted in ancient Greek civilization, as Theano and her daughters continued the Pythagorean school after the death of her husband.

Parmenides and Women

Unlike Pythagoras, who left no extant works, the thinker Parmenides of Elea (ca. 515–445 B.C.), often called the father of metaphysics, left a poem called *On Nature,* which deals in part with the questions of interest here. Interestingly, it is a female deity (Thea) rather than a male one who teaches him to reason: "The goddess greeted me kindly, and took my right hand in hers, and spake to me these words: 'Welcome, O youth, that comest to my abode. . . . It is that thou should learn all things" (Randall 1996, 18).

Unlike Aristotle, Parmenides posited that both the male and female contributed seed to reproduction; thus the female was more than passive and matter: "When man and woman mingle the seeds of love that spring from their veins, a formative power, maintaining the proper proportions, moulds well-formed bodies from this diverse blood." Whether an embryo becomes male or female depends on its position in the womb: "She [the goddess] placed the young males on the right side of the womb, young females on the left" (Randall 1996, 17).

The Pluralists: Anaxagoras, Empedocles, and Democritus

Aristotle disputed the writings of these pre-Socratic philosophers, often referred to as the pluralists, because unlike those monist philosophers who taught that there was one underlying substance of the universe, they believed that reality is composed of a plurality of entities. Here they differed from the dualistic Pythagoreans who considered opposites to be fundamental. Aristotle referred to these thinkers as "untrained boxers" who did not know how to think scientifically and maturely (*Metaphysics* 985a 10–16; Aristotle 1984, 2: 1558; Allen 1997, 85).

Anaxagoras (500–428 B.C.) was an astronomer. In his work *On Natural Science,* he put forth the view that the world was composed of tiny seeds organized into the Mind. He did not specifically refer to male or female, but believed "the living beings . . . to originate (first) out of moisture and warm and earth-like (substances), but later from another" (cited in Cleve 1949, 42). He was influenced by the Pythagoreans, in that he believed that the male was formed on the right side and the female on the left side of the womb (Freeman 1946, 272). Aristotle insisted that Anaxagoras was arguing that only the male provided the seed, and the female the "place" (*On the Generation of Animals* 763b 32–764a 1; Aristotle 1984, 1182). However, this was disputed by Censorius (third century A.D., who wrote, "Anaxagoras thinks that children resemble that parent who has contributed the most seed" (cited in Gershenson and Greenberg 1964, 152, fragment 274).

Empedocles of Agrigentum (ca. 490–430 B.C.) was the first Western philosopher to propound a theory of sex complementarism, meaning that male and female are different but equal, at least in reproduction. In the process of conception, both provided seed (Allen 1997, 30; Freeman 1946, 52–53). According to Empedocles, the soul had no sex identity. His double-seed theory provided an equal role to mother and father. Empedocles thought that the sex of the child was governed by heat (male side) and cold (female side). Although he did not extend the temperature of males and females beyond the physiological realm, in some ways he laid the groundwork for Aristotle's view that the female was colder and thus weaker and inferior to the male. In fact, Aristotle criticized Empedocles's theory for being "too easy-going," for it did not give reasons for "the organic differences between male and female" (cited in Freeman 1946, 194–195). As with Anaxagoras, Aristotle rejected Empedocles's theories, seeing men and women as very different and men as superior. Males were hot and therefore could produce sperm or seed, whereas females were colder and therefore inferior, could not produce seed, and played no active role in reproduction (*On the Generation of Animals* 765b 10–18; Aristotle 1: 1184–1185). Here Aristotle agreed with the Hippocratic corpus, although these writers did not focus on the superiority of the male.

Democritus (ca. 460–370 B.C.), writing around 420 B.C., argued that the female was not merely a receptacle, but that she provided seed and that the collision of the male and female seed was the cause of creation. He posited that the sex was not determined by the predominance of heat or cold, but by the female contribution of seeds (Freeman 1946, 306–307).

Aristotle disagreed with Democritus's belief that sex is determined by whether the greater quantity of seed comes from the male or the female: "For those who assign the same cause of sex as Empedocles or Democritus say what is on other grounds impossible, and those who say that is determined by the greater or smaller amount of semen coming from the male or female parent, cannot show how the female is to resemble the father and the male the mother, for it is impossible that more should come from both at once" (*On the Generation of Animals* 769a 15–25; Aristotle 1984, 1: 1190).

The Hippocratic Corpus

The Hippocratic corpus, a body of medical writings dating from the fourth and fifth centuries, also formed part of the background of Aristotle's thought. These works were written by various authors at different times, primarily on the subject of human reproduction and gynecological disorders. The major Hippocratic writings concerning women were *On Generation, The Nature of the Child,* and *The Diseases of Women.* The Hippocratics had some negative things to say about the female, in keeping with the majority view of the time. Menstruation was characterized as "mysterious, dangerous," and a "contaminating" event (Anderson and Zinsser 2000, 28). They described the theory of the "wandering womb," a powerful organ. Some scholars have argued that the wandering womb theory further contributed to the diminution of the female contribution to generation (Anderson and Zinsser, 2000, 29; King 1998, 7). It is clear that the writers of the Hippocratic corpus did subscribe to the doctrine of two seeds: The female seed was a vaginal secretion (Needham 1959, 11). However, a stronger seed produced a male, a weaker one a female. Here we can see the legacy of the earlier writers who believed that both male and female produced seed, and a foreshadowing of Aristotle, with notions of the female as the weaker being.

It has been suggested that "by concentrating on certain functions of the female," the Hippocratic writers indicated that they were operating on the assumption that she needed special treatment and was set apart from the male (King 1998, 7). Certainly they focused on the differences between men and women, describing woman as a creature entirely different from man in terms of the substance and feel of her body, which they described as cold, moist and passive, and in terms of her reproduction purpose (Cadden 1992, 11).

One expert on the Hippocratic corpus has made a good case that, according to these writers, the female was the abnormal in comparison to the normal male and that she was "structurally a sick being." The prevailing impression of the female created by these writings is that she was a "silent patient," ignorant of how her own body worked, accepting what the doctor prescribed (Hawley and Levick 1995, 136).

The Debate between Plato and Aristotle

Plato (ca. 428–355 B.C.) and Aristotle (ca. 384–322 B.C.) provided the fullest debate about the female in ancient Greece. Aristotle made the first major biological analysis of the female, basing her role in society on his biological interpretations, while Plato's views were more sociological in nature. They are crucial to the debate over whether women can do science as it has unfolded over the centuries, for their works have been the most cited by later writers. Aristotleian perspectives of the universe and of female inferiority based upon biology persisted well into the Middle Ages, if not beyond. In many ways, Aristotle's view has been more influential than that of Plato. We will first analyze the beliefs of Plato, who was Aristotle's teacher for some twenty years. Aristotle spent most of his time refuting the views of Plato, particularly the idea that the female was a mutilated male.

Plato is much more difficult to categorize than Aristotle in terms of his attitude toward women and their role in society, so much so that there is no agreement on the matter among specialists in the field. Many scholars have argued that, unlike Aristotle, Plato was inconsistent in his views on women (Dickason 1973–1974, 45–43; Peradotto and Sullivan 1984, 213–228; Bullough 1973, 58–59; Allen 1997, 57; Tuana 1994). As one author pointed out, this is not necessarily a bad thing, for it was typical of the Greeks to give both sides to the story (Wender 1984, 221). Others have posited that Plato's ideas were consistent and that he remained a misogynist throughout his life. The works in which he discussed women, the *Symposium,* the *Republic,* and the *Laws,* were simply written for different purposes. The *Republic* delineated Plato's view for an ideal society, while the *Laws* was more realistic, in the sense that he was writing for a second-best state (Osborne 1975, 447–452). Nicholas D. Smith approached the problem in a different way by arguing that although Plato was definitely more egalitarian in his thinking than Aristotle, the real difference between

Detail of Plato and Aristotle from The School of Athens by Raphael (Ted Spiegel / Corbis)

them was not their views on biology, but on the soul (Smith 1983, 467–78). Most recently, Nancy Tuana commented that after twenty years of debate on Plato and the female question, today scholars tend to see Plato's views as "sexist," but at the same time, she saw support for the perspective that Plato was the first Western philosopher to put forth "feminist" proposals for society (Tuana 1994, 4).

To make matters even more complicated, Natalie Harris Bluestone argued convincingly that there has been a tradition of sexism in the translations and commentaries of Plato's works throughout the nineteenth and twentieth centuries. She named such leading scholars as Ernest Baker, Allan Bloom, Benjamin Jowett, and A. E. Taylor. They have, in many respects, distorted Plato's writings, either ignoring or downplaying some of Plato's more progressive proposals, such as the one for women rulers. She summed up the problem by saying that Plato's "proposals for women guardians have met with overwhelming antipathy throughout the ages" (cited in Tuana 1994, 4).

Perhaps it is most accurate to state that Plato was less clear-cut on his ideas about women than Aristotle. His first statements about women are found in the *Symposium,* written before the *Republic* and the *Laws.* Here he presented Aristophanes, the comic poet, explaining the greatness of love by telling a story about the nature of man in the beginning. Originally there were three sexes: male; female; and hermaphrodite, a man-woman that was half male and half female. Males came from the sun, females from the earth, and the male-female from the moon. Zeus made male and female from all three parts. In all three sexes, each individual had four legs and four arms, and so on, all features doubled, and each was round. Zeus had to cut them in half to keep them in line (*Symposium* 189d–190b; Plato 1963, 542).

A second account of creation, one certainly more unfavorable to the female, is found in a much later dialogue, Plato's *Timaeus,* which stated that men who behaved badly in their lives would come back as women in the next one. Men have sperm, which originates in the head. The sperm produces reproductive Eros, a desire for procreation. As far as the woman is concerned, Plato repeated the Hippocratic notion of the wandering womb, which travels throughout the body and creates havoc unless it is satisfied through sexual intercourse. However, *Timaeus* also described the gods creating "in man one animated substance, and in woman another," in both sexes originating in the head, but then traveling to "the organ of generation" and for both sexes making that organ (the penis as well as the womb) behave "like an animal disobedient to reason" until the desire for sexual intercourse is satisfied (*Timaeus* 90d–91e; Plato 1963, 1209–1210). Once again, Plato is not clear-cut in his views.

The leading concept in Plato is the role of the soul, which is sexless. It determines the identity of male and female rather than the material aspects of generation. Plato did not devote much attention to the topic of generation and sex differences. In his *Republic,* he hypothesized that if there is a difference between male and female, it is only that "the female bears and the male begets," and so unimportant did he consider that difference that he said that if indeed that is the only distinction, "we shall say that no proof has yet been produced that the woman differs from the man for our purposes, but we shall continue to think that our guardians and their wives ought to follow the same pursuits" (*Republic* 454e; Plato 1963, 693). This is very radical indeed, for the place of the woman in classical Athens was in the private sphere. Plato would challenge this by allowing guardian women access to employment in public careers, including the sciences. He wrote, "women of the guardians . . . must take their part with the men in war and other duties of civic guardianship and have no other occupation" (*Republic* 457b; Plate 1963). Official posts were to be open to men as well as women (*Republic* 460b; Plate 1963). If men and women were both working, then the question arose of who would look after the children, the traditional female role. The children would be taken care of by special caregivers: "And the children thus born will be taken over by the officials appointed for this, men or women or both, since I take it, the official posts too are common to women and men" (*Republic* 460b; Plato 1963).

Women in Plato's Republic and Symposium

Plato's *Republic* is his greatest work of philosophy and his second longest next to his *Laws*. It is written in the form of a dialogue, and it begins with a Socratic conversation on the topic of justice before providing an in-depth debate about the topics of wisdom, courage, and moderation. The *Republic* provides Plato's plan for an ideal society with detailed accounts of human knowledge and the kind of educational program by which it can be achieved by both men and women. The dialogue concludes with a review of various types of government, an explicit description of the ideal state in which only philosophers are fit to rule, and an attempt to prove that justice is preferable to injustice.

During Plato's time, education was exclusively male. In his *Republic,* Plato was revolutionary in the sense that he stated that both men and women have the same value and should therefore receive a similar education. He restricted this education to the ruling class, or guardians. These women should receive the same education as men: "For the production of a female guardian, then, our education will not be one thing for men and another for women, especially since the nature which we hand over to it is the same. There will be no difference" (*Republic* 456d; Plato 1963, 695). In the *Laws* as well as in the *Republic,* he argued that women of the ruling class, like men, should receive instruction in gymnastics, music, mathematics, astronomy, and metaphysics (*Republic* 5, 452a, 456d, 526b; *Laws* 747a, 804e, 809c). The fact that Plato believed in teaching females the subjects of science, philosophy, and mathematics seems to imply that he must have believed that women were capable of abstract reasoning and thus had the capacity to be scientists. He certainly saw a broader role for women, at least those of the ruling class, than Aristotle.

Plato looked for the best and the brightest to be in charge regardless of sex. In his ideal state, women as well as men could qualify to be guardians. They could perform the same tasks: "And we must throw open the debate to anyone who wishes either in jest or in earnest to raise the question whether female nature is capable of sharing with the male all tasks or none at all, or some but not others, and under which of these heads this business of war falls. Would not this be that best beginning which would naturally and proverbially lead to the best end? For the best," he said (*Republic* 453a, 692). This statement must be understood in the context of his day, a society trying to protect itself against hostile neighbors. He argued that women would become more equal to men if they received similar training (*Laws* 794c–d, 1366).

Plato did believe, like Aristotle, that women were physically weaker than men, "But the natural capacities are distributed alike among both creatures, and woman shall naturally share in all pursuits and men in all—yet for all the woman is weaker than the man" (*Republic* 455d; Plato 1963, 694). As Thomas R. Martin asserted, "The inclusion of women in the ruling class of Plato's utopian city-state represented a startling departure from the actual practice of his times. Indeed, never before in Western history had anyone proposed—even in fantasy—that work be allocated in human society without regard to gender" (Martin 1996, 181). Thus, although Plato acknowledged that there were differences between men and women, these differences did not mean that women could not be trained in the art of warfare, especially in the "use of the spear and shield" (*Laws* 749d).

Evidence to support the view that Plato believed the female to be capable of rational thought may be found in the *Symposium*. Here he introduced a female rather than a male figure using dialectical reasoning to discover wisdom. This person was Diotima of Mantinea. Her method of reasoning was the Socratic one: question and answer. Socrates claimed that he received this method from her (*Symposium* 201d–e). Although her subject matter was love, in some ways, she propounded a scientifically based method to "prove" her theories. She argued that one must have a reason for something to be knowledge: "How can it be knowledge without a reason?" (*Symposium* 202a; Plato 1963, 554).

Women in the Laws

The *Laws,* the last work of Plato, was written shortly before he died. In this work, the plans for a second-best society (rather than an ideal one, as in the *Republic*) were sketched. The *Laws* contained some very advanced thinking. In many ways, it was the most radical of his works. In the first place, Plato advocated a similar education for both sexes, and although girls and boys must be separated from age six for educational purposes, the girls may share in the same instruction as the boys (riding, archery, and so on). "My law will apply in all respects to girls as much as boys: the girls must be trained exactly like the boys [in the arts of war and music]" (*Laws* 804e; Plato 1963, 1376). To prove his point, he used the case of the women living near the Black Sea, Sarmatian women, who were as good as men with the bow and arrow. "It is pure folly that men and women do not unite to follow the same pursuits with all their energies" (*Laws* 805a; Plato 1963, 1376). Plato even raised the possibility of women serving in the military, suggesting that the term of military service "for women—whatever military employment it may be thought right to impose on women," should extend from the end of her childbearing years to the age of fifty (*Laws* 785b; Plato 1963, 1360).

As Susan Moller Okin remarked, "By the time he came to write the *Laws*, Plato had come to notice that female nature was not fairly represented by the depraved and stunted women of his own society" (Okin 1979, 22). Plato argued his case for equal education in much stronger terms here than in the *Republic*. "There must be complete association of the female sex with the male in education as in everything else. In fact, we may treat the matter from some such standpoint as this. If women are not to take their part along with men in all the business of life, we are bound, are we not, to propose some different scheme to them?" (*Laws* 805c–d; Plato 1963, 1376–1377).

Consistent with his views on female education and their capacity to reason, Plato admitted women as well as men to his Academy. Evidence for female students may be found in Diogenes Laertius's *Lives of the Philosophers*. He wrote that "and many others, among them two women, Lastheneia of Mantinea and Axiothea of Philus, who is reported by Dicaerchus to have worn men's clothes" (Diogenes Laertius 1941, 1: 317). The Church Father Clement of Alexandria corroborated this in his work. Female participation in the school outlived Plato, and in the third century a woman even became director of the Academy, Hipparchia, wife of Crates.

Aristotle's Reaction to Plato

Aristotle reacted against Plato's radicalism and was much closer to conventional fifth-century Athenian thought. Women were inferior beings in every sense of the word, not just physically as with Plato, but intellectually, anatomically, and ethically. Most scholars have attributed Aristotle's explanations for female inferiority to his focus on the differences between male and female biology. Many scholars have written about Aristotle's view of woman as a defective man (Horowitz 1976; Allen 1997; Okin 1979; Harding and Hinitkka 1983). Even those scholars who believe that Aristotle meant that "males and females do not differ in species" have still stated that he saw the female as somehow inferior to the male (Deslauiers 1998). They argue that Aristotle's biological theories concerning generation led to his views about female inferiority and male superiority. A recent contributor to the debate has posited that the real reason for Aristotle's insistence on the rightness of woman's subordinate position in society was not his focus on her reproductive function, but his belief that women were "controlled by their emotions rather than reason (logos)" (Saxonhouse 1991, 38). Whatever Aristotle believed to be the most important reason for female inferiority, biological or emotional, there seems to be a general consensus that Aristotle considered the female species to be inferior to the male.

According to Aristotle, the female was a deviation from the norm, and the male was the norm. He wrote this in his *On the Generation of Animals:* "The first departure indeed is that the offspring should become female instead of male; this, however, is a natural necessity" (767b 7–9; Aristotle 1984, 1: 1187). For Aristotle, the female was a "mutilated male" lacking in the "principle of the soul." In other words, the female was a defective or incomplete male. She was produced when something went wrong, when nature did not follow its path properly (737a 26–31; Aristotle 1984, 1: 1144). The normal body was a male body. The female was an inferior form, too cold to transform blood into semen and thus unable to reach perfection (Aristotle, 775a 14–20; 765b 15–20).

Women were thus deficient and lacking in comparison with men. The characterization of the cold and wet female and hot and dry male seems to have been a traditional one and was certainly articulated in the Hippocratic corpus, but Aristotle went further than the Hippocratic writers in making these differences evidence of the superiority of the male. Females did not mature as quickly as males in the womb because of lack of heat, and this he saw as a defect. However, females matured faster out of the womb, and this also he saw as a flaw. As one expert concluded: "Women can't win with the supposed 'empiricist'; all apparent differences between male and female are attributed to the 'natural deficiency' of the female sex" (Horowitz 1976, 205). In order to understand Aristotle's reasons for this view, one must examine his theories concerning generation.

Aristotle formulated a biological theory for the basis of male superiority. In his view, the fact that the female did not contribute to conception meant that she was inferior to the male. In the following passage, he refutes the idea of his predecessors that females contributed to generation, or reproduction:

We may safely set down as the chief principles of generation the male [factor] and the female [factor]; the male as possessing the principle of movement and of generation, the female as possessing that of matter. One is most likely to be convinced of this by considering how the semen is formed and whence it comes; for although the things that are formed in the course of Nature no doubt take their rise out of semen, we must not fail to notice how the semen itself is formed from the male and the female, since it is because this part is secreted from the male and the female, and because its secretion takes place in them and out of them, that the male and the female are the principles of generation. . . . Now it is impossible that any creature should produce two seminal secretions at once, and as the secretion in females which answers to semen in males is the menstrual fluid, it obviously follows that the female does not contribute any semen to generation; for if there were semen, there would be no menstrual fluid; but as menstrual fluid is in fact formed, therefore there is no semen. (716a 5–23; Aristotle 1984, 1: 1112–1113)

If the female did not provide the seed, then all she supplied was the womb, the place where the fetus grew, and the matter that provided nourishment for the fetus, in the form of menstrual blood. "It is clear that the female contributes the material for generation, and that this is in the substance of the menstrual discharges and they are residue" (727b 31–33: Aristotle 1984, 1: 1130). The uterus was a passive receptacle.

Aristotle took his theory of the male (active) and female (passive) roles in the reproductive process and applied it to the psychological makeup of woman and by extension, to her role in society. Because only men produced semen, this meant that they were "effective and active," while the female was "passive" (729a 25–34; Aristotle 1984, 1: 1130). The following passage from the *History of Animals* explains Aristotle's view on the nature of woman:

In all cases, excepting the bear and leopard, the female is less spirited than the male. . . . With all other animals, the female is softer in disposition, is more mischievous, less simple, more impulsive, and more attentive to the nurture of the young; the male, on the other hand, is more spirited, more savage, more simple and less cunning. The traces of these characteristics are more or less visible everywhere, but they are especially visible where character is more developed, and most of all in man. The fact is, the nature of man is the most rounded off and complete, and consequently in man the qualities above referred to are found most clearly. Hence woman is more compassionate than man, more easily moved to tears, at the same time is more jealous, more querulous, more apt to scold and to strike. She is furthermore, more prone to despondency and less hopeful than the man, more void of shame, more false of speech, more deceptive, and of more retentive memory. (608b 1–15; Aristotle 1984, 1: 948–949)

And what of the reasoning faculties that human beings alone possessed? According to Aristotle, both male and female possessed a soul with the ability to reason; however, in the female the irrational power dominated. This is the opposite of the male. Furthermore, although the woman, unlike the slave, has a "deliberative faculty," it is "without authority" (1260a 14; Aristotle 1984, 2: 14). Women are not able to control themselves physically and psychologically through the exercise of reason the way men can. Therefore, the woman must submit and obey.

In terms of leadership roles, Aristotle turns to "nature" to find the answer. "All things rule and are ruled by nature." The male is the "natural ruler." Men thus were better fitted to command than women (except in some cases where their union has been formed contrary to nature), and the older and fully developed person than the younger and immature. The female is "irrational," the male "rational" by nature, so it is logical that the male commands (1259b 32–1260a 10; Aristotle 1984, 2: 1999).

Aristotle criticized the Spartans for allowing women a military role. He blamed the women for the Spartan defeat in the Theban invasion: "The influence of the Lacedaemonian women has been most mischievous. The evil showed itself in the Theban invasion. . . . They were utterly useless and caused more confusion than the enemy" (1269b 31–38; Aristotle 1984, 2: 2015).

The crucial point of Aristotle's thought for the debate about women in science is that the biological inferiority of the female extended to all aspects of her being, including her use of reason and her decision-making abilities. The inferior female sex, emotional, passive, and submissive by nature, is not capable of reason. Aristotle's system, very different from Plato's more positive interpretation, was the one that dominated for at least a thousand years.

Going against the Grain: Pioneering Female Scientists

Aristotle's worldview was predominant in the Western world; nevertheless, amazingly, there were women who, by their actual achievements, proved that women were capable of everything Aristotle said they could not do. Moreover, they were accepted by their society as thinking women. In addition to the Pythagorean women mentioned earlier in this chapter, the following women went against the prevalent ideology of the times and by their works demonstrated that women could reason and thus practice science. The most renowned of these women was Hypatia of Alexandria, but there were others who are less well-known.

The first of these women was Aspasia (ca. 470–410 B.C.) of Milesia, the hetaira, or highly cultivated courtesan, who was Pericles's mistress and later wife. Our knowledge of her is derived completely from what contemporaries wrote about her, for she left nothing by her own hand. According to a number of ancient sources, she taught rhetoric to Pericles and philosophy to Socrates. In addition she was herself a gifted speechwriter (Plato 1963, 188; Wender 1984, 222).

In his life of Pericles, Plutarch wrote of Aspasia's brilliance and of her salon, attended by philosophers such as Anaxagoras (Plutarch 1915, 3: 93). Some scholars attest that women were also members of her "salon." The education of women was important to her, and she was the first educator of women after the Pythagoreans (Allen 1997, 29). Her significance is that she demonstrated through her considerable intellectual abilities that women could indeed reason.

Hypatia of Alexandria: An Exemplary Woman Scientist

Most scholars have believed that Hypatia lived from A.D. 370 to 415, although her most recent biographer, Maria Dzielska, disputed this and dated her at about 390 (Dzielska 1995, 67). Her information is based on the letters of Synesius of Cyrene, one of her students, who knew her well. The life, teachings, and scientific contributions of Hypatia go against everything Aristotle had had to say about women and their inability to reason. What we know about Hypatia is that she was a mathematician, philosopher, and astronomer. Her father, Theon, worked in the same fields; he taught her what he knew, and they collaborated on various experiments. She did not live in Greece, but in Greek-speaking Alexandria in Egypt. Alexandria in Hypatia's lifetime was the center of the scientific and philosophic world, which may well explain why she was accepted as a scholar, inventor, and teacher (Dzielska 1995, 9, 67–72).

Hypatia ran a school where she taught philosophy. The fifth-century church historian Socrates Scholasticus described her significant role as teacher and philosopher, saying that Hypatia "surpassed all the philosophers of her time, and succeeded to the chair of the Platonic

Profile of Greek mathematician Hypatia (Bettmann / Corbis)

school that had been led by Plotinus and explained all branches of philosophy to her listeners. She had many students" (cited in Ménage 1984, 73). She taught subjects as wide-ranging as ethics, ontology, mathematics, and astronomy. Astronomy was her specialty. She lectured and wrote commentaries on the works of other major thinkers (Dzielska 1995, 54–55).

She was visited by the leaders of the city of Alexandria and taken seriously as a scientist and philosopher. Again Socrates wrote: "On account of the majestic outspokenness at her command as a result of her education, she maintained a dignified intercourse with the chief people of the city, for all esteemed her highly, and admired her for her sophrosyne" (cited in Dzielska 1995, 41). The Greek word "sophrosyne" means self-control, prudence, and soundness of mind. Interestingly, Aristotle observed many times that the female was incapable of sophrosyne.

Her major contribution to science was her commentary on the *Syntaxis Mathematica,* the major work of the second-century A.D. astronomer Ptolemy Claudius. Ptolemy was the leading astronomer of the ancient world, whose view that the Sun revolved around Earth remained intact until questioned by Copernicus in the sixteenth century. Mary Ellen Waithe made a convincing case that Hypatia's thinking about Ptolemy's theory concerning the position of Earth in relation to the Sun may well have influenced Copernicus's thinking. Apparently Copernicus had made detailed studies of all the ancients' works when he visited Italy (Waithe 1987, 1: 188–189). In addition, Hypatia wrote a commentary on the *Canon of Astronomy* by the third-century A.D. algebraist Diophantus, and *Conic Sections* by the second-century B.C. mathematician Apollonius of Pergaeus. Two of her three commentaries have survived and scholars seem to think that with more digging, the missing one, the commentary on Pergaeus's *Conics,* will be found. As an inventor, she is credited with inventing the astrolabe and the hydroscope used to determine the gravity of liquids (Ménage 1984, 28; Waithe 1987, 1: 175–181).

Hypatia's role was a very public one. She lectured both in public and in private. In public, she would have lectured in halls; in private, in her home to a select group, all male. Her biographer makes it clear she was not out preaching on the street corners. Many of her students came from places far away (Dzielska 1995, 57–58). In her sixty years, she accomplished much in both philosophy and science. Her life and achievements contribute significantly to the case that women can do science. Hypatia's life came to a tragic end in A.D. 415, when she was brutally murdered by a group of Christian monks. Her flesh was mutilated and her remains were burned. Her death presents the perfect symbol of the end of the classical world, the end for a long time of the possibility of disinterested scientific inquiry.

$$ $$

2

The Medieval Woman in Science: Contradictions within the Church and the University

The Roman Catholic Church was the most important institution in Western civilization during the Middle Ages. Wealthy and powerful, it rivaled secular authorities and controlled knowledge and education. In order to understand the attitude of the church toward women, it is necessary to provide some historical background on Christianity and its teachings.

Early Christianity

Christianity is based upon the teachings of Jesus and his disciples found in the New Testament of the Bible. Although the Christian church later became an institution that subordinated women, it did not start out this way. Jesus himself taught by example that women were not inferior. He treated women as equals and permitted them to have a role outside the family. In fact, he encouraged them to leave their families and homes behind them and follow him (Zinsser and Anderson 2000, 68–71). Not only did Jesus consider women as equals, they played prominent roles in his life, death, and resurrection (see Matthew 27:55; Mark 15:40, Luke 24:10; John 19:25). Even Paul, who in some of his teachings taught that women should have only a subordinate role, summed up the early Christian view of women when he stated: "There is neither Jew nor Greek; there is neither slave nor free; there is neither male nor female; for you are all one in Christ Jesus" (Galatians 3:28). Sixteen out of Paul's thirty-six teaching colleagues were female. Women continued to play an important dominant role in Christianity throughout the first century A.D. (King 1997).

If Jesus and the early Christians preached an egalitarian and positive message about women, how, why, and when did this attitude change? In the first place, even the early Christian teachers were not

Adam and Eve *by Lucas Cranach the Elder (Burstein Collection / Corbis)*

always encouraging about women. Although Paul may have said that male and female were one in Christ, he had plenty to say elsewhere that paints a different picture. Like Aristotle, he preached that women should be silent and that they "should be subordinate" (1 Corinthians 14:34–35). Insofar as knowledge is concerned, "If there is anything that they desire to know, let them ask their husbands at home" (1 Corinthians 11:7–8). In addition, in contrast to Jesus, Paul emphasized the myth of Adam and Eve, stating that Eve was made from Adam's rib and that "man is the image and glory of God; but the woman is the glory of man." In the light of this, he would not allow women to take on the teaching role as Jesus had done: "I permit not a woman to teach or to have authority over men; she is to keep silent. For Adam was formed first, then Eve; and Adam was not deceived, but the woman was deceived and became a transgressor" (1 Timothy 2:11–13).

One can compare Aristotle's view of women as inferior based on biology with the Christian view based on myths about creation and the Fall. Whether on the basis of science or religion, there was no place for women to be teachers or in positions of authority. In 1 Timothy 3:2–3, 11, Paul sets out the attributes for bishops, all of whom were men. They should "be above reproach, the husband of one wife, temperate, sensible, dignified, hospitable, an apt teacher, no drunkard, not violent but gentle, not quarrelsome, and no lover of money." The only mention of women in the chapter is as the wives of bishops: "Even so must their wives be grave, not slanderers, sober, faithful in all things. This attitude took hold and persisted in the church. More-over, as Christianity spread, becoming accepted and no longer a for-eign and detested sect, things began to worsen for women. In effect, the institutionalization of this religion during the late Roman Empire marked a complete change in the attitude toward women (MacDon-ald 1999, 236–253).

Therefore, the exclusion of women from a role of authority as priests dates from the apostolic age of Christianity. It must be kept in mind that the impact of the apostles was great, that they were Jewish and men of their time and thus considered women to be inferior be-ings. Thus, the principle of equality preached by Jesus, ironically also a Jew, was quashed by his disciples and followers. The Church Fa-thers, as the authoritative teachers of the early centuries of the Chris-tian era are called, inherited and expanded this tradition.

Christianity and the Roman Heritage

The teachings about the nature of woman accepted by the Christian church were to a great extent already present in Roman society. An-cient Rome, for the most part, was a man's world. The government was run by men and for men. Women were inferior and subordinate. The leading institution in Roman society was the family, with the fa-ther at its head. At the time of marriage, a woman became part of her husband's family and assumed the legal status of a child; her husband took control of her dowry and thus had complete control over his wife. In terms of education, the girls of the upper classes were pro-vided with literary training. The rationale for women's education was linked to motherhood (Lefkowitz and Fant 1992, 75); mothers needed enough education to supervise their children's tutors and de-velop their moral character. There was hostility toward learned women. The early Church Fathers, who flourished during the late Roman Empire, inherited these attitudes toward women (Bullough 1973, 81–85).

The Early Church Fathers

The ideas of the early Church Fathers have strongly influenced the Western view of women. Around the fourth century, these male the-ologians began to restate the more negative views of women. By way of introduction, a few general remarks can be made about their ideas. Most basically, they separated men from women in terms of reason and physical strength. Women were considered to be irrational and weak, whereas men were rational and strong. Because men were strong, they had the right to dominate women. For the most part, the Church Fathers stressed the submission of woman to man. Isidore of Seville, last of the Church Fathers in the West, summed up this predominant attitude when he wrote, "Women are under the power of men because they are frequently spiritually fickle. Therefore, they should be governed by men" (cited in Bullough and Brundage 1996, 85). Leadership and public roles, most importantly the priesthood, were thus denied to women. They were relegated to the home. A common argument used in support of this was that Jesus was baptized by a man rather than a woman. If Jesus had intended women to be priests, then Mary rather than John would have been the baptizer (Daniélou 1961, 11, 19).

Before discussing in more detail the major ideas of the Church Fathers, we should examine the ideas of the most important precursor who influenced their thinking, Philo of Alexandria. His life dates are usually given as 20–15 B.C. to A.D. 45–50 (Seland 1995). He was a Jew who reinterpreted the Old Testament in the light of Pythagorean, Platonic, and Stoic ideas. The major source for his ideas about women was the second chapter of Genesis. For Philo, the female represented sexuality, lust, and desire (Horowitz 1979).

The Christian thinker Origen (ca. 185–254), another Alexandrian and a Church Father, was significant for his dissemination of Philo's views to the more influential Church Fathers such as Jerome and Ambrose. He praised men for their "spiritual masculinity," while women were reproached because of their "spiritual femininity" (Horowitz 1979, 193). Origen was also important for his influence on the thought of the Church Father Saint Augustine and the later theologian Saint Thomas Aquinas.

TERTULLIAN

Tertullian (160–ca. 240) was born in Carthage of Roman parents. He was a jurist who converted to Christianity around 190. Although he preached perfect spiritual equality between male and female, this did not prevent him from depreciating the value of women. He considered women to be in a state of "manifest inferiority" (Metz 1985, 69). According to Tertullian, women should wear the veil; they should be hidden to cover their evil. Woman (in the person of Eve) was guilty of original sin and thus opened the door to all evil. As Tertullian put it: "The sentence of God on this sex of yours lives on . . . it is necessary that the guilt should live on also. You are the one who opened the door to the Devil, you are the one who deserted divine law" (Tertullian 1959, 118).

SAINT BASIL OF CAESAREA

A contemporary who held an opposing view was Basil of Caesarea (ca. 329–379), also a Church Father. He put forth the belief that a woman's soul was as good as a man's and was also God-like. His ideas were similar to those of Jesus, who stated that women had spiritual equality to men. Both men and women were capable of good works. And both sexes were virtuous. Basil's conclusions about women were cited by the French feminist Marie Le Jars de Gournay in her treatise, *L'Egalité des hommes et des femmes* (Equality of Men and Women), written in 1622 when she was trying to justify female equality (Gournay 1988).

SAINT CLEMENT OF ALEXANDRIA AND SAINT AMBROSE

Clement of Alexandria (d. ca. 215) was a Greek theologian who wrote in the second century. He was a Christian apologist and a leader of the Alexandrian community. Details concerning his early life are sketchy. His parents were pagan Athenians. He became a Christian through the influence of one of his teachers, Pantaenus. Although he agreed with other Church Fathers that men were superior to women, he put forth a less misogynist view of women than most at the time. Briefly, he believed that women and men share the same nature and both can achieve perfection. However, he did state that men are usually better at everything than women (Clement of Alexandria 1996).

Saint Ambrose (ca. 339–397) was bishop of Milan for twenty-three years, from 373 until his death in 397. His parents were Roman and his father had been a praetorian prefect of Gaul. He had practiced law and had been a governor of the province of Aemelia-Liguria before becoming a bishop. During his tenure as bishop, Ambrose made Milan the most significant see in the West (Ambrose 1954, 1: v–vii).

Ambrose's fullest statement about women is contained in his work *On Paradise* and in his letters. In *On Paradise,* he inquired as to why God created woman and why it all went so wrong. The response to the first question is that women were created to keep the human species alive, even though, through the act of generation, she would lead her husband into evil. Woman was the source of all evil and the "agency" for man's Fall (Ambrose 1954).

Ambrose borrowed a great deal from Philo, in particular his belief that the male brain was rational, while the female brain was emotional (Clark 1998, 20–21). This meant that the male was superior to the female, although there was a close union between the two. Following this view of woman, Ambrose saw the female role as one of supporting the male. As the man is the stronger of the two, the woman should serve him and be subject to his authority and his advice. This was how a woman would enter paradise (Ambrose 1961, 301–305).

Ambrose reiterated these views in his letters, for example in his letter to the priests of the church at Vercelli: "Let a woman show deference, not be a slave to her husband; let her show she is ready to be guided, not coerced" (Ambrose 1954, 361). He clearly articulated the female role when he cited Saint Paul's letters to the Corinthians in a letter to Irenaeus: "Let your women keep silence in the churches, for it is not permitted them to speak, but to be submissive, as the Law says." Women were only allowed to learn through their husbands and at home. There is no public role for women, nor should they hold any position of authority: "But if they wish to learn anything let them ask their husbands at home." To this, he added that "women should not teach, or exercise authority over men" (Ambrose 1954, 436).

He criticized women for wearing color on their cheeks, for it "created an image of ugliness and deceit" (cited in Horowitz 1979). Further, women should be veiled and only men should engage in warfare (Ambrose 1954, 437). As Gillian Clark argued, men were identified with reason and women with desire in many of these early Christian thinkers. Ambrose, she contended, took his views about female irrationality from Philo (Clark 1998, 20–21).

Saint John Chrysostom

Saint John Chrysostom (ca. 347–407) was bishop of Constantinople during the late fourth and early fifth centuries. His ideas with respect to women are contained in his biblical homilies. According to John Chrysostom (or Golden-Mouthed, a name given to him after his death), there are the rulers (male) and the ruled (female) in human relationships. This view is based upon his reading of Genesis, chapters 1 to 3. Male and female are not created at the same time. Man is created first and is therefore superior to woman. John applied this view of the sexes to their appropriate roles in society. Women are meant to be in the household; they are prohibited to teach and preach in public. To cite John: "To think of women being shared in common or performing activities appropriate to men rendered humans inferior to the beasts" (cited in Clark 1979, 11).

John also opposed giving women military training, as Plato had recommended. This was "unnatural" for women. He wrote: "Plato's sin lay in imagining that women could and should do the same work as men." This was not the natural order of things and would "turn everything upside down" and "throw everything into confusion" (cited in Clark 1979, 12).

SAINT JEROME

Jerome (ca. 347–420) was primarily a translator, scholar, and biblical commentator. His views concerning the nature of women were similar to those of the other Church Fathers. Nevertheless, he wrote treatises on the education of girls and recommended the study of Greek and Latin (Clark 1979, 73). In fact, he admitted that many of the women in his circle had better language skills than he did. He refers to a certain Marcella who would replace him as a teacher of the Bible when he journeyed to Jerusalem. His ideal woman was a virgin, an ascetic. Marriage, he believed, was polluting and childbearing disgusting. Women would never achieve equality, however, and were denied full leadership roles (Radford Ruether 1974, 175).

Detail showing Saint Jerome from St. Jerome in His Study, *attributed to Joos van Cleve (Burstein Collection / Corbis)*

Jerome drew upon classical authorities such as Virgil to support his suppositions about the nature of women. He cited Virgil's *Aeneid* to back up his claim that women were of a changeable nature: "Varium et mutabile semper femina," meaning "Change is always woman" (cited in Radford Ruether 1974).

His treatise written against Jovinian, who opposed the ascetic movement of which Jerome was a leader, was his strongest statement against women. A good part of the book is dedicated to the disadvantages of marriage. He claimed that a woman was the cause of her husband's misfortunes. He used the example of Solomon who had "suffered" women and wives more than most and quoted him as saying: "Like a worm in wood, so an evil woman destroys her husband. . . . It is better to dwell in a wilderness than with a quarrelsome and passionate wife." Jerome himself wrote, "Any man who has been married knows how rare it is to find a wife without these vices" (cited in Hanna and Lawler 1997, 188).

Augustine (354–430) wrote several treatises that contributed to the debate about the nature and role of women. His ideas, although based on the Bible, were clearly influenced by the medical treatises of the day. This is particularly the case when he was writing about women and reproduction. Several passages from his *City of God* contain references to women and reproduction. There is a direct correlation between the female body and female inferiority. She is the receptacle for male sperm and provides nourishment for the embryo that grows from it (Borresen 1981, 42). The fact that the female body was visibly different meant there were fundamental differences between male and female and to deny this "would be a manifest absurdity" (Augustine 1982, 14, 22).

Augustine's *City of God* does much more than discuss women's role in reproduction, however, and together with *Two Books on Genesis against the Manichees* and *On the Literal Interpretation of Genesis,* it gives a picture of women as human beings and their role in society. Augustine believed that man and woman were both created on the sixth day and were equal before the Fall, and unlike Aristotle, he did not see woman as a defective male. In addition, he wrote: "You created man male and female, but in your spiritual grace, they are one. Your grace no more discriminates between them according to sex than it draws distinction between Jew and Greek or slave and freeman" (Augustine 1972, 1057). But Augustine argued that the sin of Adam was brought on by Eve's lust. Woman allowed herself to be seduced and then tempted (Augustine 1982, 167). In other words, Eve was responsible for the first sin. Augustine's emphasis on Eve was a continuation of the classical myth of Pandora, who released vice and passion into the world. His views were greatly influenced by the writings of Philo of Alexandria and Saint Ambrose (Power 1996, 131).

Augustine is close to Ambrose in his tract *Two Books on Genesis against the Manichees.* The subjection of woman to man is the normal ordering of things. Woman must be dominated and governed by man. Woman is by nature passive. The role of woman is to help man. He governs; she obeys. He is ruled by divine wisdom, she by man. Here Augustine invokes Saint Paul: Man's ruler is Christ; woman's is man (Augustine 1991, 15, 111). Woman is on the earth to produce children and to be man's helpmate. This role is appropriate for her because she has a weaker mind and is more childlike than man (Augustine 1982, 171).

Parts of *On the Literal Interpretation of Genesis* are more favorable to women. Here Augustine celebrates the union of male and female as instituted by God. If woman is made from man, that is a sign of the love that should unify male and female. However, he still argued that even before the Fall, woman was made to be submissive to man, although not ruled by him. He did believe that woman, inasmuch as she was a human being, "had a rational mind and . . . was made to the image of God" (Augustine 1982, 99, 171).

ISIDORE OF SEVILLE

Saint Isidore of Seville (560–636) was a Spanish archbishop, theologian, and Church Father. His encyclopedia, *Etymologias,* made a significant contribution to the diffusion of Christian views of women. In this work, men and women are defined in terms of strength (man) and weakness (woman): "Both differ in bodily strength and weakness, the man's strength being greater, the woman's less, so that she may be subject to the man . . ." (Isidore of Seville 1964, 50).

Women were also discussed in Isidore's major theological treatise, *Sententiae (Sentences)*. In his interpretation of the creation story, Adam and Eve are created together: Woman is made from man's rib, or side. Man is made in God's image, woman in that of man, which explains why man rules woman. Woman is created for the sole purpose of assisting man (Isidore 1998, 39).

Medical and Scientific Writers

Medical and scientific writers of the early Christian era and Middle Ages reinforced and complemented Christian views on the nature and role of women. Their views, along with those of the Christians, have persisted throughout Western civilization. This section will highlight the major ideas of the more well-known writers of this genre. All basically put forth similar views: that the female was inferior to the male due to the respective nature of their reproductive organs and that women needed to be kept under male authority (Bullough 1973, 485–501).

TRANSITION FIGURES

Soranus was a Greek physician who flourished in second-century Rome. He died circa A.D. 130. His influential work, *Gynecology,* put forth the view that females were different from males in that their reproductive organs differed (Cadden 1992, 27). Females did produce sperm; however, the male sperm was stronger, and thus the male was the more powerful of the two beings. The female role was to be a mother (Soranus 1956).

The Greek philosopher and physician Galen was born around A.D. 129 or 130, the year of Soranus's death. He was the most influential of the medical writers considered here during his own time and well into the Middle Ages. Like Aristotle, Galen thought that females were a less than perfect version of the male, but unlike Aristotle, he claimed they produced semen (Cadden 1992, 33–35). Here he agreed with Soranus. Although he posited that the uterus took an active role in reproduction, in his *On the Usefulness of the Parts of the Body,* Galen stated that "the female is less perfect than the male for one, principal reason—because she is colder; for if among animals the warm one is the more active, a colder animal would be less perfect than a warmer" (Galen 1968, 2: 628–630).

Muslim physicians and writers such as Avicenna (d. 1037) and Averroes (d. 1198) came out of the flourishing Islamic civilization that had kept Western thought alive when Western Europe was going through the Dark Ages. Avicenna was a Persian medical writer whose work was translated into Latin in the twelfth century. He is significant because his medical writings influenced such Western thinkers as the Dominican theologian Albertus Magnus, who was Thomas Aquinas's teacher. Avicenna argued that the male power was stronger than that of the female, an idea that he borrowed from Galen. He wrote that the process of reproduction was akin to making cheese—the male sperm was the clotting agent of the milk, while the female sperm acted as a coagulating agent. Thus, the male sperm, as the stronger part, was the more significant (Avicenna 1999, 1: 96, 230).

Averroes echoed these ideas in his *Commentary on Plato's Republic.* He believed that men and women do differ, but in degree. What this meant was that "men were more efficient than women." He did concede that women might excel in music, but the men must write the music and the women perform it (Averroes 1956, 164–165).

Saint Thomas Aquinas

Thomas Aquinas was a thirteenth-century doctor of the church. Aquinas took medieval Catholic theology and synthesized it with Aristotelian biology. His views of women were similar to his predecessors' in the sense that they were negative. In fact, he wrote in an era when the church was attempting to increase its power over women.

Although Aquinas used Aristotle's belief that woman was an imperfect male, a being outside nature, Aquinas did dispute Aristotle's view that women were simply misbegotten males. Females were to be included in the family of man for the purpose of reproduction. In other words, females did have a role or function in nature. This idea is

Saint Thomas Aquinas (1225–1274), Italian theologian and philosopher (Bettmann/Corbis)

found in his *Summa Theologica:* "But as regards human nature in general, woman is not misbegotten, but is intended by nature, and ordered for the work of generation. . . . Therefore in producing nature, God formed not only the male, but also the female" (cited in Borresen 1981, 315, 172). Woman was created from the side of man. Women were passive, while men were active. This follows from the Greek view that the woman's womb was merely a receptacle. Power rests in the male sperm (cited in Bullough 1973, 175). As theologian Rosemary Radford Ruether aptly argues, "Aristotle brought to Thomas a complete biology as well as an androcentric anthropology, which gave a 'scientific basis' to the anti-female tradition inherited from the Fathers" (Radford Ruether 1974, 216).

Women were, however, naturally inferior and thus subjected to men: "For good order would have been wanting in the human family if some were not governed by others wiser than themselves. So by such a kind of subjection woman is naturally subject to man, because in man the discretion of reason predominates." Because the female's role is reproductive and this function is on a lower level than the male's role, which is thinking, woman is subject to man (Aquinas 1947, 466–467). Woman is defective in reason, inferior to man, and thus subjected to him. Woman is in many ways like a child, under her husband's authority as a child is under the authority of her father (cited in Bullough 1973, 174–175). For these reasons, she was barred from the priesthood, as she is mentally incapable of holding a position of authority.

Aquinas followed his predecessor Tertullian in accepting the idea that women were evil and the cause of original sin. Remember that Tertullian held that women, as creatures who were responsible for all evil in the world, were also dangerous and irrational. Aquinas held that celibacy was preferable to marriage, since "nothing so casts down the manly mind from its height as the fondling of a woman" (cited in Bullough 1973, 174–175). Marriage was almost a necessary evil for the preservation of the species. Even in the family structure, Aquinas imitated Aristotle in the sense that the family was hierarchical in nature with the male at the head. "As the philosopher says [citing Aristotle's *Ethics*] the human male and female are united, not only for generation, as with other animals, but also for the purpose of domestic life, in which each has his or her particular duty, and in which the man is the head of the woman" (Aquinas 1947, 467). Women were to be kept out of the public sphere.

Women of the Convents

Although women never achieved equality in the church, life in the monastery offered them some access to knowledge, and for a time, even power. Western monasticism dates from the fourth century. The first Western monk, according to Jerome, was Athanasius of Alexandria, who visited Rome on two occasions, 335–337 and 339–346. The earliest known monastic rule was written by St. Benedict (ca. 480–550), who is commonly known as the father of Western monasticism (Lawrence 1984, 10–12).

WOMEN IN EARLY MONASTICISM

A woman named Macrina founded one of the earliest convents; she was the sister of St. Basil and in fact introduced him to monasticism. Her establishment dates from the late fourth century. Macrina transformed a family establishment into a monastic community. Many women followed the lead of Macrina and founded monasteries. They were able to assume positions of power unthinkable by the Church Fathers. Many became abbesses. What is important for the subject of this book is not so much what the abbesses did, but the fact that they were able to hold power and perform male roles. Most scholars have agreed that the degree of power an abbess possessed depended on the convent (Tucker and Liefeld 1987, 144). From the sixth to the twelfth centuries, some even assumed a position of equality with men (Bell 1973, 96). Early examples of such women were Saint Salaberga and Saint Fara. Both founded convents in France, with Salaberga founding seven convents in all and Fara founding the double monastery (Bateson 1899, 154). The double monastery was a religious community for both men and women in which the sexes lived apart but had one supervisor, most commonly a monk (male).

For the purposes of this book, what matters most is the access to knowledge that was possible in these institutions. Nuns were taught how to read and write. Literacy at this time was defined as the ability to read Latin for religious purposes. Men encouraged such learning for nuns, especially Saint Columban, a seventh-century missionary of the Irish church. He and other missionaries traveled throughout Europe advocating education. Education at this time was concerned more with the resolution of conflicts between the flesh and the spirit than with science even in the broadest sense, the pursuit of reliable knowledge. Thus subjects such as medicine, philosophy, and music were allotted secondary position.

The contemporary texts do not distinguish between male and female when discussing education. Women, they believed, could become male, or "virulized," through education, and such a transformation brought them closer to God. The ideal woman, according to men like Columban, was "the one who acquired masculine qualities and overcame the weakness of her sex" (Columban, cited in Anderson and Zinsser 2000, 184). Examples of such women were Hilda of Whitby in England and Gertrude in Gaul (Riché 1976, 325–329, 457). Hilda founded her monastery in 657. According to the Venerable Bede, she ardently advocated education and learning, and in fact her establishment was a center of learning and power, and kings and princes sought her advice (Lawrence 1984, 52).

Saint Leoba may be cited as a further illustration of a woman of intelligence, power, and significance in the early church. She was an abbess and a scholar at the abbey of Wimborne in Germany in the eighth century. For her sex and her era, she was very well educated. She was trained in the classics, theology, and canon law. According to her biographer, she was "extremely learned" (Rudolf 1954, 215). She was friendly with some of the most powerful male churchmen of her day, such as the bishop and missionary to the Germans, Saint Boniface. It was Boniface who named Leoba and her nuns to help him convert the Germans of Saxony (Radford Ruether and McLaughlin 1979, 99–130).

The phenomenon of the double monastery, which flourished in Europe from the seventh to tenth centuries, encouraged female education. Wealthy, aristocratic women who had their own land inherited from their families usually founded these establishments. They were exclusive, in the sense that learning was only available to the upper classes. Girls from the lower orders were admitted only as servants. Learned women who took care to educate their nuns governed these communities. They were in control of their own destiny and named their successors. Thus opportunities for learning existed in the convents for a short time in the Middle Ages. They provided women with a life outside the traditional one of marriage and children. However, with the reforms inaugurated by Pope Gregory VII, who was pope between 1073 and 1085, the limited education women did receive there was reduced. His reforms were not good for women, in the sense that he encouraged the fear of women, and they affected the position of women in schools and the new universities (Ogilvie 1986, 9).

During the eleventh century, the double monasteries reappeared in a changed form during a time of monastic revival. Unfortunately, there was no renaissance for women. Their power was gone, and nuns became subject to male control. Part of the reason for this change was a renewal in the old attitude toward women, dating from the Church Fathers, that women were a threat to salvation and thus should be shunned. In addition, at this time there was a new emphasis on the sacraments, the Eucharist in particular. Since women were prohibited from celebrating the mass, this tendency further marginalized them. Lay donors to monasteries desired to reap the spiritual benefits from their gifts, which consisted of having private masses said for their souls, and women obviously could not provide these benefits. Women in the new double monasteries could only be servants, especially in the new communities, such as the Cluniac monasteries founded throughout France. These women were not educated and were given only menial duties (Lawrence 1984, 178–179).

THE EFFECTS OF REFORM

During the twelfth century, in about 1140, John Gratian (d. 1160) consolidated Pope Gregory's reforms by the codification of canon law. Gratian was a theologian and canon law expert at the monastery of Saints Felix and Nabor at Bologna. Gratian himself held the misogynist view of women typical among Christian theologians of his time. Women were inferior to men and were required to be completely servile to them.

Canon law is defined as the "complex of juridical norms enacted and enforced by the competent authorities of the Catholic Church." More specifically, from the period of the fourth century, it included "all disciplinary laws enacted by the Synods as distinct from Imperial legislation" (Rocca 1959, 3). Canon law was based on civil (primarily Roman) law, canons of church councils, papal decretals, the Bible, and the Church Fathers. Gratian, in order to "prove" the inferiority of women in his compilation of canon law, reproduced much from St. Paul, Roman law, and the most influential Fathers: Augustine, Jerome, and Ambrose. Woman is "the body of man" (cited in Metz 1985, 381), said Gratian, basing himself on St. Paul's Epistle to the Ephesians 5:22, 24; 1 Timothy 2:14; and 1 Corinthians 11:7–10 and 14:34–35.

Woman was thus in a position of dependency and should be subjected to male authority in all realms of life. From Augustine, Gratian took the notion that the natural order of things was that woman was created to serve man. Women could not teach or exercise public functions, such as playing the role of witness. The role of judge, which women had exercised in some ancient cultures, including biblical Israel, was now barred to them. According to canon law, only men could be ordained as priests. Eve was portrayed as the source of all evil, and the female body as dangerous. All previous female contributions to knowledge, that is, to science in the broadest sense, were forgotten. What made *Gratian's Decree,* as his compilation of canon law was called, significant was that for the first time views that had been around for some time were codified into a formal legal code. They were no longer simply the beliefs and opinions of a handful of churchmen, however influential; they were now formalized into law.

THE FOUNDING OF UNIVERSITIES AND THEIR IMPACT ON WOMEN

In addition to the setbacks women faced with the codification of canon law, they were further hindered in their attempt to do science by the establishment of the university, an institution that grew directly from the church. Universities began either as monasteries or cathedral schools—all-male institutions at Paris, Oxford, Bologna, and Padua. Once again, the church played a pivotal role in the exclusion of women from science. This time, it was in the form of the institution of the university. With the exception of the Italian model, which was for the most part secular in nature, the university systematically excluded women from science.

From the end of the twelfth century, the institutional home of science was the university. Historians posit that the development of modern science began with the establishment of these universities (see Lindberg 1978, 120). The chief subjects studied in the university were math, astronomy, and logic. The universities at Paris and Oxford reached their pinnacle in terms of scientific importance during the thirteenth and fourteenth centuries when the Bologna and Padua universities took them over. The southern universities such as Bologna and Padua allowed greater lay involvement, including some married professors. Apparently, in one case, a professor of canon law at Bologna named Giovanni d'Andrea allowed his daughter, Novella, to lecture for him from behind a curtain if he had to miss class. Christine de Pizan recounted this story in *The Book of the City of Ladies*. Scholars seem to have accepted it as true. (See Labalme 1980, note 49, p. 114.)

The faculty of arts in the Italian universities was associated with medicine rather than theology. However, even the Italian universities were not free from the influence of the church as they were ultimately under the control of the pope (Noble 1992, 167). Unlike their northern counterparts, some Italian universities admitted women before the late nineteenth century. However, these women did not study science. There is evidence that a certain Elena Cornaro received a philosophy doctorate from Padua on June 25, 1678. (There is a copy of the document in the Archivio Antico dell'Università di Padove, MS 365, fols. 24v–26v; see Labalme 1980, note 53, p. 115.)

Still, the fact that universities grew out of the monastery and the cathedral school meant that women were barred from attending and thus from being exposed to the sciences. As Achille Luchaire has adeptly argued with respect to the French situation, "the university was a brotherhood almost entirely composed of clerics; masters and students had the tonsure; collectively they constituted a church institution." Further, he posited that rather than being centers of free thinking, the "universities were ecclesiastical organizations and were organized accordingly" (Luchaire 1912, 72–73).

In England, at Oxford and Cambridge, the situation was very similar to that of the Continent in that only males were admitted until the nineteenth century. The monastic legacy was present both in the communal life of the students and in the fact that there was a strong presence of both regular clergy, monks who lived according to a rule, and secular clergy, the parish priests who lived amongst the ordinary folk (Cobban 1999, 1–3).

The founding of the Franciscan and Dominican orders in the twelfth and thirteenth centuries reinforced the celibate, all-male world of the university. Prominent scholars such as Albertus Magnus, Thomas Aquinas, and Duns Scots emerged from these orders. These and other similar orders, which were all-male and generally misogynistic in outlook, "shaped European education for centuries . . ." (French 1985, 160).

Although the church-sanctioned fear of women that was institutional-ized by canon law negatively affected the opportunities women had to learn and decreased their independence in the convents, scholarship for women did continue. One example from the later twelfth century comes from Hohenburg in Alsace, where the abbess Herrad (?–ca.1196) authored or was in charge of the writing of an illustrated encyclopedia called the *Hortus deliciarum* (Garden of Delights). It was an all-encompassing work in terms of subject matter and included sections about astronomy and geography (Ogilvie 1986, 9). The work was written for her nuns between 1160 and 1170.

The works of Saint Hildegard of Bingen (1098–1179) represent the high point of scientific or knowledgeable writings by a woman of the Middle Ages. What is interesting is that she was active during the period of the reform movement. Her life and work are illustrative of the contradictions within the church. She operated within the exist-ing and often confining parameters of the church, yet had a great deal of freedom. Perhaps this was due to the fact that she did not question ultimate authority. She wrote in one of her major scientific works, *Causae et Curae* (Causes and Cures) that the nature of woman is "weak and fragile and a vessel for man" (cited in Newman 1987, 128). Her activities and other writings reveal that she really believed the opposite.

One of her biographers suggested that there were a number of reasons that the church tolerated and even revered Hildegard, even though she was a female authority figure functioning in a male-domi-nated system that had no use for intelligent women (Flanagan 1998, 13–15). In the first place, she never claimed to be speaking on her own behalf. She maintained that, through her visions, she was speak-ing for God. She revealed these visions in a letter written in 1146 to Saint Bernard, abbot of Clairvaux: "Father, I am greatly disturbed by a vision which has appeared to me through divine revelation. . . ." As she continued, she belittled herself as a woman, saying that although she is "indeed more than wretched in my womanly condition, I have from earliest childhood seen great marvels which my tongue has no power to express but which the Spirit of God has taught me that I may believe" (Hildegard of Bingen 1994, 27). In her work *Vitas* (Life), Hildegard related that when her works and visions were made known to the church of Mainz, "all agreed that they came from God and from the gift of prophecy which the prophets spoke forth in former times" (cited in Flanagan 1998, 13). Second, it could be argued that Hilde-

German composer and abbess of St. Rupert's Mount, Hildegard von Bingen (1098–1179), whose writings were inspired by visions. (Hulton/Archive by Getty Images)

gard was following the tradition of female prophets in the Bible. The fact that God chose women to be prophets was not seen as contradicting their inferior status: God tended to speak through the weak rather than the strong.

Hildegard of Bingen was the tenth child of a noble family, Spanheim, and, as was the custom of the day, she was placed in a convent at the age of eight. The convent was Benedictine and located in Disibodenberg, near Bingen, hence her name Hildegard of Bingen. Bingen is situated close to Mainz. Her education was minimal at best: She was taught a reading knowledge of Latin by another nun, her aunt Jutta, who cared for her. Her visions began at the age of five (Flanagan 1998, 44). When Jutta died in 1136, Hildegard became abbess of the community.

Soon after Jutta's death, Hildegard had a vision that told her to establish her own convent; it is called Rupertsberg. Rupertsberg is located in the Rhine Valley. From here, Hildegard wielded considerable power. In addition to her religious or theological works, *Scivias* (Know the Ways of the Lord) and *Liber vitae meritorum* (The Book of Life's Merits), she wrote several scientific and medical treatises. It is her medical and scientific works, *Liber subtilatum diversarum naturarum creaturarum* (The Book of Subtleties of the Diverse Nature of Things), *Physica* (Natural History), and *Causae et Curae* (Causes and Cures), that have been the most controversial. In the early part of the twentieth century, an eminent historian of science, Charles Singer, even doubted her authorship because she used both German and Latin words in her scientific works. Scholars today have proved they are indeed her works. In recent years, most Hildegard scholars have agreed that she was the first female contributor to the debate on the nature of woman during the Middle Ages. Bernhard W. Scholz wrote that she "was the first medieval woman to reflect and write at length on women" (1980, 361); Barbara Newman, the first scholar to write a full-length study of Hildegard, asserted: "We may boldly claim Hildegard as the first Christian thinker to deal seriously and positively with the feminine as such . . ." (1987, xvii). Further, she seemed to grasp the workings of the human body and offered many herbal remedies that German scientists and doctors still see as of value today. Two Germans, Wighard Strehlow and Gottfried Hertzka, a medical doctor and a chemist, have written a book entitled *Hildegard of Bingen's Medicine,* published in 1988.

The major subjects dealt with by Hildegard in her medical work are reproduction and generation, male-female sex differences, and female disorders of the body. Although she did not propose anything new in her scientific works, she remains important, for her male contemporaries took her contributions to science seriously in her day. Given the attitude toward women and their ability to reason, this is incredible.

Her contribution to the contemporary debate lies in the fact that she saw female nature in a much more positive light than Aristotle and the Church Fathers. They did influence her, especially Saint Augustine, but her interpretation was different. Her creation story is similar to that of the Fathers: Eve was created from Adam's rib. In agreement with the classical authors, she wrote that Eve was colder and moister than Adam. Where Hildegard was original and different in her story of creation was in her emphasis. Whereas most Christian writings focused on the evil nature of Eve, as seen in her role in bringing about the first sin, Hildegard did not focus on the Fall. In other words, the evil nature of Eve was not central to her works as it was to the Church Fathers. Moreover, she held Adam and Eve equally responsible for the Fall and attributed most of the blame to the Devil. She explained the Fall in Vision Two of the *Scivias:* "Eve . . . was invaded by the Devil through the seduction of the serpent for her own downfall . . ." (Hildegard 1990, 77; see document section for full text). Hildegard believed that Mary superseded Eve, so she tended to emphasize the goodness of Mary rather than the evilness of Eve (Cadden 1992, 74–75). Hildegard thus viewed females in a much more positive light than her predecessors.

Hildegard came much closer to seeing male and female as equal than her male contemporaries did. Woman, according to Hildegard, is man's helper. They are different but equal. She stresses the interdependence between male and female rather than the superiority of one and the inferiority of the other. "Man cannot be man without woman, and woman not woman without man. . . . One complements the other and in the union of love they become one" (cited in Scholz 1980, 375). Neither is superior in terms of intelligence or morality. She wrote: "Woman was created for man's sake and man was made for woman's" (cited in Newman 1987, 99). Hildegard saw a natural dependency between the sexes, each with its own strengths and weaknesses. Man is superior in terms of physical strength—he was made from the earth—while woman possesses practical handicraft skills (Newman 1987, 96). Woman was made from the air.

Extant correspondence testifies to the fact that Hildegard was taken seriously by both secular and ecclesiastical authorities of her day. About four hundred of her letters remain. The majority of these were written to other members of the church, such as heads of monastic orders, bishops, archbishops, and even popes. She wrote, for example, to Popes Anastasius, Hadrian IV, and Alexander III on different matters, from criticizing Anastasius for his tolerance of "depraved" individuals to voicing complaints about her former monastery of St. Disibodenberg (Hildegard 1994, 44–46). She was approached for advice on topics as diverse as theology, monastic discipline, and church organization. Pope Eugenius took a very positive attitude toward Hildegard and her works. He read Hildegard's *Scivias* to members of the Synod of Trier. Bernard of Clairvaux asked this same pope to name Hildegard as a prophet (Hildegard 1994, 31).

In the secular realm, Hildegard corresponded with the Holy Roman Emperor Frederick Barbarossa, Count Philip of Flanders, and German king Conrad III of the Holy Roman Emperor (who led the German crusades). She gave advice to all three about secular and spiritual matters (Flanagan 1998, 158–159).

Hildegard of Bingen was a medieval nun who went against everything the church taught about women at the time: She was the leader of a community; she was a preacher; and she was a writer about many subjects, including science. She was the first female German scientist and medical writer. All of her works were done as God's creation rather than her own and thus accepted at the time by male authorities. The prominence of women like Hildegard was short-lived. With the reforms in the monasteries and convents during the twelfth century, women's voices were effectively silenced. We do not hear again from women until the time of Christine de Pizan in the 1400s.

The Querelle des Femmes:
The Debate about Women

The *querelle des femmes* (quarrel about women) was a debate, fought out principally in France, over the role and value of women in European society, that raged for over three hundred years in the form of thousands of tracts, treatises, and pamphlets on the nature of woman and her role. This chapter covers the first and second periods of the debate, the first spanning the thirteenth through the fifteenth centuries, but focused on one central writer, Christine de Pizan, and the second including the sixteenth century. The revival of the debate in the seventeenth century will be covered in a later chapter.

Christine de Pizan

Christine de Pizan (1364–1430) is European history's first feminist writer, in the sense that she consciously wrote against the contemporary misogynist views of women. She is the dominant feminist figure during the fourteenth and fifteenth centuries (Albistur and Armogathe 1977, 53). Although not a scientist herself, de Pizan wrote about scientific subjects and argued on behalf of women's reason and women's capacity to be scientists.

Christine de Pizan was the daughter of Thomas de Pizan, doctor, astrologer, and counsellor of the Republic of Venice. In 1368, four years after Christine's birth, the family moved to France, where Thomas became private counsellor and court astrologer to King Charles V. The most striking aspect of de Pizan's childhood was that she was able to get a scientific education in spite of her father's disagreement. As de Pizan herself wrote, "My father was a grammarian and philosopher who did not think there was any value in teaching women science" (cited in Albistur and Armogathe 1977, 54). However, he did believe in teaching girls literature. Christine's mother was not much better. She thought that girls should occupy themselves

with chiffons and prevented Christine from furthering her scientific education. Her mother's views were conventional, in that she wanted to provide her daughter with domestic training in preparation for marriage (Albistur and Armogathe 1977, 54).

At the age of fifteen, Christine was married to Etienne de Castel, notary and secretary to Charles V, who was ten years her senior. He encouraged her studies. She read Thomas Aquinas's works, including his view of the creation of women, which she rejected. She believed that the creation of the soul preceded that of the body; therefore male and female were equal (Richards 2000, 201–202).

Unfortunately for Christine, her husband died in 1389 during an epidemic. Her father had already died in 1386, so Christine was left alone at age twenty-five with no means of support and with three children and two young brothers. In this situation, she became a writer to support herself and her family. In addition to her participation in the debate, she wrote ballads and was the official biographer of Charles V, who had died in 1380. Throughout her life, she wrote on diverse subjects in many genres (Pizan 1982). What is of concern here is not the complete corpus of her works, but her contribution to the debate about the nature and role of women in society.

The Pre-Renaissance Debate: The Roman de la Rose and the Querelle des Femmes, Round One

The first stage of the great debate about the nature and role of women was inaugurated by a work written by two different authors in thirteenth-century France. This stage of the debate, known as the *querelle de la rose* (Debate of the Rose), started with the publication of an allegorical poem about love called the *Roman de la rose* (The Romance of the Rose), a major work of medieval literature. In fact, one scholar observed that "no literary production of the Middle Ages was more widely discussed than the *Roman de la rose*" (McDowell Richardson 1929, 12–13). The poem was written by two authors almost forty years apart, the first part in 1225 by Guillaume de Lorris (1212–1237), about whom we know almost nothing. The poem celebrated courtly love, and thus took a respectful attitude toward women. The lady symbolized by the rose, by the conventions of courtly love, was at liberty to demand feudal obedience from her lover. Lorris died before he could complete the entire poem.

The second part of the poem was written by Jean de Meun, who took an entirely different view toward women. De Meun was part of a new generation of writers who did not celebrate courtly love. He was a product of the University of Paris, educated in the law, medicine, theology, and philosophy. He turned the courtly love poem into an attack on women in the form of a fable, portraying them as vicious, perfidious, and evil animals that must be controlled. The rose should be possessed by a man and bear children (McLeod 1976, xvii–xxv; Campaux 1865, 8–9). It was this continuation of the poem that set off the *querelle de la rose,* which involved almost all the French writers, poets, and philosophers of the day, as well as their readers. The major participants on the misogynist side in the *querelle de la rose* were Jean de Montreuil, provost of Lille; Gontier Col, the king's secretary and humanist; and his brother Pierre Col, canon of Paris and Tournay. According to one of the participants in the debate, Pierre

Col, approximately 7,000 people took part in the debate (Rigaud 1973, 63).

On the other side of the dispute, defending women, we find Christine de Pizan, the only female who participated in this debate. De Pizan entered into the debate with her *Epistre au dieu d'amours* (Epistle to the God of Love), written in 1399. In this poem, de Pizan portrayed a group of outraged women who had asked the God of Love to transmit their complaints to an assembly of gods. Their main concern was the moral rehabilitation of women—they discussed the responsibility of each sex in love. They did not state that all women were virtuous, but that not all women were bad as claimed by de Meun in the *Roman de la rose*. There were good and honest women as well as the not so honest. De Pizan sent copies of her letter to many important figures, Jean de Montreuil, Gontier Col, and even Queen Ysabeau of Bavaria and Guillaume de Tignonville, provost of Paris and counsellor to King Charles VI (Piaget 1858, 73). Her goal was to "sustain the honour and praise of women" (McLeod 1976, 68). For the first time, de Pizan defended the intellectual capacity of women. The ideas contained here were more fully developed in her later work, *Le Livre de la cité des dames* (The Book of the City of Ladies, 1404–1405) (Rigaud 1973, 64). Pierre Col responded to de Pizan's *Epistre au dieu d'amours* (Epistle to the God of Love, 1399) in a letter outlining the incapacity of women. Col accused her of forgetting to guard her modesty (Langlois 1919, 29–48).

The quarrel continued with Gontier Col, who wrote to de Pizan in 1402 asking her to retract her ideas. She refused. In the meantime, Jean de Gerson, theologian and chancellor of the University of Paris, had written his *Vision faite contre le roman de la rose* (Vision Made against the Romance of the Rose), which was not intended primarily as a defense of women, but which in fact included such a defense. The Col brothers responded to Gerson and to de Pizan's letters. They recommended that Christine de Pizan "should not conduct herself like a weak writer of poison pen letters and be left blinded by her pride" (BN MS franc. 1563 fol. 185, cited in Piaget 1858, 70). For their part, de Pizan and Gerson soon after replied to Pierre Col, stating that he would find the arguments answering his attacks already present in a letter she had written to Jean de Montreuil. De Pizan was tired of all the debates, which could be endless. She wished that de Meun's friends would leave her in peace. She felt they could continue their dispute with Gerson. In their joint letter, Gerson defended de Pizan as a "remarkable and virile woman" (Letter dated 2 October 1402 MS 835, cited in Piaget 1858, 72).

These exchanges prompted de Pizan to expound her views in a fuller form. She asked herself why so many clerics and learned men despised women. She wrote that one could not read one book without at least one to two pages of slander against women. Thus she decided to write her own books. The most important of these to the debate under consideration here were *Le Livre de la cité des dames* (The Book of the City of Ladies, 1404–1405) and *Le Livre des trois vertus* (The Book of the Three Virtues, 1405). Here she protested against the treatment of her gender. She created a city of women that was aided by three female deities: Reason, Uprightness, and Justice. In this city, women would be educated. She argued that women were as capable as men of learning, and this learning included scientific learning.

De Pizan asked Reason whether God had ever wished to ennoble the mind of Woman with the loftiness of the sciences. Did God provide women with a "clever enough mind for this"? De Pizan went on to state how much she wanted to know the answer, for men were claiming that "women can learn only a little." Lady Reason replied: "You know quite well that the opposite of their opinion is true. . . . If it were customary to send daughters to school like sons, and if they were taught the natural sciences, they would learn as thoroughly and understand the subtleties of all the arts and sciences as well as sons. . . ." She concluded with the premise that women were actually more capable than men of inquiry: "Just as women have more delicate bodies than men, weaker and less able to perform many tasks, so do they have minds that are freer and sharper whenever they apply themselves" (Pizan 1982, 62–63). Although women have at least equal intelligence to men, women know a great deal less than men do. When de Pizan asked Lady Reason why this is the case, Reason responded that society's expectations of women are that "it is enough for them to perform the usual duties to which they are ordained. . . . The public does not require them to get involved in the affairs which men are commissioned to execute . . ." (Pizan 1982, 64).

To further argue her case for women scientists, de Pizan's Goddess of Reason provided many examples of female scientists and inventors from antiquity: Proba the Roman who had mastered the liberal arts, Sappho the poet, Minerva the inventor of machines for making cloth and a harness and armor from iron (Pizan 1982, 65–73). When she wrote about Sappho's achievements, de Pizan borrowed heavily from one of the few male proponents of women during the late Middle Ages, Boccaccio. Boccaccio's *De claris mulieribus* (Concerning Famous Women, 1355–1359) was a compendium of 104 famous women and their lives, the first collection of biographies of women (Boccaccio

1963, ix). He was one of the few men of his time who considered women to be capable of intellectual pursuits. De Pizan quoted him on Sappho: "From what Boccaccio says about her, it should be inferred that the profundity of both her understanding and of her learned books can be only known and understood by men of great perception and learning, according to the testimony of the ancients" (Pizan 1982, 67).

De Pizan, unlike other writers of her time, held that education for females should be all-inclusive. Even though Boccaccio wrote about famous women, he still restricted female education to subjects of a religious nature. Another near contemporary, Leonardo Bruni (1369–1444), a well-known Italian humanist and secretary to the papal chancery from 1405, thought girls' education should be moral in nature (Bell 1976, 178). De Pizan's opinion was that girls should be sent to school at an early age with their brothers—this would benefit the boys, given that the girls' minds had a "freer and sharper understanding" (Pizan 1982, 74).

De Pizan was not only the first proponent of female education in France, she was the first woman in history we know of who supported herself by her pen. *The Book of the City of Ladies* is her most popular work. Copies were owned by Queen Elizabeth I, Marguerite of Navarre (sister to Francis I, king of France), and Mary Queen of Scots.

In *The Book of the Three Virtues* (1404), de Pizan addressed women from all classes, from noble and bourgeois women to women of the lowest order. She assigned an education and career for these women depending upon their class. For instance, a noblewoman should study the Bible, Seneca, common law, and the laws of warfare. Middle-class women should be taught how to manage estates.

To return to the debate, in May of 1402 de Pizan continued it with her *Dit de la rose* (Tale of the Rose). She continued to denounce de Meun's attitude in this pamphlet. At this stage, an important ally came to her side, Jean de Gerson, who wrote a long treatise (*Tractatus contra Romantium de Rosa* [Treatise against the Romance of the Rose] 1402) expounding his views on women and condemning the *Roman de la rose* for its injustice to women. Gerson's intervention on de Pizan's behalf temporarily brought the debate to a conclusion, until Martin Le Franc, canon of Lausanne, played an important role by taking the same side as Gerson in poetic form in the *Tractatus* in *Le Champion des dames* (The Champion of Ladies), a poem of 24,000 verses. Le Franc was born around 1410 in the county of Aumale in Normandy. After completing his studies in Paris, he became an assistant to the Council of Bâle in Arras in 1435. We do not know the date of publication of his *Le Champion des dames,* but scholars usually date its composition between 1440 and 1442. We do know that it was reissued in 1530 (Piaget 1858, 10–18, 32).

Le Franc came to the defense of women in a similar fashion to de Pizan, and attacked all those who slandered them. His work, subtitled *Contenant la défense des dames contre Malbouche et ses consorts et victoires d'icelles* (Containing the Defense of the Ladies Against Bad Mouth and His Consorts and Their Victories), played a major part in the debate. Le Franc brought together all the arguments for and against women. One of the main reasons why women were attacked so much in the later Middle Ages was the tremendous influence of the church thinkers and Roman law upon clerics, who were the major writers. Le Franc not only opposed the views of de Meun, but also those of the Church Fathers, including Augustine, Tertullian, Gregory, Ambrose, and Jerome, which constituted the orthodoxy of the time. In essence, argued Le Franc, de Meun provided nothing new in his arguments, but merely elaborated upon the works of the Church Fathers. Le Franc wrote much about women and reason in *Le Champion des dames.* He wrote that women were "welcome" in the house of reason, that "women defend reason which they hide well." He continued to argue that "reason is a sage and good woman . . ." (Le Franc 1968, 25).

The quarrel was not resolved during Christine de Pizan's lifetime. It would be renewed during the Renaissance. Almost one hundred years after the initial publication of LeFranc's *Champion,* the Toulousian poet Gratien du Pont replied to Le Franc in a long poem, *Controverses des sexes masculine et feminine* (Controversies of the Male and Female Sexes), published in 1534. This violent invective against women stated that "woman as Eve's daughter was vain, flirtatious and full of infinite lies." In the 1541 edition du Pont wrote that woman was the "chief cause of the Fall of humanity, original source of the first sin, and had contributed nothing to mankind (du Pont 1541, 180).

The Renaissance and Women

The historical era known as the Renaissance is often dated from approximately 1350, when it can be seen as beginning in Italy, to 1650. During these years, a great deal changed in terms of how people perceived the world. For men, the period of the Renaissance meant freedom for the individual, a spirit of inquiry, reason, and a questioning of traditional values. Renaissance humanist Pico della Mirandola summed up this attitude in his *Dignity of Man,* where we read about the perfection of man, of man as the greatest creation of God (Pico della Mirandola in Perry, vol. 1, 1999). One would have expected this attitude to transfer itself to women. Unfortunately, this was not the case. The period of the Renaissance was not a liberating time for women.

Joan Kelly stressed this view—that there was no Renaissance for women—in her groundbreaking work, "Did Women Have a Renaissance?" Kelly responded to this question in the negative by asserting that there was no renaissance for women, at least not during the era commonly referred to as the Renaissance (Kelly 1984, 19). She attempted to demonstrate that, far from the freeing experience that men enjoyed during the fifteenth and sixteenth centuries, women experienced a contraction of freedoms in both the public and private spheres (Kelly 1984, 20). Women's sexuality was more tightly regulated; women's economic and political roles were more narrowly limited. Education was negligible and not designed to prepare women for the public sphere (see Chapter 4 of this book for details on education), and the ideological framework of society, highly patriarchal in nature, did not allow women the same freedom as men. Thus, rather than a period of liberation, the Renaissance actually meant a step backward for women. The debate during the sixteenth century focused on the differences between male and female.

More recently, historian Merry E. Wiesner inquired as to whether or not the Renaissance decreased women's freedoms. In order to answer this question, she asserted that one cannot simply accept the traditional meaning and connotations of the word "freedom" because that definition was developed around the male interpretation of freedom (Wiesner 1986, 1). Instead, Wiesner attempted to discern how women living during the Renaissance would have viewed freedom. She developed the idea that "'freedom' to them meant the ability to participate in public life" (Wiesner 1986, 3). Based on this new definition of freedom, Wiesner went on to find that women's access to public life decreased during the Renaissance and therefore they lost freedom in that sense.

During the Renaissance, traditional female roles were stressed. There was much emphasis on marriage and the family. Traits such as obedience, female chastity, modesty, beauty, and humility were stressed as female virtues. Catholic celibacy had been a failure. The more and more highly educated students of the classics, called humanists, and the Protestant Reformers agreed that women's role was first and foremost in the family. The Black Death, an epidemic of the bubonic plague, had left Europe's population devastated, and thus increased importance was placed on the female reproductive role. At the same time, during the first half of the sixteenth century, we find the growth of female influence, especially in the fields of literature and politics, but not in science. The influential women of the period were concentrated in the royal and aristocratic courts of France, England, Spain, and Italy, and included women such as Marguerite d'Angoulême, Jeanne d'Aragon, Vittoria Colonna, Louise Labé, Anne of Brittany, Anne Boleyn, Catherine de Médicis, Mary Stuart, and Queen Elizabeth I (Le Franc 1914, vol. 2, 270).

Throughout the Renaissance, education was the subject of discussion for many critics and writers. One of the most significant of these was the Spanish scholastic Juan Vives, who wrote *De institutione feminae Christianae* (On the Education of a Christian Woman) in three books published in 1523. Vives was the humanist who paid the closest attention to education. He was employed by the court of Catherine of Aragon, and he drafted an educational proposal for Mary, Catherine's daughter. For Vives, whose ideas were typical of the age, female education meant preparation for marriage. He was adamant that women should remain in the private rather than the public sphere. Intellectual education should play a part in women's education, but emphasis should be placed on the domestic arts such as sewing and cooking. He wrote: "I am of the opinion that we should take care of the education of young girls more than is generally thought. . . . They should be taught to be modest and sober" (cited in Rousselot 1881, 37). Serious education during the Renaissance meant a humanist education, in other words the study of the classics, which at the time meant all the learning connected to Greek and Latin. As Catherine R. Eskin recently noted, most women were not taught Latin, a necessity for education during the Renaissance. Latin was exclusively taught to males: "By cutting off access to Latin, the educational system effectively cut off women from the only education that was valued in Renaissance society" (cited in Whitehead 1999, 110).

The Protestant Reformation of the sixteenth century brought about changes in education with a belief that everyone should be able to read and interpret the Bible. This was particularly true in German states and cities where laws were passed that instituted universal education. Protestant Reformers like Martin Luther believed that girls should receive a Christian education for the purpose of raising Christian children (Rousselot 1881, 37–38).

The *querelle des femmes* was renewed with great ardor during the sixteenth century, when France began to fully experience the Renaissance. A possible explanation for this renewed enthusiasm may be the rediscovery of classical texts and of the work of the Church Fathers. As indicated earlier in this chapter, the debate about women was fought out most vigorously in France. The classical views of women as deformed males and the Roman legal notion of the female as fragile still held great currency in France. The medical community taught that something had gone wrong during gestation to produce a female. Theologians, in particular monks and priests, taught that women were evil and more inclined to sin than the male sex (Screech 1958, 6).

The Querelle *during the Renaissance, Round Two*

The *querelle* continued throughout the period of the Renaissance and involved almost all French as well as other European writers, in addition to their readers. Renaissance writers concerned themselves more exclusively with the access of women to knowledge than the late medieval writers, who had been for the most part more concerned with love and morality. But as we have seen, even in the late Middle Ages, Christine de Pizan and Martin Le Franc began the change, as the first two writers to question whether women were indeed inevitably inferior and intellectual weak in comparison to men. Thus de Pizan and Le Franc had introduced the question of female capacity to absorb and even create knowledge to the *querelle*.

Lula McDowell Richardson argued that there were three distinct periods of the *querelle* during the sixteenth century: between 1500 and 1542 when arguments were theological in nature; between 1542 and 1560 when they were characterized by Neoplatonic ideas of gallantry; and finally, toward the last quarter of the century, when writers turned their attention to the question of female education (McDowell Richardson 1929, 80). There were three prevailing attitudes during the century: women were at best a necessary evil; women were of some value, albeit limited; women were as good as men, with some writers even arguing for female superiority (McDowell Richardson 1929, 80).

As the sixteenth century opened, the woman controversy became more serious in nature. It benefited from the progress of knowledge, especially the rediscovery of writings from antiquity, developments in medicine and all observational sciences, and the new emphasis on juridical studies. Most treatises that dealt with women in the sixteenth century were negative. The major contributors to the debate during the first half of the sixteenth century were André Tiraqueau, Rabelais, Jean de Nevizan, Erasmus, J. de Pontalais, Roger de Collerye, Pierre Gringore, Guillaume de Postel, Heinrich Cornelius Agrippa, and Gratien du Pont.

At the beginning of the century, a French jurisconsult (specialist in questions of the law), André Tiraqueau (1488–1558), led the antifemale group of writers. Although an often forgotten figure today, Tiraqueau was a leading legal humanist in his time. In 1513, he published his *De legibus connubialibus et iure maritale* (Concerning Conjugal and Moral Law), which formed part of a commentary on the local customs of the city of Poitou. The title of the entire work has been translated as *The Laws of Marriage Commentary on Matrimonial Laws of Poitou*. This work became a massive text in legal scholarship. It was reissued in 1515, 1524, and 1546 (LeFranc 1914, 2: 266–267). Tiraqueau's *De legibus* intensified the *querelle* because of its violence and its use of arguments and theories based on ancient texts that were hitherto unknown to most participants in the debate. Tiraqueau used extensive citations from authoritative sources such as the Bible; classical authors, including Aristotle, Homer, and Plutarch; the Church Fathers; and medieval writers like Albertus Magnus to prove his thesis that women were weak, fragile, humid, and sickly. Tiraqueau cited 276 authors in total in his work, ranging from the ancients to modern doctors and historians (Barat 1904, 150).

Tiraqueau's major hypothesis was one that was now commonplace in the literature: Woman is inferior to man; she must obey man; this is the natural order of things. Strength and reason belong to man, not woman (Tiraqueau 1569, 6–31). Further, Tiraqueau argued that women were easily deceived; they were followers of new cults and "helpers of heresy." Because of woman's nature (weak, imbecilic, loving of domination), she should not become involved in legal disputes in legal or customary courts (Tiraqueau 26, 31). Tiraqueau, who was a friend of Rabelais, had a tremendous influence on his thought as well as that of Erasmus. Both borrowed ideas from him concerning women.

The French humanist and medical doctor François Rabelais (1483–1553), now chiefly known for the outrageous humor and biting satire of his fiction, was part of a group of humanists, primarily jurists, who met at Tiraqueau's residence in Fontenay-le-Comte. He had been acquainted with Tiraqueau since his youth and had collaborated with Tiraqueau on the second edition of *De legibus,* published in 1524 (Barat 1904, 150–151). Rabelais's views followed Tiraqueau's almost to the letter: Woman is inferior to man and must obey him;

this is the way of nature. The female sex is fickle and impertinent in nature. The only possible reasons for their creation are for pleasing man and for the perpetuation of the race (Rabelais 1870–1873, 69). Chapters 30 and 31 of Rabelais's *Tiers Livre* contain a summary of *De Legibus*. Woman's role is to be wife and mother. Women have meditated evil against men since the beginning of the world because they wish to control men. "The women, at the beginning of the world or soon after, conspired together to flay the men alive completely, because the men want to lord it over them everywhere. . . . O the great frailty of the female sex! They began to skin man, or flay him as Catullus puts it . . . over six thousand years ago, and yet they have still got only to the head of it" (Rabelais 1992, 310). In spite of all this antifeminism, Rabelais does, in one section of *Pantagruel,* advocate female learning and even teaching the queen of the sciences, theology, to women (Screech 1958, 26). This was very daring for his era and something not even the more liberal Montaigne advocated later in the century. The more common attitude was that propounded by Tiraqueau, who wrote about Marguerite of Navarre's writings on theology, "You would hardly believe they were done by a woman at all" (Tiraqueau 1546, 101).

Tiraqueau's work, along with that of another jurisconsult, Jean de Nevizan (d. 1540), figured among the most-read writings of the first thirty years of the sixteenth century (Le Franc 1914, 2: 261). Jean de Nevizan was the author of *Sylvae nuptialis libri sex* (Silvae Book of Sex and Marriage), written in Italian and published in Paris in 1521, then Lyons in 1526 and 1572, Venice in 1570 and 1584, and Cologne in 1656. The first two books of his work, *Non est nubendum* (Not to Be Married), examined the reasons to avoid marriage; the next two, *Est nubendum* (To Be Married), provided reasons in favor of it. Nevizan based a good deal of his work on Plato and Cicero and used their arguments for avoiding marriage. The main significance of Nevizan here is the influence that he exerted on writers such as Rabelais and François de Billon (Le Franc 1914, 2: 262–263).

The famous Dutch humanist Desiderius Erasmus (1469–1563) also contributed to the debate. His views were somewhat ambiguous. He was certainly not a feminist, in the sense that he did not believe in equality for women, or for a role for them outside the traditional one (Rummel 1996, 9). On the one hand, Erasmus did state that all men are tyrants and gave a voice to women in his *Minor senatus* (The Little Senate) in which the ardent Cornélie exposes the injustices of which women are victims: "Men are all tyrants and they treat us like toys; . . . they make us do their laundry and their cooking and make sure they exclude us from everything else which they keep for themselves" (cited in Reynier 1929, 5). On the other hand, in his *Institution of Marriage,* which appeared in 1526 and was dedicated to the queen of England, Erasmus wrote that "woman is an inept and ridiculous animal. . . . Woman is always woman meaning she is stupid" (cited in Le Franc 1953, 272). He tended to group women together with the other undesirables of society: "the uneducated mob," "women and superstitious people," "children, old people and women whose tongue is less controlled because their mental powers are weak" (cited in Rummel 1996, 9). He did not believe in educating women as a way of making them able to think for themselves, but as a means of keeping them out of mischief and as a form of entertainment (Thompson 1965, 115–131, 149–152).

Sixteenth-century French philosopher and author Desiderius Erasmus (Library of Congress)

Writing four years after the new edition of Martin Le Franc's *Champion des dames* (Champion of Ladies), published in 1530, was the advisor to the king of Navarre and local official from Toulouse, Gratien du Pont. He continued the misogynist debate with his huge poem, *Controverses des sexes masculine et feminine* (Controversies of the Male and Female Sexes, 1534), a reply to the *Champion.* It was a violent invective against women characterized by the usual arguments: Man is superior; man has superiority over woman in all things; woman has no place in heaven nor even in hell. Insofar as the pursuit of scientific inquiry was concerned, women were fickle and incapable of contributing anything positive or profitable to humanity (Le Franc 1914, 2: 274–76). Perhaps because of the growing influence of females in European courts, du Pont was convinced that female domination in the social milieu was becoming a serious danger in society (Le Franc 1914, 2: 275).

FEMALE APOLOGISTS

What about the other side of the debate? Were there any female apologists during the Renaissance? Shocked by the violence of language used against women by Tiraqueau and Rabelais, a writer by the name of Aymery, or Amaury, Bouchard came to the defense of women by writing a treatise entitled "On the Immortality of the Soul," which was never published. It dealt with women's role, as part of an apology for ideal love and beauty (Le Franc 1953, 276). Bouchard, also a legal humanist, did publish a riposte to his friend Tiraqueau entitled *Foeminei sexus apologia adversus A. Tiraquellum* (An Apology for the Female Sex, 1552). However, even he could not resist putting women down, commenting that to treat women as equals would be "indulging in a most excusable pretence" (Bouchard 1552, 38).

Jean de Marconville responded to this work in 1564 with his influential *L'Heuré et le malheur du marriage, ensemble les lois connubiales de Plutarque* (The Hour and the Misfortune of Marriage, Together with the Marriage Laws of Plutarch), which was hostile to women and continued the tradition of treatises on the question of marriage, conjugal law, and morality (Ascoli 1906, 35).

Around the middle of the century, the celebrated mystic and mathematician from the Collège de France, Guillaume Postel (1505–1581), contributed to the debate in his *Les Très merveilleuses victoires des femmes du nouveau monde* (The Very Marvelous Victories of the Women of the New World, 1553). This work was dedicated to Marguerite de France, duchess of Berry. There is some controversy among scholars as to how to interpret Postel's views. The earlier scholars tend to see him as a defender of women, whose ideas foreshadow those of the Saint-Simonians of the nineteenth century, with their belief that the female role was to regenerate society (Gustave Brunet 1869, x; McDowell Richardson 1929, 101). More recently, Michael Andrew Screech has posited that "it is a striking indication of the basic misogyny of the sixteenth century that he could be mistaken as a defender of the rights and dignities of women" (Screech 162). Postel's work was one of the few that directly addressed the issue of women and science. Most writers in the Renaissance were still concerned with theological matters, although they did touch upon the question of female reason or the lack of it. Postel wrote that "women were incapable of science and that science is not made for women." He seemed to indicate that because of their ignorance, which was due to a lack of education, women could not do science: "science cannot be understood by women because they do not have adequate instruction" (cited in Ascoli 1906, 49).

Heinrich Cornelius Agrippa de Nettesheim (1486–1535) added something new to the debate. Born in Cologne in 1486, Agrippa tried to prove female superiority over 450 years ago. He was a doctor, philosopher, and astrologer, in addition to being secretary to Maximilian of Austria. He mastered eight languages and earned a doctorate in civil and canon law (McDowell Richardson 1929, 91). Denounced as a heretic by the Franciscans before Marguerite of Austria, Agrippa wrote the treatise *De nobilitate et praecellentia foeminei sexus* (A Treatise of the Nobility and Excellence of Womankind) to win her favor. It was written in Latin in 1509 and presented to Marguerite in 1529, then translated into French in 1537 (Prost 1881, 1: 166). The pamphlet was published in English in London first in 1542 and then again in 1652, 1670, and 1684. Marguerite, for her part, was a learned woman who had written several works of prose and poetry.

Profile of Heinrich Cornelius Agrippa de Nettesheim (1486–1535), a German occultist philosopher and doctor of law (Hulton / Archive by Getty Images)

In this pamphlet by Agrippa, we find the nature of woman discussed from the theologian's perspective. Agrippa deals first with the biblical account of creation, arguing that things were created in order of rank, since human beings, who are obviously superior to animals, were created last. The Bible also said that man was created before woman: Eve was the last creature to be formed in Paradise and directly by God. God gave man and woman the same form and the same nature. Agrippa even argued that original sin came from Adam rather than Eve, a radical departure from previous writers. Following the views of Galen and Avicenna, Agrippa posited that the female contributed more substance and intelligence to the offspring than the male. He contended that women have even been able to conceive without men—witness the example of the Virgin Mary (Agrippa 1726, 37, 75, 118). All of these points were made in an effort to prove female superiority.

Agrippa is significant for his comments concerning female intelligence and accomplishments. Women have proved their intelligence in fields such as philosophy and mathematics. He used examples from antiquity such as Theano and Dama (wife and daughter of Pythagoras); Diotima, who instructed Socrates; and students of Socrates such as Philesia and Axioca. He also named the poet and dialectician Sappho (Agrippa 1726, 127–129). The major issue that he addressed is why women, who are endowed with a natural ability to reason, have been reduced to the simple tasks of the household.

> The tyranny of men which prevails everywhere, has deprived females of the freedom with which they were born; . . . the current legal system and custom enforce the subservient role of women. For the woman, as soon as she is born, is from her earliest years detained at home in idleness, and as if destitute of the capacity for higher occupations, is permitted to conceive of nothing beyond needle and thread. Then when she has attained years of puberty, she is delivered over to the jealous empire of man, or shut up forever in a shop of vestals. The law also forbids her to fill public offices. . . ." (Agrippa 1726, 147–148)

Finally, he argued that the lack of access to education held women back from achieving the same as men in society.

A similar line was taken by French writer François de Billon (1522–1556) at midcentury. De Billon was a secretary to Cardinal Guillaume du Bellay, and it was through him that Billon met Rabelais. Both accompanied du Bellay to Rome in 1547, and it was here that Billon wrote his tract entitled *Le Fort inexpugnable de l'honneur du sexe féminin* (The Indisputable Proof of the Honor of the Female Sex) in 1550. It was published in 1555. To Billon, Rabelais was the most misogynist writer of his day (Billon 1970, xi). Billon was determined to defend women's intellectual abilities; in his treatise, he accused the misogynists of making every possible effort to propagate the idea of the fragility of the female sex, which made it impossible for her to have any "capacity for science and virtue." He criticized the "doctors who wanted to judge women as less perfect than men" (Billon 1970, 7). Billon disagreed with vehemence. What Billon attempted to do was to prove that women did have a capacity for science by providing long lists of female scholars. He argued that throughout history, one finds the same names: those from antiquity, those in Boccaccio's *De mulieribus*. Contemporary examples of women scholars were more difficult to find (Billon 1970, 32–39).

The apparent intellectual inferiority of women was not, however, something that they had been endowed with by nature; it had resulted from a cultural phenomenon: the lack of instruction. Billon did assert that he would prefer not to be a woman "not because females are more vile than men by nature," but because "women are prevented from the immortal light of Science because of custom." If, on the other hand, one asked women why they would like to be men, they would attribute it to "the natural desire they have to See and Know, to make use of the faculty which they were given at birth" (Billon 1970, 113–114). The champions of women's scientific ability looked beyond the traditional implications of the male-female couple. Even though they were deprived of an education, they argued, women could surpass men, for they were gifted in science. They were "naturally more capable of 'subtle innuendos.'" As well, they had the faculty of prophecy, of magic—they were privy to secrets of nature and God's designs that men were not (Postel 1553 16).

The Female Contribution: The Lyon School

During the period of the Renaissance, there was a group of women centered in Lyon who followed in Christine de Pizan's footsteps. The most well-known of these was Louise Labé. Labé was born in 1493 in Lyon, a city filled with Italian ideas. Her father, a wealthy artisan, was determined to give her a good education in the tradition of the Italian Renaissance. She studied Latin and participated in the same sports as the boys. This was exceptional for a French girl at this time (McDowell Richardson 1929, 105–107). According to her biographer, Labé's "knowledge of science and virtue was equal to if not better than that of the men of her era" (Dorothy O'Connor 1926, 53–54). Labé held a salon in Lyon, where she became a confidante of Catherine de Médicis. It was a meeting place for all the cultured and learned of Lyon, a sort of academy over which she presided.

Her ideas are contained in her writings, which made her well-known among her contemporaries. She believed that women were freer to learn than they had been in the past and that they should devote themselves to knowledge to show men how wrong they had been in depriving women of this privilege. She wrote that her sex could be equal in learning and virtue to men: "The time has come for the repeal of the severe laws created by men to prevent women from applying themselves to the sciences and disciplines; it seems to me that those who have the ability should have this freedom that our sex had in previous times wanted; that is the freedom to learn and to demonstrate to men their error in depriving us of this honor. I beg the virtuous ladies to raise their spirits above their sticks and guns" (Labé, Letter to Clémence de Bourges, cited in McDowell Richardson 1929, 157, and Rebière 1897, 307).

Labé wrote a satire on love, *Le Débat de folie et d'amour* (The Debate of Madness and Love) in the middle of the sixteenth century. Her intention was to demonstrate that "folie" (the female character) was not in any way inferior to "amour" (the male character) and that amour was nothing without folie; he could not reign without her (Labé 1924, 217). Labé's works received both praise and criticism from contemporaries. Her works were praised for their technical ability, but they were criticized because, as with de Pizan, they departed from the traditional view of a woman.

During the middle of the sixteenth century we find more female contributions to the debate. Hélisenne de Crenne (ca. 1500–1552) was the author of a number of works in the middle of the sixteenth century. Among these were the first sentimental novel, *Les Angoisses douleureuses qui procèdent d'amour* (The Painful Anguishes That Proceed from Love) (Lyon, 1538); a group of letters, *Les Epistres familières et invectives de ma dame Hélisenne* (Familiar and Invective Letters from My Lady Hélisenne, 1539); and an essay in the form of a series of allegorical dreams, *Le Songe* (The Dream, 1540) (Wood 2000, 15). De Crenne was apparently the first female French novelist (Crenne 1995, 10; Wood 2000, 15). Very little is known about her life. We do know from the legal records that she was born Marguerite Briet around 1500 and that she was part of the minor nobility in Picardy (Crenne 1995, 10). She was educated in the Latin classics and was the only woman to defend her sex in the first part of the sixteenth century. The fact that she had mastered Latin was significant in itself, for as a rule girls learned only enough Latin for religious purposes. The mastery of Latin was the key to knowledge itself (Wood 2000, 67). Even though she was a literary figure whose works primarily concerned the theme of love and she did not discuss women and science in her works, de Crenne is significant for her contribution to the *querelle*. She argued that women should write (at the time, writing was considered a male occupation) and that women should put down their knitting needles. Here she echoed the ideas of Louise Labé and Agrippa.

De Crenne was not as thorough as de Pizan, but she did write a defense of women. In her work *Le Songe* (The Dream), it was woman rather than man who was convinced by Reason, one of the mythological figures. Part of the work was presented in the form of a debate between Sensuality and Reason (Wood 2000, 111). Reason repeated the contemporary view of woman, which de Crenne based upon the now familiar sources (the Bible, classical authors, and the Church Fathers), and then proceeded to destroy them by arguing that women were not irrational beings governed by their senses and emotion (Wood 2000, 68–9). On the other hand, she praised women for their glory. She still clung to the view that men were superior because they were created first, but she did argue that women could reason, itself a revolutionary statement for the time. François de Billon certainly recognized her contributions, referring to her and one of her treatises, *Les Angoisses* (The Anxieties), in his pamphlet. He argued that "in the amorous anxieties, she provided angry reply to all detractors of women" (cited in Wood 2000, 35–36). As Wood argued in her important study of de Crenne's works, "the scarcity of women involved in the debate . . . underscores Hélisennes's exceptionality." For de Crenne, "the debate meant showing in print the power and ability of the female mind" (Wood 2000, 117).

Madeleine des Roches (ca. 1520–1587) and her daughter Catherine (ca. 1542–1587) were poets who had several things to say about female intelligence and capacity to learn. Their arguments were not original in the sense that they had been made by de Pizan and others; however, they provide an insight into the opinions of two learned women of the Renaissance. Madeleine belonged to a family of notaries and was born in either 1530 or 1531; she married André Fradonnet, a procurator, in 1539. Their daughter Catherine was baptized in 1542 (Roches and Roches 1993, 16–17). Madeleine's main concern was her daughter's education. Madeleine did not begin writing until she was fifty-eight years old. Her themes were primarily literary, and she was more restrained in her feminist ideas than her daughter.

Their writings, entitled *Oeuvres* (Works), were published in 1578 and 1585 and were primarily the work of Catherine. Catherine was a distinguished *savante,* who in many ways foreshadowed the forward-thinking Marie de Gournay. In their works, the mother and daughter made an argument for female instruction in the classics such as Plutarch and Seneca, for women were "more sober, chaste and peaceful than men" (Roches and Roches 1993, 36). Further, they argued that the major reason why women were frivolous and flirtatious is that they had not been exposed to learning: "When women have been properly guided and developed by wise reading, they will desire to do nothing which is unreasonable. . . . Allow them to read and their knowledge is increased" (Roches and Roches 1993, 36b). "It seems that women are either stupid or wise; however, I would be of the opinion that if you allow them to read . . . they will at least not be kept idle in the home" (Roches and Roches 1993, 36b).

Women had been kept ignorant, they suggested, for the reason that learned women became arrogant and proved to be disdainful of their husbands. According to men, "learned woman is a monster who will never help men when they are in need of it" (Roches and Roches 1993, 37b, 38, 38b). The work by this mother and daughter team was not original, but the opinion of two educated, intelligent, and wise women. Mother and daughter both died in 1587.

Ideas about women did not change significantly during the later Middle Ages and the Renaissance. Women were still considered to be weak, fragile, inferior to men, and thus subordinate to them. The *querelle des femmes* did change in its emphasis from a debate about chivalric love to one about female intelligence and woman's access to knowledge. For the first time in the late fourteenth century, we see a woman enter into the debate and make some cogent arguments about women and science. Christine de Pizan was not only a pioneer but also someone to whom men listened and whom they even repeated, as Agrippa did. During the period of the Renaissance, we see the debate change again and become more serious in nature. Once again, women enter the debate, but primarily as women of letters rather than scientists. In this century, ironically, it was only men who argued in favor of women's capability in the sciences.

At the end of the century, in 1596, we do find the scholar Henri Estienne writing that women could take an active role in the public sphere. He wrote specifically on behalf of female participation in politics. If women sat on councils, men could benefit from their views. Women had mastered mathematics and philosophy, he argued; why could they not participate in politics? (Clément 1894). In the next century, we will witness a dramatic increase in the number of men and women debating whether women are capable of understanding science.

4

The Debate about Education
and the Inferiority of Women

The issue of female education was by no means new at the opening of the seventeenth century. As Professor Ian Maclean, a Renaissance scholar at All Souls College, Oxford, in his study of women and the Renaissance, commented, "The question of whether or not women should be allowed to cultivate their minds is not new . . . and in the sixteenth century there are several eloquent pleas for the right to study." However, he continued, "the debate about female education in the seventeenth century is . . . more vehement in tone and more prolific in texts" (Maclean 1977, 53).

During the seventeenth century, an intense debate raged over the question of female education. On the one hand were the men and women who promoted the education of girls, particularly in science and academic education, and on the other were the men and women who opposed this idea. Those on the opposing side were more concerned with the moral education of girls than with training them for a public role. The debate about education concerned not merely the question of whether or not women should be educated. It involved several issues such as the female capacity for learning, the type of education girls should receive, the amount of education, and so on.

Promoters of Female Education

The principal exponents of the proeducation side of the debate were Marie le Jars de Gournay, Johann Amos Comenius, Anna Maria van Schurman, Madeleine de Scudéry, Bathsua Makin, Poulain de la Barre, Lady Mary Chudleigh, and Mary Astell. These writers were at odds with the prevailing ideology articulated by most theorists who put forth the view that women were not to be educated for the public sphere. Underlying the various arguments they gave for education and their beliefs on the nature of education women should receive were the views they held on the nature and role of women.

MARIE LE JARS DE GOURNAY

Marie le Jars de Gournay (1565–1645) was one of the most advanced thinkers of her era and one of the strongest proponents of education for women. This French writer, editor, and translator was born in 1566. She was self-taught, learning Latin and reading literature on her own. She also had a keen interest in science, studying physics, history, geometry, and alchemy at a time when these subjects were reserved for men (Albistur and Armogathe 1977, 1:125)

Marie le Jars de Gournay (her name is often shortened to de Gournay in the literature) is best known as the editor of Montaigne's essays. She met Montaigne in Paris in 1588 when she was eighteen. This was the start of their collaboration on his *Essais*. He was thirty-two years older than she, and she became his adopted daughter in the intellectual sense. However, she was also the author of a number of her own works on education and linguistics. Her major works about women are entitled *L'Egalité des hommes et des femmes* (The Equality of Men and Women, 1622) and *Grief des dames* (The Ladies' Grievance, 1626). Her chief arguments concerning female education are contained in her *L'Egalité des hommes et des femmes*. She dedicated this work to Queen Anne of Austria, who was the daughter of Philip III of Spain and Marguerite of Austria.

Montaigne's views on the intellectual capabilities of females and their role in life were never very consistent. On the one hand, he believed that women were unfit to rule and incapable of understanding theology. According to Montaigne, women's purpose was to tutor small children until they reached the age of reason. In other words, they should act as nursemaids, or nannies. The reason for this limited role was their feeble intelligence. The combination of knowledge and the understanding of knowledge was impossible for women. They could accumulate facts, but they could not make the connections necessary for understanding (Montaigne 1937, 467). Thus, here he did not advocate an intellectual education for girls, arguing that women did not have the capacity for it. He criticized women who desired "to imitate thinkers, for they do not possess, in any sense, the necessary intellectual faculties to assimilate the discourses; they listen and repeat them without comprehending anything" (Montaigne 1937, 467).

Montaigne developed a limited educational plan reserved for a small group of elite women. They would read poetry, history, and philosophy but would be kept away from science. He quoted Plato's passage in the *Republic,* which promoted education, the exercise of public functions, and vocations for both men and women. Further, Montaigne argued in *Essais* that "the male and female are cast in the same mold: except for education and custom the difference between them is not great" (Montaigne 1937, 870). Perhaps Montaigne's positive views of the female mind and capacity were a result of years of intellectual work with Marie de Gournay. De Gournay cited the same chapter from Book V of Plato's *Republic* and referred to the same statements of the Greek cynic philosopher Anthistene on the lack of difference between the sexes. She paraphrased Montaigne when she wrote: "The human animal is neither male nor female." The sexes, she wrote, were created solely for the continuation of the human race. She distinguished the reproductive organs in the sexes, but believed that their only function was reproduction and that they were not related to intelligence (de Gournay 1989, 74–75). Man and woman are one. In fact, she argued that "man and woman are so united that man is more woman than man" and vice versa (de Gournay 1988, 121). She quoted the Bible to substantiate her thinking that "man" was a generic term that included male and female (de Gournay 1988, 121). She also invoked Plutarch and Seneca as authorities on the equality of the sexes. From Plutarch she derived the idea that male and female virtue are the same. Seneca believed that females are gifted with the same vigor and faculties as males (de Gournay 1988, 118).

The central point of de Gournay's *Egalité* was the idea of a natural complementarity between the two sexes. There is neither inferiority nor superiority between them. This idea situates her in the direct lineage of Platonic thinkers. She used three kinds of writers to back up her ideas: the Church Fathers (Paul, Jerome, and Basil), classical authors (Plato, Socrates, and Aristotle), and Renaissance writers, her recent predecessors (Erasmus, Agrippa, Politien, Boccaccio, and Castiglione) (de Gournay 1988, 61).

Marie de Gournay fought for the intellectual freedom of choice for women. She railed against female ostracism from society. In addition to defending women, she sketched the prejudices against them that had been propagated during the Middle Ages and were still very much in vogue. In particular, she was concerned about the limits placed on women taking a public role. She made reference to Saint Paul, saying that if he had been a woman, he would have been required to establish his church through peregrinations, conversations, and assistance. In other words, he would have been forced to work behind the scenes and not independently (de Gournay 1988, 58–59).

In some ways, she was Christine de Pizan's successor in the sense that she reaffirmed the intellectual equality between male and female when she wrote that "if the custom was to put little girls in school where they would learn the Sciences like boys, they would learn as perfectly and understand the subtleties of all the arts and the sciences" (de Gournay 1989, 52–53). Like de Pizan, she supported herself through her writings, as she never married and she lacked an independent income. Marie de Gournay decried the persistent portrayal of the female as frivolous, gossipy, jealous, lying, and so on. This was the medieval legacy. Once again, education was the key. She acknowledged a difference in access to education by those of different social classes and countries. The Italians were superior to the French and the English here, but only women in the upper classes, such as the queens and princesses, were educated (de Gournay 1988, 117).

Johann Amos Comenius

Perhaps the most advanced argument promoting the education of both boys and girls during the seventeenth century was put forth by the clergyman and educational reformer Johann Amos Comenius (1592–1670). He was well ahead of his time with respect to his ideas about general education and the education of girls. Comenius was one of the few writers of the seventeenth century who directly addressed the question of science education and women. In addition to his promotion of science education for both sexes, he proposed an international language and a reformed religion. Comenius did not dwell on the issue of the nature of women, as had many writers in the past; he was concerned with universal education. In that sense, he did not question the intellectual abilities of females. He placed scientific knowledge on the same level as religious knowledge, an attitude that put him far ahead of anyone else at this time. He worked for a universal system of education, thus offering equal opportunities to women. He held that the cultural progress of a society is dependent equally on men and women. Women were not inferior to men. Nor were they any different in nature except in their obvious physical dissimilarities (Comenius, in Sadler 1969, 113).

Comenius was born in 1592 in Moravia into a family who were members of the Unity of Moravian Brethren, a Protestant sect. Comenius became a teacher and at age twenty-four, in April 1616, was ordained a pastor in this religious group (Dobbie 1995, 12). Comenius's homeland suffered greatly during the religious wars between Protestants and Catholics in the Thirty Years' War from 1618 to 1648. By 1627, the people of the kingdom of Bohemia were forced to become either Protestant or Catholic by the Hapsburg emperor. The only alternative was to flee the country, which Comenius did. He spent the years from 1628 to 1641 in Poland where he was involved in education. It was during this time that he wrote his *Opera Didactica Omnia* (The Great Didactic, 1657), which contained the clearest statement of his educational project (Murphy 1995, 8–14).

Comenius's goal was to improve the state of education for both males and females. *The Great Didactic* explained that education

Johann Amos Comenius (Bettmann / Corbis)

in groups was superior to individual tuition, which was more the norm at this time. The subtitle of his most important work on education, as it was translated, indicates the aims and intention of the book: "A certain Inducement to found such schools in all the Parishes, Towns and Villages of every Christian Kingdom, that the entire Youth of both Sexes, none being excepted, shall Quickly, Pleasantly and Thoroughly Become learned in the Sciences, pure in Morals, trained in Piety, and in this manner instructed in all things necessary for the present and for the future life. . . ." This work contains thirty-three chapters on the theory and practice of education. Comenius hoped to apply these ideas to his own country initially and later the world (Prévot 1881, 24). He thus aimed at propagating the idea of public and universal education for both sexes: "The following reasons will establish that not the children of the rich or of the powerful only, but of all alike, boys and girls, both noble and ignoble, rich and poor, in cities and towns, villages and hamlets, should be sent to school" (Comenius 1967, 66).

In support of his proposal, he put forth the view that all human beings were endowed with a rational faculty, so that it did not make sense to educate some and not others (Comenius 1967, 66). In terms of female education, he made it clear that women could and should be educated: "Nor can any sufficient reason be given why the weaker sex . . . should be altogether excluded from the pursuit of knowledge (whether in Latin or in their mother tongue)" (Comenius 1967, 67). Further, he put forth the bold view that women were intellectually superior to men: Women were "endowed with equal sharpness of mind and capacity for knowledge (often more than the opposite sex)." Even more boldly, he considered that female education would serve as preparation for careers, including scientific ones, other than marriage and raising children, for women "are able to attain the highest positions, since they have been called by God Himself to rule over nations, to give sound advice to Kings and princes, to the study of medicine and of other things which benefit the human race" (Comenius 1967, 43).

As he designed curricula and programs for his public schools, he put more stress on science education than most of his contemporaries. Comenius was in many ways influenced by the ideas of Francis Bacon when it came to his stress on the inductive scientific method. In fact, Comenius described Bacon as the single most important influence on his views concerning the sciences. In his *Via Lucis* (The Way of the Light, 1641), Comenius commented that Bacon had been the individual "to whom we owe the first suggestion and opportunity for common counsel with regard to the universal reform of the sciences" (cited in Murphy 1995, 71).

Comenius, however, did not believe in the strict specialization between the disciplines, particularly the arts and the sciences, that characterizes modern education. He believed that science had a moral component and thus science would be integrated with Christian values. He wrote "that a true knowledge of the world of Nature will be a key to the mysteries of the Scriptures, and here we rest upon a solid foundation. . . . For Nature and Scripture serve the other, as commentator and interpreter, Scripture speaking in more general terms, and Nature in particular instances" (cited in Murphy 1995, 126).

In many ways Comenius foreshadowed John Locke in his emphasis upon sensory perception. He wrote:

> Everything should, as far as possible, be placed before the senses. [The reasons for this are threefold:] Firstly, the commencement of knowledge must always come from the senses. . . . Secondly, the truth and certainty of science depend more on the witness of the senses than on anything else. . . . We do not trust a conclusion derived from reasoning unless it can be verified by a display of examples. . . . Science, then, increases in certainty in proportion as it depends on sensuous perception. (Comenius 1967, 184–185)

The sciences that he included in his curriculum were physics, geometry, geography, arithmetic, mineralogy, and mechanics.

Comenius traveled to England to discuss the issue of science in education at the invitation of the influential educational writers Samuel Hartlib, John Drury, Robert Boyle, and John Pell. He advised this group that science should be the basis of all educational programs and for all people (Phillips 1990, 31).

ANNA MARIA VAN SCHURMAN

Linguist and scholar Anna Maria van Schurman was born into a wealthy noble family of Cologne in 1607. She was tutored at home, except for two months at a French boarding school, and began her education at the age of two. She was the first woman to attend a Dutch university, the University of Utrecht; she wrote a Latin treatise in the form of a dissertation in 1641. This dissertation was concerned with the question of women's suitability and capability for higher education (Schurman 1998, 4–5). Van Schurman is significant for many reasons, but perhaps the most important is that her writings were read throughout the Netherlands, and they sparked a serious debate on women's intellectual abilities and their education (Schurman 1996, 1–2). She was well known in her day. She corresponded with many of the learned noblewomen and men of her day, including queens of Sweden and Poland. Her most extensive correspondence was with Princess Elisabeth of Bohemia, who was the daughter of Elizabeth Stuart. They discussed matters of scholarship in their letters. She also knew the famous French philosopher René Descartes (Schurman 1998, 6–7). One eulogist, Paul Jacob, who was a member of the Lyon Parlement, the highest court of appeal in France, wrote that "she was a girl born for the glory of her sex and for the confusion of our own." He praised her knowledge of foreign languages, the arts, and the sciences (Jacob n.d., 115).

Van Schurman's ideas about the education of women are contained in her chief work, which has two titles. On the title page of the first edition appears *Nobiliss. Virginis Annae Mariae A Schurman Dissertatio, de Ingenii Muliebris ad Doctrinam, & meliores Litteras aptitudine* (A Dissertation on the Aptitude of the Female Mind for Science and Letters). The second title, found in the text, is *Problema practicum, num foeminae christianae conveniat stadium litterarum* (A Problem, Relating to Active Life, on the Question of Whether the Study of Letters Is Fitting for a Christian Woman) (Schurman 1996, 43). This work, often known as the *Dissertatio,* was published in 1641 in Leiden. In 1659, an English edition was published as *Whether it is Necessary for Women to be*

Educated or Not; The Learned Maid; Or, Whether a Maid May be a Scholar?
The Learned Maid. Some of van Schurman's correspondence with a
leading Calvinist theologian, Andrea Rivet, was published with this
work. In 1648, a collection of her writings, including both her correspondence and her *Dissertatio,* was published under the title of *Op-
scula.* Her dissertation is based upon a refutation of many of Rivet's
views on this subject. It was written from November 1637 to March
1638 (Schurman 1996, 25). The *Dissertatio* was a particular genre of
writing in a medieval scholastic formula in which arguments for and
against a question were presented and debated. Experts agree that she
was the first Dutch woman to put forth arguments in support of
higher education of women (Schurman 1996).

Van Schurman's arguments in favor of education for women
were primarily academic in nature. She did not propose a school and
write curricula as did Comenius. She wrote of education in moral
terms: "Ignorance and idleness cause vice" (Schurman 1650, 36). She
believed in learning for learning's sake and that "whoever by nature
has a desire for arts and sciences is suited to arts and sciences; women
have this desire, therefore women are suited to arts and sciences"
(Schurman 1650, 35). She did not advocate education for women of
the lower classes, but rather for ladies of the leisure classes (Schurman 1650, 35).

In addition to this work, Schurman wrote letters to the theologian André Rivet, which were published under the title of *Question
célèbre* (The Celebrated Matter, 1649). In many ways, the most interesting and telling debate took place between Rivet and van Schurman
between 1637 and 1640. She argued that rather than following "bad
custom, we should listen to the voice of reason. If we appealed to the
witnesses of antiquity, the examples of past centuries and the authority of great personages, we would be persuaded to the contrary."
However, women such as Marie de Gournay had already proven that
man and woman are equal and she was not going to "bore her readers
with repetition." She asserted that "it is enough to study the sciences. . . ." She believed that women could and should make a valuable contribution to society rather than be left to atrophy. In fact, she
maintained that it was necessary for the happiness of women that they
focus on studying theology, abstract subjects, and the sciences (Schurman 1646, 15–19).

In response to a letter in which she had tried to prove that "the
spirit of women is as capable as the spirit of man for doing the arts
and the sciences," Rivet indicated his admiration for her abilities
when he wrote, "you yourself have surpassed them [men]" (Rivet to

Schurman 1646, 43–44). But he went on to say that "although you have shown us this with grace, your persuasions are futile. . . . You may have many admirers, but none of them agree with you." According to Rivet, van Schurman was completely on her own. Not even women agreed that women should be educated in the arts and sciences. He then went on to outline his view of the female and male roles: Women were destined for one thing and men for another. Addressing the question of women in science, he admitted that some women were capable of the higher sciences. Which "sciences" did he include? Letters, philosophy, all those connected to languages, but not law, medicine, or theology (Rivet to Schurman, 1646, 43–49).

In a letter almost two years later, van Schurman posed the question of whether or not in this century it was suitable for a girl to apply herself to the study of letters and the knowledge of the arts. To Rivet, she replied that he had misunderstood what she wrote—that women are in fact more suited for study than men. She cited Marie de Gournay and an Italian who wrote in the same genre, Lucretia Marinella (Schurman 1646, 71–74).

Although van Schurman did not recommend education for all women, only those of the leisured classes, she nonetheless wrote an important defense of woman's mind and its suitability for scholarship in both the arts and the sciences.

Madeleine de Scudéry and Louise de Lambert

A number of noblewomen also thought and wrote about education at this time. One French author of the seventeenth century, Marie Madeleine de Scudéry (1607–1701), commented on the lack of seriousness about female education. She wrote, "Speaking truthfully, there is nothing more injurious to our sex than to say that woman is not obliged to learn. . . . There is nothing more bizarre than to see how the education of women operates. We see that they are nothing more than flirts and they are not permitted to learn seriously" (Scudéry 1650–1654, 2: 675). She advocated teaching females how to read and debate, and to reason. One of her early works, *Les Femmes illustrés* (Illustrious Women, 1642), an account of the contributions of some prominent women poets, authors, and scientists, resembled Boccaccio's *Famous Women*. Her work is a defense of women and their intellectual contributions throughout history.

Not only was de Scudéry a great novelist—her most famous work is *Artamène, ou le Grand Cyrus* (Artamene, or Large Cyrus), published between 1649 and 1653. She held her own salon called *Le*

Samedi (Saturdays) where some of the seventeenth century's great intellects met to discuss ideas (France 1995, 752–753).

A contemporary to de Scudéry was Louise de Lambert (1647–1713). She held a salon in her home, the Hôtel de Nevers, which was a meeting place for the intellectual elite. Her views on education are found in the advice she wrote to her daughter, entitled "Avis d'une mère à sa fille" (Advice from a Mother to Her Daughter, 1726–1782). She reiterated the common view that the education of girls had been neglected and all attention had been paid to boys. Girls, she claimed, "had been abandoned to their governesses." She detested the idleness of the women of her class and thought that they should put their minds to something useful such as history, both ancient and modern, and the learning of languages. Although her views were moderate—religious teaching is a must for good conduct and girls should stay away from the "extraordinary sciences"—she did address the issue of education or training of one's mind (Lambert 1761 1: 98, 101–103, 146).

Bathsua Makin

Bathsua Makin (1608?–1675) is known for the shorthand system she developed, for her plea for the serious education of girls, and for taking up the cause of women (Salmon 1987). Makin was tutor to Princess Elizabeth, daughter of King Charles I of England, during the English Civil Wars, until 1650 when the princess died at age fifteen. Very little is known about her life even though according to one scholar, "she was one of the most learned women of her time" (Brink 1980, 87). We do not even have the correct date of her birth, for her records are lost. Her parents, John and Mary Pell, died when she was a child. Her father had been an Anglican minister. We know that her brothers, John and Thomas, were born in 1611 and 1612. Both brothers attended Cambridge, with only one graduating, the mathematician, John. He went on to pursue a career as a mathematics professor, holding chairs in Amsterdam and Breda, and was responsible for inventing the division sign (Teague 1998, 11). Thomas was a gentleman of the bedchamber to Charles I (Brink 1980, 87). Bathsua Makin must have received a decent education, for she worked as a royal tutor—not as a governess—a post usually reserved for males (Salmon 1987, 307). We know that she taught her pupil French, Latin, Italian, Greek, and Hebrew (Teague 1998, 61). She was certainly surrounded by educated men, for most of her acquaintances were medical men.

Makin was acquainted with the works of both van Schurman and Comenius, which presumably influenced her own; she met Comenius in 1641 (Teague 1998, 60). Makin and van Schurman corresponded, although Makin's letters are lost. Van Schurman's letters from 1640 refer to Makin's work as a royal tutor.

Recent scholars including Mary Prior have maintained that Makin's feminism was of a conservative nature, that Makin was not putting forth a case in favor of gender equality; however, if women could gain access to a good education, they could perhaps obtain further rights (Prior 1985, 229). Like Mary Astell and Comenius, Makin was committed to the improvement of female education. To this end, she opened a school at Tottenham High Cross, in London, with a schoolmaster, Mark Lewis. Apparently, this school, for both boys and girls, was an expansion of an existing school. The school's textbooks were based on Comenius's theories of education. Subjects for tuition included the standard female fare of music, singing, and accounting, in addition to many languages. There is no mention here of the sciences. Makin's treatise on education, "An Essay to Revive the Antient Education of Gentlewomen" (1673), was written as an advertisement for the school. She addressed it to Mary, daughter of James, duke of York. In the treatise, Makin protested against the prevalent opinion of the low breeding of women, as well as against the ideas that women are not endowed with reason and are therefore not as capable as men, and that education of women will turn the world upside down and "it will set the whole world in a flame" (cited in Teague 1998, 109). Like many who had contributed to the debate about female education before her, she listed women scholars, such as linguists, orators, logicians, and so on, dating from ancient times to the present. She cited van Schurman's contributions to female education and scholarship as further proof that women could reason (cited in Teague 1998, 117). And like van Schurman, she was committed primarily to the education of "gentlewomen" (cited in Teague 1998, 22).

She argued that women were not educated in seventeenth-century England so that they could be kept in a submissive state: "We cannot be so stupid as to imagine, that God gives Ladies great Estates, merely that they may Eat, Drink, Sleep, and rise up to Play. . . . Poor Women will make but a lame excuse at the last of the day for their vain lives; it will be something to say, that they were educated no better. But what Answer Men will make, that do industriously, deny them better improvement, lest they should be wiser than themselves, I cannot imagine" (cited in Teague 1998, 28).

She also wrote about science education: In a section of her work entitled "Some women have understood the mathematics," she explained that "the mathematics require as much seriousness as any art or science, yet some women have attained an extraordinary knowledge" (cited in Teague 1998, 120). Here she included sciences such as astronomy, theology, and alchemy as well as mathematics. She provided examples of female scientists of the past. A sampling of these includes Hypatia; Fabiola and Marcella, Roman biblical scholars; Anna Maria van Schurman; and finally, Isola Navarula, "proficient in philosophy and theology" (cited in Teague 1998, 121).

Although Makin was learned herself and advocated education for upper-class females, she did not argue in favor of a public role for women. She wrote: "There are other ends of Learning, besides pleading in the Hall, and appearing in the Pulpit" (cited in Teague 1998, 33).

Poulain de la Barre

The French theologian and Cartesian thinker Poulain de la Barre (1647–1723) was the "most outspoken and relevant feminist of his day" (Rowan 1980, 279). He was educated at the University of Paris where he obtained a bachelor's degree in theology in 1667. He was the author of several treatises on women, which will be considered in Chapter 5. Here we are concerned with his ideas about female education. They are contained in his pamphlet, *De l'éducation des dames pour la conduite de l'esprit* (1674) (On the Education of Ladies for the Conduct of Their Minds in Sciences and in Manners). Poulain was revolutionary in the educational program he proposed, for it was weighted heavily in favor of the sciences, particularly in subjects such as biology and physics, which were almost universally forbidden to women at this time. His goal was to develop critical thinking, which most commentators believed was beyond the reach of females: "You have a mind, use it and don't sacrifice it blindly to anyone. . . . Observe, judge and examine everything without scruples." His curricula included the study of all the sciences in addition to the Bible. The usual fare of domestic arts was excluded. He was the only writer at this time to consider education for women as a preparation for a job outside the home, including professions such as teaching, medicine, and the law (Poulain de la Barre 1674, 229, 300, 315).

Lady Mary Chudleigh

Lady Mary Chudleigh (1656–1710), poet, feminist, and philosopher, also deserves attention for her contribution to the education debate. She was apparently a follower of Mary Astell's ideas and may have known her personally (Erickson in Todd 1989, 143). Although Chudleigh did not write extensively and exclusively on the education of women, she did indicate the importance of it in her poetry. Her contribution came in the form of a poem, *The Ladies Defence: or the Bride-Woman's Counsellor Answered: A Poem. In a Dialogue between Sir John Brute, Sir William Loveall, Melissa, and a Parson* (1701). The poem was written in response to a sermon delivered at a wedding by John Sprint, whom Chudleigh considered to be a misogynist. The themes of the poem were the negative views of women by men and within the church, female inferiority, and lack of education for women. The following passage indicates her views on both education and the current role of women:

> 'Tis hard we shou'd be by the Men despis'd,
> Yet kept from knowing what wou'd make us priz'd:
> Debarr'd from Knowledge, banish'd from the Schools,
> And with the utmost Industry bred Fools.
> Laugh'd out of Reason, jested out of Sense,
> And nothing left but Native Innocence:
> Then told we are incapable of Wit,
> And only for the meanest Drudgeries fit:
> Made Slaves to serve their Luxury and Pride,
> And with innumerable Hardships try'd,
> 'Till Pitying Heav'n release us from our Pain,
> Kind Heav'n to whom alone we dare complain.
>   (Chudleigh 1701)

MARY ASTELL

Mary Astell (1666–1731) was born in Newcastle-upon-Tyne in 1666. Very little is known about her early life. She was not a member of the upper class; her father was a coal merchant. She was educated by her uncle, a Cambridge University graduate, and she is considered by many scholars as "the first widely read, expressly feminist polemicist" (Todd 1989, 18–19; Hill 1986, 1). Both of her parents were dead when Mary moved to London at age twenty, where she began to write anonymously. She never married and was apparently supported throughout her life by a series of wealthy female friends (Hill 1986, 6–14). Mary Astell's goal was to establish a religious community for "Ladies of Quality" (Astell 1997, xi).

Astell's reputation as a feminist rests on her ideas contained within her treatise, *A Serious Proposal to the Ladies for the Announcement of Their True and Great Interest,* of which Part I was published in 1694 and Part II in 1697. Astell's educational ideas were influenced by her contemporaries. Women, she wrote, were barred from the advantages of education from a very young age. Because women's education was poor, women's minds were not trained properly, and this led to poor judgment. Women, therefore, made the wrong decisions in life (Astell 1997, 52–3). In order to right this wrong, Astell intended to found "a religious community, retreat or retirement" for "Ladies of Quality." Each woman would bring a dowry with her, which would be used to fund the school (Astell 1997, 54). Astell was significant to the debate about women for several reasons. She advocated a career for women outside the home and the convent. She also believed that wealthy women who did not marry should donate their dowries to an educational institution for girls.

In her *Some Reflections on Marriage* (1700), she explained that the principal reason women were considered to be inferior to men was that boys "have much Time and Pains, Care and Cost bestowed on their education," while "Girls have little or none." Further, she argued that boys "are early initiated in the Sciences, are made acquainted with ancient and modern discoveries, they study Books and Men, have all imaginable Encouragement; not only Fame, a dry Reward now a-days, but also Title, Authority, Power, and riches themselves, which Purchase all Things, are the Reward of their Improvement." On the other hand, girls "are restrained, frowned upon, and beat, not for, but from the Muses; Laughter and Ridicule, that never-failing Scare-Crow, is set up to drive them from the Tree of Knowledge" (Astell 1730).

She continued by refuting the "natural inferiority" of women by giving examples of the achievements of prominent women in the Bible such as Deborah: "Where shall we find a nobler Piece of Poetry than Deborah's Song? Or a better and greater Ruler than that renowned Woman, whose government so much excelled that of the former Judges? And though she had a Husband, she her self judged Israel, and consequently was his Sovereign, of whom we know no more than the Name. Which Instance, as I humbly suppose, overthrows the Pretense of Natural Inferiority." She goes on to praise further women from the Old and New Testaments to prove her point (Astell 1730).

Scholars do not know much about the connections between the different female proponents of intellectual equality and education. We do know from Anna Maria van Schurman's collected writings published in 1638 that Bathsua Makin, Anna Maria van Schurman, and Marie de Gournay corresponded with one another. Van Schurman mentioned de Gournay's work by name in her own, stating that the latter had already proven, on the basis of ancient testimony, examples from past centuries, and on the authority of great personages, that men and women are equal (Schurman 1646, 15). In addition, we have a letter written by van Schurman to Sir Simonds d'Ewes in 1645 indicating van Schurman's influence on Makin's ideas about the education of women (Wilson and Warnke 1989, 174). In fact, Mary Astell and Bathsua Makin modeled their ideas and educational programs on the ideas and work of Anna Maria van Schurman. Van Schurman and Makin each had a particular plan to improve female education.

The Other Side of the Debate: Educating Women to Be Wives and Mothers

The principal educator of girls in seventeenth-century France was the Roman Catholic Church in the form of the convent school. The most important order involved in education was the Ursulines, which was established in 1592 during the Counter-Reformation. By the close of the seventeenth century, their convents numbered three hundred (Barnard 1971, 40). Most educational theorists, including those discussed below, were both critical and praiseworthy of the education the nuns provided. The convents brought girls up to be modest and honest, but they provided little in the way of intellectual training. Religious education was the most important aspect of the curriculum at the convent schools. Those involved in the reform of education at this time, such as Fénelon and Madame de Maintenon, sought to make some changes to the education nuns provided.

FRANÇOIS DE SALIGNAC DE LA MOTHE-FÉNELON

During the seventeenth century, there was increased interest in pedagogy in France. This focus on pedagogy was intimately connected to the "woman question" and its relation to the development of the salons discussed in Chapter 5. The prevalent view was that education, rather than nature, made women inferior and condemned them to a state of perpetual frivolity. This was the view of Fénelon, who was the most important French contributor to the education debate during the seventeenth century. He was a tutor and advisor to the Duc de Bourgogne, the Dauphin's eldest son, and later archbishop of Cambrai. He was interested in the education of both males and females and wrote extensively about this subject. Not only did he prescribe various curricula, he also set forth a psychological theory of childhood based upon his view of human nature. He wrote that "human nature is neither good nor bad; it has no inclination to go either way" (Fénelon 1966, 8). What he was asserting was that human nature could be made either good or bad depending on education. Education was the key to making people either good or bad. Thus, in many ways, Fénelon believed that education was at its heart moral.

In 1687, Fénelon published his treatise on female education entitled *Traité de l'éducation des filles* (Treatise on the Education of Girls).

Although Fénelon was serious about educating females, he was primarily interested in training future wives and mothers. In essence what Fénelon was promoting was character formation rather than education as we understand it today. His chief grievance against women at the time was their "vanity." To correct this character flaw, they were to be taught "Christian modesty" (Fénelon 1966, 69–70). In addition to forming modest, Christian women, Fénelon advocated a submissive, silent role for women. He wrote: "A girl must not speak unless it is really necessary, and even then with an air of hesitance and diffidence" (Fénelon 1966, 73–74). This is an interesting comment, for Fénelon criticized the long periods of silence imposed on the girls by the Ursuline nuns at their schools (Barnard 1971, 40).

He rejected what he saw as the idle role that women played in the society of his day and spoke of the urgent need to improve female education:

> Nothing is more neglected than the education of girls. . . . People imagine that this sex should be given little instruction. The education of boys is regarded as a most important matter because of its bearing on the public weal. . . . As for girls, it is said, there is no need for them to be learned . . . it is enough for them to know how one day to look after their households and obey their husbands without asking why. . . . If girls do not learn how to live seriously, they will not learn how to think; they will not know how to do calculations, history, geography, grammar; they hardly know how to read correctly and write legibly. (Fénelon 1966, 1)

Fénelon set forth what he saw as the purpose for educating women. His views here are based upon two central premises: that women are intellectually weaker than men and that women's occupation is the home. Since women were "weaker and less curious than men; is it desirable to educate her just to turn her head?" They "should not govern, they should not be involved in war nor enter the sacred ministry." Therefore, there was no point in teaching women politics, military arts, jurisprudence, philosophy, or theology. Most of the mechanical arts were not suitable for women either (Fénelon 1966).

He outlined the role of women in society in chapter 11, "Instruction des femmes sur leurs devoirs" (The Duties of Women). He asked what jobs a woman had to perform and answered that her most important role is the education of her children: boys until a certain age, girls until they married or became nuns. She should teach girls domestic chores, good morals, household economy, and how to keep track of farm revenue. The subjects to be studied by girls were reading, writing, and the four rules of mathematics, so that she would know how to keep track of her household accounts (Fénelon 1966, 75–77).

MADAME DE MAINTENON

Madame de Maintenon (1635–1719) is also usually considered to be "antifeminist" in her views (Rowan 1980, 273). It is certainly true that Madame de Maintenon did not contribute significantly to the debate and was very traditional in her views, but she should be given some mention here, for she is responsible for the evolution of education for women in France. She was the governess to Louis XIV's children and later his wife. Her attempt to resolve the problem of female education was the establishment of a girl's school, the Maison Royale de Saint Louis at Saint-Cyr in 1686. She wanted to take some positive steps in eliminating female ignorance, and her school was in many ways a reaction against the traditional convent education in France. Ironically, the school returned to the church in 1693 (Albistur and Armogathe 1977, 153). The double objective of the school was to educate the daughters of the lesser nobility and to train primary school teachers.

In common with Fénelon, Madame de Maintenon was critical of the Ursulines, yet at the same time, she sought their assistance when she was setting up her own school at Saint-Cyr. The major difference between Madame de Maintenon and the Ursulines lay in their beliefs about the development of rational faculties. Madame de Maintenon was much keener to develop them than were the nuns; as she wrote, "All possible means—even games—are used to develop their reason" (Barnard 1971, 227).

Madame de Maintenon's views on education are found in her correspondence, *Lettres et entretiens sur l'éducation des filles* (Letters and Conversations on the Education of Girls, 1686). Her curriculum excluded more subjects than it included. The "Prospectus of Saint Cyr" listed the aims and objectives of education for girls. The first point is to "make them Christians" and following on that premise "they are to be instructed in religion" and they "are taught that there is nothing on earth so important as the reception of the sacraments" (Maintenon in Barnard 1934/1971, 226). Madame de Maintenon followed in Fénelon's path, but she limited his program in terms of reading, grammar, and the study of the law. She was in no way a feminist, stating: "Our memory is as good as men's, but we have less judgment; we

are more foolish, flippant and less inclined towards serious things"
(cited in Rousselot 1881, 41). She continued to prescribe a religious
and moral education, specifically banishing the physical, or natural,
sciences and mathematics from her curriculum. Permitted subjects of
study were reading and writing, but these took the form of copying
religious works. No original thought was allowed. What guided
Madame de Maintenon was her view of the female role in society.
Here she differed in no way from her Renaissance predecessors: The
end of all education was marriage. The goal of education was to train
good wives who would speak and read French well (Barnard
1934/1971, 43).

The Abbé Fleury, a colleague and friend of Fénelon, also wrote
on education. He was a famous theologian, a magistrate, and a mem-

ber of the French Academy. Abbé Fleury's views were similar, in the sense that he believed women were less capable of applying knowledge and had less patience in reasoning than men. In addition, they were less courageous and less firm, and the constitution of their bodies did not help them either. On the plus side, he argued that they were more vivacious, and that they had more softness and modesty (Fleury 1686, 339–340). He reasoned that because women were not destined for important positions in society and therefore had more leisure time on their hands and thus more chance for their morals to be corrupted, women were in need of education. His curriculum was fairly broad in scope: religious studies without theology (theology was too speculative; the female brain was not capable of this), but with plenty of moral instruction that would teach girls to be "modest, submissive, and humble." He included reading and writing and enough basic arithmetic to keep the household accounts (Rousselot 1883, 274–275).

What we see in the seventeenth century is a growing debate about the education of women. Most participants in the debate, however conservative, saw the need for some kind of an education for women. Comenius was the most modern in the sense that he did not make any distinction between male and female, in terms of both learning capabilities and the type of subjects to be taught. Marie le Jars de Gournay fought for intellectual freedom of choice for women and underscored the restrictions on women's right to speak in public. By the end of the century, much had been debated concerning the ideals of female education. Except for a few voices, the prevailing view was to educate women for marriage.

The Cartesian Debate

The seventeenth century in France was in many ways a century of contradiction. On the one hand, we find Cartesian philosophy and those who, based upon this philosophy, put forth arguments in favor of women doing science. In addition, for the first time women in general had some access to science through the popularizers of science such as Fontenelle. On the other hand, the ideology of absolutism, which characterized the *grand siècle* (great century), as the seventeenth century in France is traditionally called, enforced tenets of order, obedience, and paternalism. Subordination of wife to husband was seen as implying the moral and intellectual inferiority of women. One of the chief exponents of this view was the French bishop, Jacques-Benigne Bossuet (1627–1704), a major theoretician of the divine right of kings. He reiterated the old arguments concerning female inferiority that woman was pulled from a superfluous side of man, a side that God had created for that purpose (Bossuet cited in Rebière 1894, 291). In addition, when dealing specifically with science, he wrote: "This is the principal reason for which, if I am not mistaken, we exclude women from the sciences, because when they are able to acquire them, they hardly prove effective in them. . . ." He even went so far as to say that exposing women to science was an "enterprise too dangerous" (Bossuet cited in Rebière 1894, 299).

The concept of female subordination was clearly enunciated by the lawyer Antoine de Courtin (1622–1685) in his *Traité de la jalousie ou moyens d'entretenir la paix dans le mariage* (Treatise about Jealousy or Methods of Bringing Peace to Marriage, 1685). He claimed that "no society can subsist without the subordination of the parts which compose it. Nature has imposed this law of marriage . . . putting the natural right of empire in the hands of the man because of the nobility of his sex and imposing by necessity an indispensable respect and obedience of the woman because of her weakness." He continued by comparing the family of man to a monarchical state where there is only one in command (Courtin 1685, 1–8). The man of letters and critic Jean-Louis Guez de Balzac (1597–1654) referred to women who aspired to learning as *femmes doctes* (learned women), using *docte* as a pejorative term to suggest that such women were infatuated with their own knowledge. Balzac was one of the original members of the French Academy (Timmermans 1995, 331).

The Précieuses and Science

During the seventeenth century, women who attempted to gain access to any kind of learning were ridiculed, even if their reasons for learning were less than to obtain knowledge for knowledge's sake, as in the case of a group of women in France known as the *précieuses.* This small group of women from the upper classes met in private homes where they hosted salons. They were known at the time by the term "précieuse," coined by Molière and other male writers, meaning pretentious lady. Molière claimed that these ladies who frequented and held salons were not really interested in true learning. He mocked them in his plays, *Les Précieuses ridicules* (The Pretentious Young Ladies,1656–1658) and *Les Femmes savantes* (The Learned Ladies, 1672). They were "ridiculous" women who existed only "through the prism of comic degradation . . . which in Molière's era was called *le ridicule*" (Stanton 1981, 112–113). He ridiculed these women the way in which he ridiculed the bourgeoisie in general. Part of the reason why he mocked them was that he did not see them as serious about their pursuit of knowledge. They were dilettantes and superficial. But what access did women have to serious learning?

Less cruel and perhaps more accurate was the description of these women by Baudeau de Somaize, who wrote *Le Grand dictionnaire des précieuses* (The Great Dictionary of the Invaluable Ones, 1661) and said of these women that they were "literate but not learned" (cited in Harth 1992, 79–80). According to Somaize and another commentator, Abbé de Pure, author of *La Prétieuse ou le Mystère des Ruelle* (Prétieuse or the Mystery of the Lanes, 1656), these women "set about to reform French orthography—their principal goal was language and the art of conversation, to find new expressions and new words" (cited in Richards 1914, 7).

What we do know is that the salons produced some women of a degree of learning unusual for their day, including Madame de Scudéry, Madame de Sévigné, and Madame de Maintenon. The salons were composed of a small number of upper-class women, noble before 1648, and middle class afterwards. The change in class had to do with the Fronde. The Fronde (1648–1653) was a series of rebellions against the regency government of Louis XIV because of rising taxes. It took its name from the slingshots that children used to throw stones at carriages. The rebellion was aimed against the king's advisors rather than the king himself and was led by the nobility and the Parlement of Paris (highest court of appeal), who demanded a greater participation in politics and lower taxes. After the Fronde, the nobility lost a great deal of its previous power.

These women of the salons were concerned with education and the right of women to choose their own husbands (Shaw 1984, 25–26). Their principal focus was the literary arts and language rather than science; however, science was a subject of interest to them, and they were mocked for this. The Abbé de la Roque, writing in the *Journal des Savants* (4 March 1686), complained about all the social problems associated with the introduction of scientific concepts to women. These problems involved young ladies rejecting marriage proposals (cited in Gibson 1989, 39, 156–157). Many authors did not make the distinction between literature and science at this time (Timmermans 1995, 123).

The theologian, lawyer, and satirist Nicolas Boileau-Despreaux (1636–1711) wrote an entire satire, entitled *Satire X, Satire contre les femmes* (Satire against Women, 1694), on this sort of female *salonnière* in general, and one in particular, a Madame de la Sablière, who had attempted to make a study of astronomy. Madame de la Sablière, or Marguerite Hessein de la Sablière (1636–1693), held one of the most important salons in the seventeenth century at her home in Paris. Concerning her attempts to do science, Boileau commented: "An astrolabe in her hands, she makes it her pleasure to follow Jupiter the entire evening. . . . Her science, I believe is nothing more than something to occupy her days. . . . Nothing escapes the look of our Curious one. But who follows her footsteps? She is a Précieuse" (Boileau 1966, 73). These authors celebrated the traditional female qualities of beauty, politeness, and softness. Boileau satirized women who aspired to literature, whom he called précieuses, and those who occupied themselves with science, whom he referred to as savants. Science was even considered bad for a woman's character.

Madeleine de Scudéry, who held a salon and was a literary giant in her own right, also had little use for the savantes and précieuses. She felt that they were pedantic and had only learned to sing their own praises. A true "savante," she wrote, did not do that (Scudéry

1656, vol. 10, 350). It was not female learning that she opposed, but the pretension of these women and their reasons for learning:

> I would like it to be said of a person of my sex that she knows a hundred things of which she makes no boast, that her mind is extremely enlightened, that she has an exquisite knowledge of beautiful literature, that she speaks well, writes properly and that she has a savoir-faire, but I wouldn't like it said of her that she's a learned lady. It's not that she who refuses to be dubbed savante can't know as much and more than she who has been given that terrible name, but that she knows how to make better use of her mind, and that she has learned how to conceal cleverly what the other so inappropriately displays. (Cited in Harth 1992, 87)

Another who wrote against the savantes and précieuses was Samuel de Chappuzeau (1625–1701). In his *Académie des femmes* (1661), the husband of a pedantic *cartésienne* orders her to destroy all her books and perform her domestic duties (Gibson 1989, 39, 156).

Descartes and Cartesian Dualism

The single most important philosopher, mathematician, and scientist of this period was René Descartes (1596–1650). Descartes was a skeptic who did not accept received authority, which meant that religious authority was no longer acceptable when one was searching for scientific truth. Reason was the foundation of all knowledge. Descartes put forth the first thoroughly mechanistic view of the universe, based completely on matter and motion. The sun and stars were at the center of a rotating vortex of matter holding the planets in their orbits. Descartes's first work on the scientific method, *Règles utiles et claires pour la direction de l'esprit en la recherche de la vérité* (Rules for the Direction of the Mind, 1628), was unfinished. His next and more famous work, *Discours de la méthode pour bien conduire sa raison et chercher la vérité dans les sciences* (Discourse on the Method of Rightly Conducting Reason and Seeking the Truth in Sciences), was actually written before 1633 and the church's condemnation of Galileo's *Dialogue*. Galileo had made improvements upon the telescope. Because of the church's excommunication of Galileo, Descartes understandably was hesitant to publish his work. It was not published until 1701.

Descartes searched for truth through deductive reasoning. His goal was to demythologize the views of Aristotle and the scholastic philosophers that had persisted to his time. Reason was his concern, as he explained in Part V of the *Discourse on Method*:

> From the description of inanimate bodies and plants, I passed to animals, and particularly to man. But since I had not as yet sufficient knowledge to enable me to treat of these in the same manner as of the rest, that is to say, by deducing effects from their causes, and by showing from what elements and in what manner nature must produce them, I remained satisfied with the supposition that God formed the body of man wholly like to one of ours, as well in the external shape of the members as in the internal conformation of the organs, of the same matter with that I had described, and at first placed in it no rational soul, nor any other principle, in room of the vegetative or sensitive soul, beyond kindling in the heart one of those fires without light, such as I had already described, and which I thought was not different from the heat in hay that has been heaped together before it is dry, or that which causes fermentation in new wines before they are run clear of the fruit. For, when I examined the kind of functions which might, as consequences of this supposition, exist in this body, I found precisely all those which may exist in us independently of all power of thinking, and consequently without being in any measure owing to the soul; in other words, to that part of us which is distinct from the body, and of which it has been said above that the nature distinctively consists in thinking, functions in which the animals void of reason may be said wholly to resemble us; but among which I could not discover any of those that, as dependent on thought alone, belong to us as men, while, on the other hand, I did afterwards discover these as soon as I supposed God to have created a rational soul, and to have annexed it to this body in a particular manner which I described. (Descartes 1961, 27–28)

René Descartes (Library of Congress)

As stated above, Descartes's method of reasoning is known as the deductive method—this is quite different from Bacon's method of inductive reasoning, which was formulated earlier in the seventeenth century. Descartes's method is based on a series of rules, summarized here: In the first place, one is to accept nothing as true which one does not clearly recognize as such—in other words, one must avoid preconceived notions and prejudices (for example, religious ones). Second, one must divide each problem into as tiny parts as possible in order to resolve it. Third, one begins with the simplest objects and moves to the more complex (France 1995).

Descartes did not specifically address the female question in his works. However, his philosophy is important to the debate because of the universality of its message. For Descartes, the thinking mind was more real than the body. He explained: "I had after this described the reasonable soul, and shown that it could by no means be deduced from the power of matter, as the other things of which I had spoken, but that it must be expressly created; and that it is not sufficient that it be lodged in the human body exactly like a pilot in a ship, unless perhaps to move its members, but that it is necessary for it to be joined and united more closely to the body, in order to have sensations and appetites similar to ours, and thus constitute a real man." Descartes put forth the idea of dualism, or the separation of body and mind or soul. He found that the thinking function in man was separate from the soul. In the course of his thinking, he found that God had "created a rational soul, and . . . annexed it to this body in a particular manner . . ." (Descartes 1961, 35–36).

Previous to Descartes, commentators had considered that because of the physical differences between male and female, women were inferior in both body and mind. With the Cartesian distinction between body and mind, previous views that stressed sex-related theories of mind and body came to be seen as erroneous. In addition, his idea that all humans have reason implied equality between the sexes. Writers like Poulain de la Barre, whose ideas about female education were discussed in Chapter 4, used these Cartesian views in an attempt to prove that women were equal to men in all capacities and thus were fit to be scientists.

Not everyone, of course, accepted the Cartesian worldview, and even Descartes himself was not really a feminist. Scholars are divided over this issue and disagree on whether Descartes explicitly stated that women were inferior. Some have argued that Descartes admitted spiritual equality between the sexes, while others have contested this view (Hoffman 1977, 60–61; Alcover 1981, 72). One piece of evidence that is often used to illustrate Descartes's view on female intelligence and capabilities is a letter he wrote to a Father Vatier, in which he said that he had omitted the more difficult philosophical arguments when trying to prove the existence of God because he wanted women to understand something from his book (Descartes to Father Vatier, 22 February 1638, in Descartes 1953, 991).

Genevieve Lloyd read this letter as evidence that Descartes wanted to open up knowledge to women. She maintained that his remarks should not be seen as denigrating the intelligence of women, that they must be put in the context of the times. Further, she argued that the fact that Descartes wrote his *Discourse* in the vernacular rather than in Latin is further evidence to support the view that he was truly interested in extending knowledge to women. Latin was the language of male education in schools. Since women were educated at home, if at all, the majority were excluded from Latin. Lloyd concluded that "the accessibility of the new method even to women was thus a powerful symbol of the transformation which it marked in the relationship between method and autonomous, individual reasoning" (Lloyd 1984, 44).

It has also been argued that Descartes's objective was not to discuss female intelligence but to refute scholastic philosophy. He was not particularly concerned with the question of male and female intellectual equality, and the notion of accessibility was not his main interest (Harth 1992, 9; Delon 1978, 83–84, Scott 1988).

By his rejection of Aristotle and the scholastics who followed Aristotle, Descartes had freed himself from a theoretical handicap, which allowed for a more profound feminist reflection. He had freed himself of the burden of the belief that God had made two different sexes with two different functions. However, Descartes did not confront the differences between the sexes directly in his major works.

Descartes was, however, involved with the intellectual life of two women, Queen Christina of Sweden (1626–1689; ruled 1640–1654) and Princess Elisabeth of Bohemia (1618–1680). He taught Christina philosophy when he was living in Sweden at her request. They began their lectures at five in the morning at her request. Christina herself was greatly interested in the arts and sciences. To promote them, she founded the Accademia dell'Arcadia and held several salons for literary and philosophical discussions. She was also a scholar of some note: She wrote a number of books, including *Letters to Descartes* and *Maxims*. In addition, she dabbled in the sciences, especially in astronomy and archaeology, employing both in her own laboratory and conducting archaeological excavations (Masson 1968; Stolpe 1966).

With Princess Elisabeth of Bohemia, mentioned in Chapter 4 as a correspondent of linguist and scholar Anna Maria van Schurman,

Queen Christina of Sweden (Underwood & Underwood/ Corbis)

Descartes conducted a philosophical correspondence. Elisabeth of Bohemia was the daughter of Elector Palatine Frederick V and Elisabeth Stuart, herself the daughter of James I of England. She was educated at home and received an education that went well beyond what most girls received at the time. She studied Latin, Greek—her knowledge of Greek was so great that her family called her La Grecque (the Greek woman)—and some of the natural sciences. As Margaret Atherton pointed out, "Only rarely was a woman able to acquire the training necessary to enter into philosophical discussions, whose full participation required a knowledge of Latin and French or English" (Atherton 1993, 2). In a letter dated 21 May 1643, Descartes indicated his respect for Elisabeth's intellectual abilities: "The favor with which Your Highness has honored me, in granting me to receive her commands in writing, surpasses anything I had ever dared hope for." Commenting on her writings, always in the form of letters, Descartes wrote, "it is your clemency that has wished to compensate for that flaw [a flaw in him] by placing the traces of your thoughts on paper, where, rereading them several times, and accustoming myself to consider them, I am indeed less dazzled, yet have only so much more the admiration for them, recognizing that they do not seem ingenious merely at first sight, but proportionate more judicious and solid the further one examines them" (Atherton 1993, 12–13).

In a good Cartesian manner, Elisabeth questioned Descartes's methodology and philosophy. Gender is rarely mentioned in these letters. She did hint at female physical inferiority in one letter; however, her primary concern was Descartes's metaphysics. She focused on the mind-body duality, doubting Descartes's notion of the soul: "There are properties of the soul, unknown to us, which could, perhaps, overturn what your Meditations persuaded me of with such good arguments: the non-extension of the soul" (1 July 1643, in Atherton 1993, 130).

There is some disagreement among scholars as to the nature of the relationship between Descartes and Princess Elisabeth. On the one hand, it has been argued that she was the inferior party, a novice in comparison to the great philosopher. On the other, the fact that Descartes dedicated one of his works, his *Principles of Philosophy,* to her has been seen as an indication that he had much respect for her as a scholar (Schiebinger 1989, 46–47; Harth 1992, 71). One biographer of Descartes thinks that the philosopher genuinely admired Elisabeth's intellectual abilities and very much enjoyed their correspondence (Baillet 1972, 2: 500).

The debates that took place during the seventeenth century, in the age of Descartes, as the second half of the century is often called, followed from his theories concerning mind and body. They focused on his emphasis on the rational mind. Some modern commentators have posited that his influence had a negative impact on women's access to knowledge, because his notions about reason disqualified women (Bordo 1987). Others have put forth the opposite view (Atherton 1993, 7).

Jacques Du Bosc, Poulain de la Barre, and the Equality of the Sexes

A pre-Cartesian precursor to Poulain de la Barre was a liberal cleric by the name of Jacques Du Bosc. Du Bosc was a Franciscan with a degree in theology from the Sorbonne (Whitehead 1999, 160). He was the author of a tract entitled *L'Honnête femme* (The Honest Woman), which he wrote between 1632 and 1636. Published in London in 1639 as *The Compleat Woman,* the treatise was written as a manual for the guidance of women in society and as a defense of the female sex.

As Poulain de la Barre was to do later, Du Bosc wrote that both the custom and the law were unfair to women. He advocated improving their education on the grounds of morality. In a section of the work entitled "Of Learned Women," he set out his beliefs on women and their aptitude for the sciences. He argued that "to say that the sciences are too obscure for women" in the sense that the terms are too difficult for them "is nonsense." It was a matter of communication—the sciences should be made clear and expressed in the vernacular rather than in Greek or Latin. Women would then understand them (Du Bosc 1639, 27). Science, he asserted, was no more natural for man than for woman. Here he was responding to those writers who claimed that the female impediment to science was their "wit which is not strong enough for it." Medical thinkers, who maintained that the fragility of the female meant she could not study sciences, were in error (Du Bosc 1639, 28). He cites examples of women from antiquity such as Aspasia, Saint Macrina (Saint Gregory's sister), and others to support his defense of women in science (Du Bosc 1639, 28). If women were sometimes lacking, if they appeared not to be as strong as men, the explanation, according to Du Bosc, was rather "modesty or some consideration, than any feebleness" on the part of the woman. Women should be permitted to read subjects such as history, philosophy, poetry, music, and rhetoric to "develop their minds." They could thus achieve a place in society—a role outside the home (Du Bosc 1639, 28–30).

As stated above, the French theologian François Poulain de la Barre applied Descartes's philosophy to prove the equality of the sexes. He followed the Cartesian method by examining everything, judging everything, and putting reason above all else (Poulain de la Barre 1674, 120). As one expert has commented, "His works were a kind of new Discourse on the Method, inciting women to adopt the Cartesian method and above all, to take from Descartes the universality of 'good sense,' especially the conclusions that the sexes were equal" (Hoffman 1977, 45). He has been called the "most outspoken and relevant feminist of his day," one whose "theories still shock by their force and modernity and by their pertinence to current arguments" (Gibson 1989, 279).

Poulain de la Barre was born in Paris in 1647, and by 1667 had obtained a bachelor of theology from the University of Paris. He was first exposed to Cartesian thought at the Académie des Orateurs where he read *The Discourse on Method*. Its ideas made him renounce his previous ideas about women. The methodology of doubt and skepticism made him reexamine his previously held prejudices about female inferiority. Poulain wrote three books: *De l'égalité des deux sexes* (The Equality of the Sexes, 1673), *De l'éducation des dames* (The Education of Ladies, 1674) and *De l'éxcellence des Hommes contre l'égalite des sexes* (Of the Excellence of Man against the Equality of the Sexes, 1675).

In the preface to *De l'égalité,* Poulain wrote that his purpose was "not to prove that women are better than men, but to provide a way of comparing the arguments for and against and then making the best decision based on the reasons on which they are founded" (Poulain de la Barre 1673, 4–5).

Part I of *De l'égalité* was concerned with contemporary and past prejudices against women. Part II challenged the prevailing view of women by employing Cartesian methodology. In his preface, he outlined his method for the book as follows: "The happiest thought comes to those who work to acquire a solid science after having been instructed in the popular method; this is to doubt that which has been taught and to desire the discovery of truth for oneself. In the progress of their research, they discover that we are filled with prejudices and that we must completely renounce them to arrive at clear and distinct knowledge" (Poulain de la Barre 1673, 1).

The prejudice that Poulain chose to address was that of the inequality of women. He gave the usual explanations for the exclusion of women from science: "Everyone, those who are learned and those who are not learned at all, and even women themselves agree and say that they take no part in the sciences and public life, because they are not capable of these duties; that they have less intelligence then men, and that they should therefore be inferior to them in everything as they are . . ." (Poulain de la Barre 1673, 1). In answer to such thinking, he summarized statements made by Church Fathers, providing quotations from Clement of Alexandria and Saint Basil that indicated that male and female were of the same nature (Poulain de la Barre 1673, 6–7).

Poulain de la Barre was enough of a Cartesian to consider that Descartes might not be the supreme authority and the absolute master in all things concerning the mind. He asserted that Descartes did not overthrow the authority of the scholastics to replace them in the role of an authority himself. Poulain adopted the aspects of Cartesian philosophy that he felt brought men and women to the truth: "I do not claim that Descartes is infallible; that all of his ideas are true and without difficulty, that we should blindly follow him. . . . I simply tell you that I believe this is one of the most reasonable philosophers we have and that his method is the most universal, natural and closest to good sense and the nature of the human spirit; and the most proper at discerning the truth" (Poulain de la Barre 1673, 325–326).

Nature did not intend women to be in a subservient position in society. Custom, not natural law, made women inferior to men. On the basis of his experience, consisting of discussions with women from all social classes, he refuted the supposed inferiority of women. In a sense he carried out his own empirical research. He also provided examples of female competence in the past, such as nuns running monasteries (Seidel 1974; Poulain de la Barre 1673, 6–8).

In one of the summaries in the margin of his text he wrote, "The mind has no sex . . . not acting differently in one sex than in the other; it is in each equally capable of the same things" (Poulain de la Barre 1673, 117). Physical differences between males and females meant nothing when dealing with the mind: "It is easy to notice that the differences between the sexes concern only the body; that being the only part necessary to the production of men, to which the mind does nothing but lend its consent" (Poulain de la Barre 1673, 109). Again on physical differences, he wrote that men are not necessarily stronger than women, even though "there be some organs in one which are not in the other. In all that, it is not necessary . . . that women have less strength and vigor than men" (Poulain de la Barre 1673, 194). This was a bold statement for its day, since most writers argued that physiological differences and supposed female weakness were the causes of female intellectual inferiority.

Having argued that women were equal to men in all ways, he then proposed that all fields of endeavor should be open to women, from the law, both civil and canon, to medicine, and to education. He was the first modern writer to advocate the right to work for both sexes (Poulain de la Barre 1673, 162).

In his *De l'éducation des dames,* he proposed a new educational program that was heavily weighted in favor of the sciences. Again, this was groundbreaking for the times. It was discussed in Chapter 4, as part of the discussion of education for women, but it was such a revolutionary work that it seems worthwhile to cover it again. He believed that the "sciences would serve as an easy and soft exercise for them [women]; they would cultivate their minds without altering their bodies and put them in a state which makes them value their merit." Geometry would provide excellent mental training (Poulain de la Barre 1674, 14). Foreign languages were only necessary for those wanting to be in the learned professions. Philosophy, particularly Cartesian philosophy, was important, as was grammar and theology, in particular the study of the New Testament. Again exceptionally, Poulain repeated the view that there was no reason why women could not serve in public functions, including government, as well as men (Poulain de la Barre 1674, 27).

In his third and final book, *De l'éxcellence des hommes*, he repeated many of the arguments that he had presented in his two previous works. The purpose of this book was to establish that women are not superior to men even though the title is misleading in suggesting that men are superior to women (Poulain de la Barre 1675, 4). He utilized opinions put forth by some of the Church Fathers (Clement, Basil, and Ambrose) to prove that men and women were of the same nature (Poulain de la Barre 1675, 9). He argued that in Genesis, one sees neither the word "inequality" nor "dependence." It is true that Adam was created first, but God created Eve in the paradise of the earth (Poulain de la Barre 1675, 16). God created the first woman in a place more remarkable than Adam and from a material more durable and stronger and even more noble—a human body (Poulain de la Barre 1675, 19). Although she was created to be man's helpmate, this did not mean that she had to be his dependent. Here, Poulain differs from his predecessors, especially the Church Fathers, who argued that her role was to obey man. It was man, rather than God, who had made woman an appendage. And throughout the ages, women themselves have become convinced of their inequality and incapacity (Poulain de la Barre 1675, 117–118). In the end, Poulain repeated what he had written in his earlier works: Women were as good as men; they could run churches and states; they were as able as men to administer the sacraments (which they still cannot do in the Roman Catholic Church); they could govern kingdoms, preside over law courts, and run armies (Poulain de la Barre 1675, 238–239).

Clearly, then, Poulain believed that women were not inferior to men. Their failings in society, in learning, in achievement, and so on, were all due to custom, tradition, and defective education. They were in every way as capable as men.

Malebranche and La Bruyère

The seventeenth-century French philosopher and Roman Catholic theologian Nicolas de Malebranche (1638–1715) was also an interpreter of Descartes. Scholars are only recently recognizing him as a leading intellectual of the seventeenth century, who synthesized the thought of Saint Augustine with that of Descartes (Nadler 2000, 1). In his *Traité de morale* (Treatise on Morality, 1684) he paraphrased Saint Paul in Ephesians 5:22 to justify his view of the female role: "Woman must obey her husband as Her Lord; she must fear and respect him, please him and run the family by dependence on his authority and designs . . ." (Malebranche 1874, 9: 229). He believed that women possessed delicate brain fibers and thus were intellectually inferior to men, that their brains resembled those of children—immature and weak. Therefore, it followed logically that they were "neither born for science, nor philosophy, nor for doing great things. . . . All abstract thought is incomprehensible" (Malebranche 1874, 3: 222–223).

He argued that since women lacked formal training in philosophy, this guaranteed their success at the new science because knowledge in philosophy was not required to do science. He envisaged women as passive and docile disciples whose aim was to understand but not question. In his *De la recherche et de la vérité* (The Search after Truth, 1674–1675) he wrote: "As a rule, women are incapable of penetrating truths which are a bit difficult to understand" (Malebranche 1874, 1: 202).

The French satirist, moralist, and member of the prestigious French Academy Jean de la Bruyère (1644–1696) wrote in a similar vein. His work, *Caractères de Théophraste, traduits du grec, avec les caractères ou les mœurs de ce siècle* (The Characters or the Manners of the Seventeenth Century, 1688), is a masterpiece of French literature. It contained a chapter called "About Women," in which he made known his views on the female character and on women's intellectual ability and education. None of his comments were very positive. Women were constitutionally defective, and that was what had turned them away from learning. He blamed female ignorance on women's character rather than on men preventing them from learning. "Why should men be blamed because women have little learning? By what laws and restrictions have they forbidden them to use their eyes, and to read and retain what they read and show it in conversation or literary effort? Is it not rather they themselves who have introduced the fashion of ignorance, either through weakness of disposition or laziness or care for the preservation of their beauty, or inherent levity which prevents them studying anything thoroughly?" (La Bruyère 1885, 74). Domestic concerns, together with the love of gossip and pleasures (except the pleasures of the mind), also contribute to their ignorance. Further, he considered that a learned woman does not serve any useful function in society, so she is "suited only for a museum of art." He did write, however, that "by nature," women were better at languages than men (La Bruyère 1885, 75–76).

Popularizers of Science: Bernard Le Bovier de Fontenelle

Popular scientific literature developed during the second half of the seventeenth century, as authors made an attempt to make science more accessible to the reading public. The popularizers did much to encourage women to pursue the sciences. However, they believed that in order to make science comprehensible to females, it had to be cloaked in a fictional form. The most significant work of this genre is Bernard Le Bovier de Fontenelle's *Entretiens sur la pluralité des mondes* (Conversations on the Plurality of Worlds, 1687). It was a popular defense of Copernican astronomy and Cartesian physics, written in the form of five dialogues between a learned philosopher and his student, a Marquise, about the various astronomical systems of Ptolemy, Copernicus, and Tycho Brahe. *Conversations on the Plurality of Worlds* was the most popular work of its day, going through thirty-three editions and translated into English, German, Dutch, Russian, Spanish, and Greek (Marchal 1997, 163).

Fontenelle (1657–1757), who lived one month short of one hundred years, was a leading intellectual of his day who was educated by the Jesuits of Rouen, a member of three Parisian royal academies, and secretary of the Académie des Sciences. He was the nephew of the French classical playwright Corneille (Gelbart 1990, xiv–xv). Before his *Plurality of Worlds,* he had authored *Nouveaux dialogues des morts* (New Dialogues on the Dead, 1683), a work that criticized accepted ideas.

As with Descartes and women, there is no agreement among scholars with respect to Fontenelle's attitude toward the female brain and its capacity for the sciences. In his *Plurality of Worlds,* the Marquise is portrayed as charming and naïve. (The Marquise is held by most experts to be based on Marguerite de Rambouillet, the Marquise de la Mésangère.) Authors such as Erica Harth, Carolyn Merchant, and Margaret Alic (Alic 1986, 79) have interpreted the philosopher's attitude toward the Marquise as one of condescension because of Fontenelle's statement about his purpose:

> I've placed a woman in these Conversations who is being instructed, one who has never heard a syllable about such things. I thought this fiction would serve to make the work more entic-

ing, and to encourage women through the example of a woman who, having nothing of an extraordinary character, without ever exceeding the limitations of a person who has no knowledge of science, never fails to understand what's said to her, and arranges in her mind, without confusion, vortices and worlds.

Further, he wrote: "I only ask of the ladies, for this whole system of Philosophy, the same amount of concentration that must be given to the *Princess of Cleves* in order to follow the plot closely and understand all its beauty" (Fontenelle 1737, 4–5). *La Princesse de Clèves,* now considered a classic of French literature, was a popular novel written by a *salonnière,* Madame de Lafayette.

Harth argued that the Marquise acts out "Descartes's letter to Father Vatier. . . . Her intellectual journey recapitulates and illustrates the historical journey of Cartesian women from active participation to effacement" (Harth 1992, 124). On the other hand, Nina Rattner Gelbert, in her introduction to a translation of the *Plurality,* praised Fontenelle for wanting to spread the secrets of the new scientific universe to women. Given the seventeenth-century view of women's intellectual capacity, "that women were included in Fontenelle's invitation to ponder and resolve the meaning of existence was extraordinary for his day. This, as much as anything else, makes the *Entretiens* an exceptional and enduring work. . . . Fontenelle, though he never wrote explicitly feminist tracts, simply gave women the benefit of the doubt" (Gelbart 1990, xxvi, xxvii). If one cites Fontenelle himself, however, one will see that he did not think women capable of serious scientific research: "For laborious serious research, for the solidity of reason, for strength and profundity, it must be men" (cited in Rebière 1894, 291).

It is also interesting to consider the viewpoint of Aphra Behn (1640–1689), a contemporary and translator of Fontenelle. Although primarily known as a playwright, poet, and novelist, Behn also had an interest in the new science of her age. Behn approved of women being instructed in the sciences. She commented many times in her works on the subject of women's inadequate schooling and their lack of knowledge of the classics. For example in her poem, "To the Unknown Daphnis on His Excellent Translation of Lucretius," she thanked the translator for making the Latin poet available to her: "Till now I curst my Sex and Education / And more the scanted Customs of the Nation / Permitting not the Female Sex to tread / The Mighty Paths of Learned *Heroes* Dead" (Behn 1973).

She dedicated her translation of Fontenelle's *Plurality* to the Right Honorable James Douglas, earl of Drumlangrig. In her dedication, she referred to herself as "a new beginner in Science." Apologizing for any mistake that might be found in her translation, she alludes to the sorry state of her education: "I hope your Lordship will pardon it in a Woman, who is not supposed to be well-versed in the Terms of Philosophy" (Behn 1993, 4: 72).

Behn explains that her motivation for translating the work is its popularity both in England and France, adding that "introducing a Woman as one of the speakers in these five Discourses were further Motives for me to undertake this little work; for I thought an English Woman might adventure to translate any thing, a French

Late seventeenth-century English playwright Aphra Behn (Library of Congress)

Woman may be supposed to have spoken" (Behn 1993, 4: 73). Her translation played an important role in the dissemination of science to women. She had even intended to write her own work of science dealing with astronomy, but her failing health prevented her from doing so (Ogilvie 1986, 107).

She did make some criticisms of the work, after first apologizing: "I am sorry I must write what some may understand to be a Satyr against him." Behn observed that the reason Fontenelle had used the character of a woman was "to make every body understand him." In other words, he believed that if he had employed a man as the student, his ideas would have been inaccessible to most, and especially to women. She insinuated that he was insulting female intelligence through this method. Further, she wrote that he had "failed in his Design; for endeavouring to render this part of Natural Philosophy familiar, he hath turned it into Ridicule; he hath pushed his wild Notion of the Plurality of Worlds to that heighth of Extravagancy, that he most certainly will confound those readers, who have not Judgment and Wit to distinguish between what is truly solid (or, at least provable) and what is trifling and airy." Finally, she took him to task for his inconsistencies in the character of the Marquise: "He makes her say a great many very silly things, tho sometimes she makes Observations so learned, that the greatest Philosophers in Europe could make no better" (Behn 1993, 4: 77).

Descartes and his followers, both male and female, did provide women with a chance to be exposed to knowledge that they had not had access to before. Poulain de la Barre provided the greatest defense of women in science. Although the access to scientific knowledge was still confined to a limited group, things did change in the seventeenth century in spite of the absolutist regime. The chemist Marie de Meurdrac and her work provide a contemporary example of a woman who was practicing science, however "popular" it may have been. Her *La Chymie charitable et facile en faveur des dames* (Charitable and Easy Chemy in Favor of the Ladies) was published in 1666. Scholars believe that her textbook may have been the first treatise on chemistry ever written. Very little is known about the author and very little research has been done on her. Some experts think that she might have been a medical doctor or a medical practitioner; if so, that means she had some sort of education unusual for women of seventeenth-century France (DeLoach in Grinstein et al. 1993, 403). Evidence for her knowledge of medicine comes from her description of medicinal uses of herbs such as rosemary (Meurdrac 1680, 58). The aim of her book was practical in nature. She wrote in the preface that initially she intended the book to be for her own private use, hoping that it would help her to retain knowledge. She indicated the inner battles she had over the role of women, speaking of her doubts about publishing, given that most authorities said "it was not the profession of women to teach, that she must remain silent, listen and learn, without displaying her knowledge," and she wrote of her fear that once men read her book they would attack her. However, she did want to teach women science: "On the other hand, I flattered myself that I am not the first lady to have had something published; that minds have no sex and if the minds of women were cultivated like those of men and that we take as much time to instruct them, then they could be equal: that our century makes women who are born for Prose, Poetry, Language, Philosophy and even government" (Meurdrac, Preface, 1680, np). Her small book was a manual to teach the rudiments of chemistry to women.

Thus, despite the persistent opposition to women acquiring knowledge by many men, women like Meurdrac demonstrated that the attempt to silence women and keep them from science did not win completely.

6

The Professionalization of Science: The Exclusion of Women

The professionalization of science in the seventeenth century had a tremendous impact on the exclusion of women from this discipline. As with the development of universities in the Middle Ages (See Chapter 2), each time the pursuit of knowledge was institutionalized, women suffered a setback. The seventeenth century witnessed the development of a new institution for men: the scientific academy. Women were systematically excluded from these institutions as they had been in the twelfth century with the founding of the university. This exclusion denied women participation in the "new science," which involved the observation of natural phenomena, experimental science, and the studies of physics, chemistry, astronomy, and so on. In short, modern science, or science as we understand it today, was born in this century. The new institutions, the Royal Society of London, the French Académie des Sciences, and similar academies throughout the European continent, formalized the study of nature. For the most part, women did not seem to challenge the continuation of their historical exclusion from science.

However, not everyone was willing to accept this latest blow to women in science. One woman who caused considerable debate and controversy was Margaret Cavendish, the duchess of Newcastle, called "Mad Madge of Newcastle" by some of her contemporaries, such as diarist Samuel Pepys, and later by Sir Walter Scott. In addition to producing fourteen books on science in subjects ranging from natural history to atomic physics, she attacked eminent scientists of her day, such as Robert Hooke, curator of experiments at the Royal Society, and she sparked a great debate at the society itself when she expected to be invited to speak to its members. At the same time, Anne Conway, who showed no interest in the burgeoning professional societies, was encouraged by the men around her to pursue her scientific and philosophical interests.

Francis Bacon and the Masculinization of Science

Francis Bacon (1561–1621), an early contemporary of Descartes, is considered by many to be the "father of modern science," even though Bacon was not a scientist himself. He is significant at this juncture because he was the inspiration behind the Royal Society of London and the founder of the inductive method of carrying out scientific research. Bacon was the son of Sir Nicholas Bacon, a courtier and the Lord Keeper of the Seal under Elizabeth I. Francis entered Trinity College Cambridge at age twelve, where he studied law. He had intended to follow in his father's footsteps, but Elizabeth did not trust him. His career turned around when James I became king in 1603. He rose to become baron of Verulam, Viscount St. Albans, and Lord Chancellor of England and was able to focus on his scientific writings, such as the *Advancement of Learning* (1605) and the *Novum Organum* (1620). In these works, he rejected Aristotle and the deductive method of Descartes and advanced the inductive method of painstaking empirical research (Porter and Ogilvie 2000, 1: 109–110).

Bacon is an important figure in the debate concerning women and science, for he advanced arguments about man's domination over nature and man's exclusive right to science in works such as *The Masculine Birth of Time,* subtitled *The Great Instauration of Man's Dominion over the Universe* and *Three Books Concerning the Interpretation of Nature. The Masculine Birth of Time* was written from 1602 to 1603; however, it was not published during Bacon's life (Noble 1992, 181). These early works foreshadowed what he would later develop in his more well-known *Essays* and *The New Atlantis* (Merchant 1980, 222–223). Bacon viewed science as power. His vision was man's mastery over nature. He wrote that the aim of science was the "restitution and reinvesting of man to the sovereignty and power which he had in his first state of creation" (cited in J. H. Robertson 1905, 188).

A number of twentieth-century feminist critics of science and of the environment have taken a new interest in Bacon's writings concerning science and nature. Nature, which is identified as female, is supposed to be controlled by Science, which is male. Carolyn Merchant wrote that in Bacon's writings, "the role of women has been reduced to near invisibility" (see Merchant 1980, 172–174, 181). Those who see Bacon as fostering a view of science that was an overwhelmingly masculine discipline with no place for women contend that his influence contributed to a bias against women that still affects the world of science in the early twenty-first century.

Bacon's goal was to regain man's domination over nature. Man, he contended, "is not a child of nature, but a superior creature" (cited in Farrington 1964, 28). Bacon blamed women, specifically Eve, for the loss of "man's dominion over the universe." He wrote that "man by the Fall fell from his state of innocence and from his dominion over creation. Both of these losses, can however . . . be in some measure recovered . . . by the arts and sciences" (cited in Farrington 1964, 29). According to Bacon, the perfect scientist was male and a patriarch: "He was clothed in all the majesty of a priest, complete with a robe of fine black cloth with wide sleeves and a cape, an undergarment of excellent white linen, and a girdle with a clerical scarf, also of linen. His gloves were set with stone, his shoes were of peach-coloured velvet, and he wore a Spanish helmet" (cited in Farrington 1964, 62, 129–130). The job of the male scientist was to control nature, which was female: Nature must be made a slave or a servant of science (Merchant 1996, 81).

Francis Bacon, seventeenth-century British philosopher and scientist (Library of Congress)

Bacon's world was entirely masculine in nature. Although he did marry, he did so to improve his situation. He simply disliked women. Bacon considered woman a hindrance to man's advancement: "He that hath wife and children hath given hostages to fortune; for they are impediments to great enterprises, either of virtue or mischief. Certainly the best works, and of greatest merit for the public, have proceeded from the unmarried or childless men; which both in affection and means, have married and endowed the public" (Bacon 1996).

Only males counted in the world of Francis Bacon. Women were to be invisible, as he required in the following passage from *The New Atlantis*:

> When the tirsan cometh forth with all his generation or lineage, the males before him, and the females following him; and if there be a mother, from whose body the whole lineage is descended, there is a traverse placed in a loft above on the right hand of the chair, with a privy door, and a carved window of glass, leaded with gold and blue; where she sitteth, but is not seen. . . . He is served only by his own children, such as are

male; who perform unto him all service of the table upon the knee, and the women only stand about him, leaning against the wall. (Bacon 1901, 122)

There is some debate over the interpretation of Bacon's science as overwhelmingly masculine. Sarah Hutton has challenged this view in her interpretation of Francis Bacon. She wrote: "I should like to reopen the question of whether Baconian science is antithetical to women and I shall do so by placing Bacon and his writing in a broader contemporary context than does Keller" (cited in Hunter and Hutton 1997, 9–10). Hutton seemed to believe that Bacon is far more "pluralistic" in his scientific method than many of his feminist critics have argued (Hunter and Hutton 1997, 12). Hutton interpreted Bacon's use of aphorisms, his use of spinning and weaving metaphors, to show that he was describing an increase of female mechanical knowledge. In addition, she explained that Bacon employed a "maternal image for natural philosophy (science), which he calls 'The Great Mother of Science.'" She admitted, however, that many of Bacon's images and fables do reflect male domination over the female (Hunter and Hutton 1997, 14). She suggested that Bacon's thought is more complex and less one-sided than some feminists have asserted. By "privileging one type of metaphor over others," critics have come to see Bacon's view as exclusively masculine (Hunter and Hutton 1997, 25). She was asking scholars to have a more multifaceted interpretation.

Scientific Societies

We know that to be actively engaged in scientific research today, scholars require institutional support and funding. This was no different in the past. Universities and, starting in the seventeenth century, formal scientific societies provided this necessary backing. Since women were barred from universities and, with the scientific revolution, academies, they were effectively kept out of science. The new science organizations provided members, usually the leading scientists of their day, with a network of corresponding societies throughout Europe and a vehicle through which to conduct the collaborative research so essential to scientific work.

The Royal Society of London and the French Académie des Sciences are certainly the most important of the scientific institutions or societies that emerged during the period of the scientific revolution. They became models for the Berlin Academy, founded at the end of the seventeenth century, and subsequent scientific societies founded during the eighteenth and nineteenth centuries. The major difference between the Royal Society and the French Académie was that the Royal Society remained a much more informal group and amateur in nature, while the French society, although it may have been begun by a group of scientists meeting privately in homes, became a government institution.

Certain key individuals were responsible for the founding of European scientific societies. In England, it was Sir Francis Bacon, whose principal ideas about the role of women and women's capacity for science are summarized above and certainly permeated the society.

THE ROYAL SOCIETY

In line with Bacon's thinking, Henry Oldenburg, the Royal Society's secretary, wrote that the goal of the society was "to raise a Masculine Philosophy . . . whereby the mind of man may be ennobled with the knowledge of Sold Truths" (cited in Keller 1985, 52). Thomas Sprat, who wrote an early history of the Royal Society, published just seven years after the founding of the Royal Society, stressed the key role of Bacon: "His works contained the best Arguments, that can be produced for the Defence of experimental Philosophy, and the best Directions, that are needful to promote it" (cited in Pyenson and Sheets-Pyenson 1999, 78). The Royal Society originated as an informal gathering of twelve men at Gresham College in London in 1660. The group called itself the Royal Society of London for Improving Natural Knowledge, and it met twice a week. Charles II granted it a royal charter in 1661 (Pyenson and Sheets-Pyenson 1999, 79). Although the society admitted members of "different Religions, Countries, and Professions of Life," it was clearly geared toward men. Only men were referred to in the section dealing with membership: "They admit Men of all Religions . . . Of all Countries . . . Of all Professions" (Sprat 1958, 64–66). The Royal Society often admitted men on the basis of their social standing in society. A man above the rank of baron, for example, could become a member without going through the same process as those of a lower social standing (Birch 1756–1757, 2: 175).

Although the Royal Society was less rigid in terms of membership than the French Academy of Sciences, women were barred from membership until 1945, when Kathleen Londsdale, who worked in the fields of crystallography, chemistry, and physics, and Marjory Stephenson, a biochemist and microbiologist, were admitted as fellows. (This information was kindly provided to me by Stephanie

Morris, Information Officer, Royal Society of London. For more information see http://www.royalsoc.ac.uk.)

The French Academy of Sciences

The history of the scientific academy in Europe is intrinsically connected to the Roman Catholic Church with all its misogynist views, especially in France. The French Academy of Sciences, founded by Jean Baptiste Colbert, Louis XIV's finance minister, in 1666, was the successor to a group led by the monk Marin Mersenne (1588–1648), a member of the mendicant order of Minims. Mersenne, a great man of learning, produced twenty-four editions of the works of his friends, including Galileo, Hobbes, and others. His greatest personal contribution to science was in acoustics, a branch of physics (Whitmore 1967, 145, 150). Mersenne was known to all the prominent scientists at the time. He was a personal friend of Descartes; he translated Galileo's *Dialogo sopra i due massimi sistemi del mondo* (Dialogue Concerning the Two Chief World Systems, 1632) and his *Discorsi* (Discourse, 1638) into French (Ornstein 1928, 140). Mersenne and his followers held weekly meetings in Paris, and they held conferences and corresponded among themselves. This group was called the Academia Parisiensis (Parisian Academy). We do not know the exact date of its establishment; however, historians date it to sometime before 1635. Although Mersenne never became a secretary of a scientific academy, "by temperament and ability, he was clearly cut out to be one" (Whitmore 1967, 150). Mersenne believed the role of the academy to be that of a great teacher. Mersenne's circle included Pierre Gassendi (1592–1652), a cleric and the chair of mathematics at the Collège Royale in Paris. The French were leaders in the field of mathematics at the time. The group consisted of not only French scientists, but also foreigners, including future members of the British Royal Society. Mersenne's group also corresponded with the Royal Society (Ornstein 1928, 142–143).

Gassendi became Mersenne's successor upon his death. At that time, the group moved to the home of Henri Louis Hubert de Montfort, another scientist and member of the Council of State. The group became known as the Montfort Academy. It adopted an informal constitution in 1657 and met on a weekly basis. This group later became the Academy of Sciences (Pyenson and Sheets-Pyenson 1999, 84), which became the most powerful scientific institution in Europe (Noble 1992, 220–222). The Academy later published the scientific activities of these groups in its early papers (Noble 1992, 144).

Females were naturally excluded from the start. The men who

composed the embryo of the French Academy were adamantly opposed to both heresy and religious enthusiasm, both of which they associated with females. In addition, given the attitude of churchmen toward female intelligence and female roles in society, it was a given that they would be kept out at all costs.

Curiously, there is not a word about women on the Academy's official Web site, which recounts its illustrious history. The official Web site of the Academy states:

> The Paris Academy of Sciences has a long and prestigious history. Created in 1666 under the aegis of Colbert, the new institution provided a forum to pursue meetings already initiated by various scholars who, working informally with such figures as Mersenne, sought to free themselves from the uncertainties of private patronage while ensuring the material means to indulge in their research. The status of Royal institution was conferred upon the institution by Louis XIV, who granted his protection to the Academy in 1699. Its history is one of rich activity, not only in terms of history of science per se. The Academy has at one time or another included the greatest French and many foreign scientists among its members, many of whom have presented their best work there. It is also prominent in the more general area of the political, economic and social history of France. (Académie des Sciences 2003)

Interestingly, the site provides a list of important dates in the Academy's history, but the date of admittance of women as members is not there.

The misogyny of the academy persisted well into the twentieth century. The case of Marie Curie demonstrates this point well. Physicist Marie Curie received the Nobel Prize with her husband Pierre in 1903 for their discovery of polonium and radium. In 1911, she received the Nobel Prize for chemistry. As a Sorbonne professor and Nobel Prize winner, Curie thought quite naturally that she would be an obvious candidate for the French Academy of Sciences. A membership in the Academy would entitle her to privileges she had not known in her career, such as presenting her latest research findings to its weekly seminar and having them published in its prestigious journal. Curie put her name into the running in 1910 to help her research group. She was a candidate for the physics section, but she lost by one vote. Both her sex and her nationality—she was Polish rather than French—hurt her (Crosland 1992, 234–235; McGrayne 1998, 29–20).

It was not until 12 March 1962 that the first woman was elected to the French Academy of Sciences as a corresponding member without

Chemist Marie Curie in her laboratory (Bettmann / Corbis)

the rights and responsibilities of full members, such as voting rights. I had considerable difficulty in obtaining this information, which I received from Mary Brodbeck, an official at the American National Science Foundation Office located in the American embassy in Paris, who contacted Claudine Pouret from the Academy. The first woman elected to the Academy as a corresponding member was a French physicist and chemist named Marguerite Perey (1909–1975). Perey was a research fellow at the Centre National de la Recherche Scientifique (CNRS) and subsequently had a chair in nuclear chemistry at the Université de Strasbourg.

The lack of women members has apparently changed within the last fifty years. Women had to wait until 1979, with the election of Yvonne Choquet-Bruhat, for a full member. The French Academy of Sciences elected its first female president as recently as December 1994. She is Marianne Grunberg-Manago, who is the head of the Biochemistry Department of the Institute of Physico-Chemical Biology at the CNRS. The academy has only 4 full and 8 corresponding women members out of a total number of 150 full members, 300 corresponding members, and 120 foreign associates (National Science Foundation Europe, 4 April 2003).

The Female Alternative to the Academy: The Salon in France

The salon, as discussed in Chapter 5, developed because females were barred from academies and universities, or formal institutions of learning and science. Women of the seventeenth century wanted access to scientific knowledge and even the chance to practice it, and thus private, informal institutions began in people's homes. These groups tended to be informal and unofficial and composed of members of the upper classes. In France, they took the form of salons in the mansions of Paris, and in England of informal meetings on the estates of the nobility. Unlike the academies and universities, such assemblies allowed women a role. Interestingly, males were a permanent fixture at the salons and eventually came to dominate them in

the eighteenth century, but females were kept out of the academies. One can trace this tradition of keeping women out of scientific societies to that begun by the universities and the cathedral schools that preceded them. This was the culture of masculinity and the ascetic tradition (Schiebinger 1989, 30–31).

The salon in France tended to be a literary rather than a scientific institution; however, by the middle of the seventeenth century, the *Cartésiennes,* or female followers of Descartes's philosophy, held discussion groups about Descartes's ideas in their homes. Apparently,

Descartes's philosophy was discussed at salons held by women, including Madame de Sablière, Madame Deshoulières, and Madame de Bonnevaux, who likely lectured on Descartes in her home. (See the lists of learned women in contemporary sources such as Marguerite Buffet, *Traité sur les éloges des illustres sçavantes, anciennes et modernes* [Treatise of Eulogies about Illustrious Wise Women Old and New, 1668], and Jean de Forge, *Le Cercle des femmes sçavantes* [The Circle of Wise Women, 1663] cited in Harth 1992, 65.) Unfortunately, these women did not leave behind them a corpus of writings. Salons, by their nature as informal meetings in private spaces, were inferior to the newly founded scientific societies and academies and could not provide the kind of institutional support that women needed to make real scientific contributions (Harth 1992, 4–5).

The English Model: Science at Home

In England, where there were no salons, there were several examples of similar scientific discussion groups or meetings that took place outside the official academy and afforded women a voice. These groups and meetings provided a place for women to discuss and practice science and, in some ways, were unofficial academies.

The Doreset Estate of scientist Robert Boyle (1627–1691) and his sisters Mary, who became Lady Warwick, and Katherine, who became Lady Ranelagh, was one example of the English model of science. Boyle, most commonly remembered as the father of modern chemistry, was a key apologist for the new science, expounding its rationale, working out its philosophical implications, and reflecting at length on the mutual relations between science and religion. He was a member of the first council of the Royal Society, a prominent lecturer on the new science, an important democratizer of science, and was particularly interested in teaching women science. Beginning in 1668, Boyle lived with Lady Ranelagh and had his laboratory in her home. His sisters assisted him with a work on medical cures and herbal remedies (Noble 1992, 199). Boyle's niece, Lady Thanet, was an amateur scientist who learned about science through her uncle (Phillips 1990, 123).

Two Products of the English Model:
Anne Conway and Margaret Cavendish

Another example of an estate serving as a center for such an informal arrangement for doing science was Ragley Hall, the home of Anne

Finch Conway (1631–1679). Ragley Hall was the intellectual center for such scientific and philosophic luminaries as Henry More; Francis Mercury Van Helmont, a friend of Leibniz; Joseph Glanvill; and Ralph Cudworth (Noble 1992, 199–200). Conway, a scientist in her own right, will be compared with Margaret Cavendish further on in the chapter; they were scientists with different strategies for gaining access to and practicing science during this era when official institutions were closed to women.

Conway was a sickly woman who suffered from terrible headaches; she wrote only one book. She received a good education at home in the classics and mathematics, tutored by her brother's teacher, Cambridge Platonist and theologian Henry More (1614–1687). More was a critic of Descartes, Spinoza, and Hobbes. Richard Popkin calls More a "major figure . . . in the Third Force in seventeenth century thought, a movement that grew out of the attempt to overcome the sceptical crisis of the time through religious activity and inspired readings of the prophecies in Scripture" (cited in Hutton 1990, 98). Anne Conway later became More's colleague.

In addition to receiving a solid education, Conway had connections to the scientific world through her father, Sir Henry Finch (Sergeant-at-Law, Recorder of the City of London, and Speaker of the House of Commons), who was part of the group that founded the Royal Society. He knew Margaret Cavendish's husband, William Cavendish, duke of Newcastle, and the mathematician and Royal Society member John Pell (Phillips 1990, 145–146). Conway made a serious contribution to science and influenced both contemporaries and successors such as the father of German science, Leibniz, and Emilie du Châtelet in the eighteenth century.

Conway's only work, *Principles of the Most Ancient and Modern Philosophy, Concerning God, Christ, and the Creature; that is concerning Spirit and Matter in general,* was published posthumously in 1690 in Latin in Amsterdam by Francis Mercury Van Helmont (1614–1698), a Dutch philosopher, mystic, and physician whom she met via More (Hutton 1994, 8). Conway wrote anonymously, so Van Helmont was credited with the work (Merchant 1980, 257; McAllister 1996, 92). Most scholars agree that Conway came up with an original philosophical synthesis that was quite different from that of her tutor, Henry More (Alic 1986, 8; Conway 1982, 16). Conway, unlike More, was one of the first philosophers/scientists to challenge Descartes's dualistic philosophy. She viewed body and spirit as one, as she explained: "I say, life and figure are distinct attributes of one substance, and as one and the same body may be transmitted into all kinds of figures; and as the perfecter figure comprehends that which is more imperfect; so one and the same body may be transmuted from one degree of life to another more perfect, which always comprehends it in the inferior" (cited in Waithe 1991, 70–71). She employed the term "monad" or particle, or "elemental matter"—in essence, her philosophy was all about substance—in a similar way to Leibniz, although Conway thought that monads had some sort of spiritual as well as physical essence (Conway 1982, 21). She identified three classes of substances: God (lacking in bodily form), Christ (with some bodily form), and all other created substances, which have both corporeal and spiritual, or mental, aspects to them (Conway 1982, 21–22).

Conway was a major proponent of the philosophy of monadology, which combined both matter and spirit. This was rather different from the mechanistic ideas of Descartes, Hobbes, and Spinoza that influenced Margaret Cavendish, our second product of the English model.

A very different group of people met in an informal academy or scientific grouping at the estate of Margaret and William Cavendish, including Descartes, Marin Mersenne, Pierre Gassendi, and Thomas Hobbes (Noble 1992, 200).

Margaret Cavendish, known as "Mad Madge" for her boldness and eccentricity, was the first Englishwoman to write extensively about natural science and philosophy. (Walter Scott in *Peveril of the Peak* called her "that old mad-woman, the Duchess of Newcastle," and "author of trash" [cited in Bazeley 1990, 5].) Between 1649 and 1668, she published in various genres: biography, autobiography, drama, poetry, romance, and science (Meyer 1955, 2–3). Although she lacked a formal education, in the sense that she did not attend school and university, Margaret Cavendish was not stopped by the conventional views about female abilities. She read Descartes and became a committed Cartesian. She also read the works of Hobbes, Henry More, and Van Helmont. She authored fourteen books published in twenty-four editions (Mell et al. 1998, 59). Whatever contemporaries and modern-day scholars think of her—mad, eccentric, fanciful, outlandish—the fact remains that she accomplished, in both word and deed, what few women dared in her day. As historian of science Londa Schiebinger has aptly pointed out, Cavendish "was not only one of the first women to produce original natural philosophy, she was also the boldest and most prolific." Cavendish made an attempt to take part in the scientific debates of her day discussing "matter and motion, the existence of the vacuum, the nature of magnetism, life and generation, color and fire, perception and knowledge, free will and God" (Waithe 1991, 5).

Margaret Cavendish was born to a privileged family in 1623 or 1624, to Thomas and Elizabeth Lucas. Her father, who died when Margaret was two, was a member of the minor nobility of St. John's near Colchester (Evelyn 1908, 3: 478; Waithe 1991, 1). In 1645 she married William Cavendish, the duke of Newcastle, who was an exiled commander-in-chief of the Royalist forces during the English Civil Wars. He was some thirty years Margaret's senior and had held considerable power in Charles I's Privy Council before the outbreak of civil war (Bazeley 1990, 1). Margaret, who had been a maid of honor to Charles I's wife, Henrietta Maria, left England with the royal family. The Cavendishes spent the period of the Commonwealth in exile in Holland, returning to England in 1660 upon the restoration of the monarchy (Smith 1998, 53).

E. Scriven, sc.

Margaret Cavendish, duchess of Newcastle and author (Bettmann/Corbis)

Cavendish was a woman who pursued scientific interests through the networks introduced to her by her husband. For example, she was admitted to the informal society of the Newcastle Circle. Her brother-in-law—Sir Charles Cavendish, a mathematician and scholar—influenced Margaret's thinking and work on science, such as her *Poems and Fancies* (Mendelson 1987, 36). Thus, Cavendish was able to do science because of her privileged position in English society, which allowed her to study, write, and have access to the Newcastle Circle. As Schiebinger has aptly put it, "Without this private philosophical network, Margaret Lucas Cavendish could not have become a natural philosopher" (Schiebinger 1991, 2). Although Cavendish benefited greatly from the contacts and knowledge gained through the Newcastle Circle, she primarily worked on her own or with her husband and other members of her family. Her brother, Lord John Lucas, was an early fellow of the Royal Society. Cavendish herself wrote that she "never had a familiar acquaintance, or constant conversation with any profest Scholar, in my life . . ." (Cavendish in Schiebinger 1991, 3). Apparently, Descartes did not speak English, and at the dinners he sat in silence. Cavendish had little or no contact with other women in the French salons (Schiebinger 1991, 4). Thus, in spite of her connections to the Newcastle Circle, she complained about leading a rather isolated and confined life.

Londa Schiebinger theorizes that Margaret Cavendish's famous visit to the Royal Society of London in 1667 was in reaction to this isolation and the exclusion of women from these societies. As stated above, the Royal Society was the home of the new science in England and of course did not admit women at this time. However, Margaret Cavendish would have made a valid candidate as she had authored six books on natural philosophy and she had donated a great deal of money to Cambridge University. Because she was female, her possible membership was not even considered. Even her request for a visit to the society caused a great tumult. Samuel Pepys recorded the event of her visit—which occurred on 23 May 1667—and the debate that led up to it in his diary of 30 May of the same year and described the "expectation of the Duchesse of Newcastle, who had desired to be invited to the Society, and was, after much debate pro and con, it seems many being against it and we do believe the town will be full of ballets [ballads] of it. . . ." Pepys continued by describing the Duchess as a "very ordinary woman" except for her "good black little eyes." Members performed various experiments in her presence, "of Colours, Loadstones, Microscope, and of liquors: among others, of one that did while she was there turn a piece of roasted mutton into pure blood—which was very rare . . ." (Pepys 1970–1983, 8: 242–243). Royal Society member John Evelyn, in his diary, described the Duchess as a "mighty pretender to Learning, Poetrie & Philosophie, & had in both published divers bookes. . . ." Concerning her visit to the Royal Society, he merely recorded that she "came in greate pomp, & being received by our President; at the dore of our Meeting roome, the Mace &c carried before him, had severall Experiments shewed before her . . ." (Evelyn 1908, 482–483). The experiments were conducted by Robert Hooke and Robert Boyle. Margaret Alic sees the Duchess's visit to the Royal Society in a rather different light from Schiebinger. Alic considered it to be a "historic moment for the scientific lady" and a "personal triumph" for Margaret herself (Alic 1986, 82). Cavendish was the only woman to visit the Royal Society for almost 300 years. Her legacy lies in her courage, her attempt to educate herself, and her popularization of science, specifically the mechanistic view of nature.

Cavendish complained about the isolation that she felt. She found fault with her own lack of formal schooling and with female ignorance in general. She wrote in 1655 to Oxford and Cambridge about her views on these matters in her dedication of her work, *Philosophical and Physical Opinions,* written in 1652 and published in 1653:

> To the Two Most Famous Universities of England, as they ought to encourage any idealistic movement for the emancipation of women, lest in time we should grow irrational idiots . . . for we are kept like birds in cages to hop up and down in our houses; not suffered to fly abroad to see the several changes of fortune, and the various humours, ordained and created by nature; thus wanting the experiences of nature, we must needs the understanding and knowledge and so consequently Prudence, and Invention of Men. (Cited in Perry 1918, 186–187)

She almost apologized for her lack of formal education; however, she did not consider that lack to be a sign that women were less intelligent than men or incapable of learning:

> As for learning, that I am not versed in it, no body, I hope will blame me for it, since it is sufficiently known, that our sex is not bred up to it, as being not suffer'd to be instructed in Schools and Universities; I will not say, but many of our Sex may have as much wit, and be capable of learning as well as men; but since they want Instructions, it is not possible they should attain to it; for learning is Artificial but Wit is Natural. (Cited in Mell et al. 1998, 59–60)

She condemned female exclusion from universities and the newly formed professional scientific societies, yet she sent copies of her works to Oxford and Cambridge. Her last work of natural philosophy, *Grounds of Natural Philosophy* (1668), was dedicated to "all the universities of Europe" (Mell et al. 1998, 59–60).

Margaret Cavendish was not always consistent in her "feminism" and, for this reason, some modern scholars such as Mary Ann McGuire, Hilda Smith, and Sara Heller Mendelson criticize her views as "outspoken if inconsistent feminism" (Bazeley 1990, 14). McGuire believed that Cavendish "was unable to shake off old ideas of woman's innate inferiority but was uncomfortable with traditional female roles" (McGuire 1978, 204). Smith called her the "most puzzling of seventeenth century feminists . . . [whose] views were at once the most radical and far-reaching and the most contradictory" (Smith 1982, 12, 75). Mendelson considered Cavendish to be "an egoist who happened to be of the female gender" (Mendelson 1987, 55). Arguments put forth by Deborah Taylor Bazeley, in her 1990 unpublished thesis, focus on Cavendish's scientific works, where one finds her "boldest feminist doctrine" (Bazeley 1990, 15). She considered Margaret Cavendish's importance as an "outspoken feminist, into such elite intellectual pre-serves as science and literary publication. . . ." She concluded that the fact that Cavendish made no attempt to reconcile her "conflicting nar-ratives" was not important. Rather, Cavendish's candid writings re-flected the struggle going on within her and within the changing na-ture of seventeenth-century England. In short, Cavendish provides an example of a pioneering feminist (Bazeley 1990, 17–18).

Nevertheless, Margaret Cavendish attempted to heighten female interest in science through her works, especially her *Observations upon Experimental Philosophy* (1688), perhaps her most important work. This piece, her fifth philosophical writing, was published with an ac-companying pseudoscientific romance, *The Description of the New Blaz-ing World* (1666). In her preface, she wrote, "Most Ladies take no de-light in Philosophical Arguments" (Smith 1998, 59). This problem, she believed, needed to be addressed. Her goal was to both instruct and entertain—a goal similar to Fontenelle's in his *Plurality of Worlds*. She was thus writing science under the guise of romance.

Her *Observations* provided a critique of the experimental science of Bacon: "I confess, I have had little faith in Such Arts, and as little in Telescopical, Microscopical, and the like inspections, and prefer ratio-nal and judicious Observations before deluding Glasses and Experi-ments" (cited in Smith 1998, 59). Margaret and William had pur-chased a Dutch microscope during their exile in Holland and she criticized the microscope and telescope as imperfect machines: "Con-cave and convex glasses, and the like . . . represent the figure of an Object . . . very deformed and misshaped: also a Glass that is flaw'd, crack'd, or broke . . . will present numerous pictures of one Object" (Cavendish 1668, 7–8). Her book covered astronomy and meteorol-ogy. The Duchess also wrote about medicine.

Anne Conway and Margaret Cavendish were two exceptional women for their era. Both were interested in and investigated the new theories explaining the workings of the universe. Cavendish shows us that one did not require a formal university education to do science. Although she complained bitterly about her lack of education and her denial of access to the university, she did occupy a privileged social position in society through her family and her marriage, which allowed her to make contacts with contemporary men of science that she otherwise would not have been able to make. She was able to practice a form of science that did not require a formal education. The new science of the seventeenth century, the science that was called natural philosophy, "did not have a weight of book-learning to support it, and it existed outside the institutions of learning." According to Sarah Hutton, this is how women like Cavendish were able to practice a form of science. Having said that, it remains true that the exclusion from the university and the nascent academies and scientific societies meant that women's science remained a private rather than public endeavor and consequently, they did not receive the support necessary to do science.

The Age of the Enlightenment:
Science as an Unsuitable Subject for a Lady

I believe that women are only lacking in the opportunity to be
instructed and to rival men; I also see that they distinguish
themselves in spite of the obstacles of education and prejudice.
I believe that they have as much intelligence as most men to
achieve success in the sciences.

— Joseph-Jérôme de Lalande, *Astronomie des dames*

During the intellectual revolution of the eighteenth century, commonly known as the Enlightenment, the debate over the different natures of male and female intensified. Some men and women of this "Age of Reason," like the author of the epigraph that begins this chapter, followed the example of the Cartesians of the previous century and indeed went even further in challenging tradition. At the same time, the attack on any departure from the traditional female role grew stronger. During the period of the High Enlightenment, a new corpus of literature was produced in England, France, and Germany, defining finer boundaries of sex differences than had been articulated in the past. As Londa Schiebinger has articulated, the arguments concerning the nature of women that began to be stated in an "impartial" or "scientific" manner during the eighteenth century continue to have an effect even now on "women's relationship to science" (Schiebinger 1986, 43).

The late eighteenth century produced three views about women's nature and abilities: (1) Women were mentally and socially inferior to men (Rousseau, Diderot, Roussel, and Kant); (2) women were equal but different (Voltaire, who actually worked with a woman scientist—his mistress Emilie du Châtelet—and was amazed to find that a woman was capable of rational thinking); and (3) women were potentially equal in both mental ability and contribution to society (d'Alembert, Helvétius, and Condorcet).

Leading the debate was the French philosophe Jean-Jacques Rousseau, whose antifeminist writings were highly influential. According to Rousseau, women's role was to devote herself to motherhood and to the service of her male partner. He considered women to be passive, weak, sensuous, and accommodating and men strong and rational. Other philosophes, including those who put together the *Encyclopédie,* echoed Rousseau's sentiments. These included men like Montesquieu and Diderot, to name two. In Germany, Immanuel Kant took up Rousseau's views. Women, he argued, had a different kind of mind than men, a mind in which abstract thinking was impossible.

Two of the few voices on the other side of the debate were the highly respected French astronomer Joseph-Jérôme Le Français de Lalande and the Marquis du Condorcet. Lalande (1732–1807) was a professor of astronomy at the Collège de France and director of the Paris Observatory. He was also member of the French Institute and several European academies. Lalande was primarily known in his day for his tables of planets. His work in calculating the distance to the moon was his first contribution to astronomy (Porter and Ogilvie 2000a, 582). Our interest in him here concerns his support for three women of science during the eighteenth century, most notably Mesdames Nichole-Reine Lepaute and Louise du Pierry in France and Laura Bassi in Italy. All three women were mathematicians and astronomers whom he encouraged and with whom he even collaborated. Lalande produced a work entitled *Bibliothèque universelle des dames: Astronomie* (Universal Library for the Ladies: Astronomy, 1786), the first history of women astronomers, which he dedicated to a woman astronomer, Madame Louise Du Pierry.

The French mathematician, philosophe, and revolutionary the Marquis de Condorcet was a prominent "feminist." Condorcet, secretary of the French Academy of Sciences many years before the revolution, promoted female education and participation outside the private sphere.

Emilie du Châtelet was certainly not the only working female scientist during the eighteenth century in France, but she is perhaps the most well-known one because of her relationship with Voltaire and her high social standing. Other less renowned women of science, yet also worthy of mention, are Madame Nichole-Reine Lepaute, Madame Louise du Pierry, and Madame Marie Anne Lavoisier. Their importance to the contribution to the debate on women in science during this period is not so much what they wrote, but what they accomplished and how they were able to accomplish what they did.

The Swiss philosopher Jean-Jacques Rousseau (1712–1778) was one of the most influential thinkers of the eighteenth century. Rousseau is credited for being among the first Western European authors to argue in favor of equality among men. However, he did not extend this equality to the fair sex. Men and women differed in their fundamental natures. Although man has been endowed by God with "boundless passions," these "passions" are controlled by reason. Women are also endowed with the same "boundless passions," but their passions are restrained by modesty rather than reason (Rousseau 1974, 323).

In addition to his writings on politics and government, which had a tremendous impact on French revolutionaries such as Maximilien Robespierre, Rousseau wrote one of the most influential works on education in history, *Emile,* first published in 1762. Here we find not only theories on education, presented in the form of a simple romance, but also Rousseau's major ideas concerning women. The book is for the most part concerned with male education and the reforms needed in the educational system of the day. Emile is the principal male character. Book 5 deals with female education by describing the education of Sophie, Emile's future wife. Although a treatise on education, *Emile* provides a clear statement about Rousseau's views on the nature of men and women, on women's role in society, and on female capabilities for science.

Rousseau was definitely not in favor of equality between the sexes. Rather he put forth the theory of complementarism: "Where sex is concerned man and woman are unlike; each is the complement to the other" (Rousseau 1974, 321). They "are made for each other," but Rousseau was clear on who was in control: "Nature has decreed that woman, both for herself and for her children, should be at the mercy of a man's judgment." Not unlike Aristotle, Rousseau argued that women are "weak and passive and timid" and men "strong and active" (Rousseau 1974, 328). These characteristics are placed in women to help them appropriately fill their proper role, which itself is dependent on men: "She cannot fulfill her purpose in life without his aid, without his good will, without his respect; she is dependent on our feelings, on the price we put on her virtue, etc. . . . . She will always be in subjection to a man or to man's judgement" (Rousseau 1974, 328, 333). The reason for this is biological: "The male is only male now and again, the female is always a female, or at least all of her youth; everything reminds her of her sex; the performance of her functions requires a special constitution" (Rousseau 1974, 324).

French Enlighten-ment philosopher Jean-Jacques Rousseau (Library of Congress)

What then, was the female role? To please her man. Rousseau explained: Woman is "made for man's delight." Sophie should be first and foremost a devoted wife and mother. She should please others and never think about pleasing herself. "A woman's education must therefore be planned in relation to man. To be pleasing in his sight, to win his respect and love, to train him in childhood, tend him in manhood, to counsel and console, to make his life pleasant and happy, these are the duties of woman for all time, and this is what she should be taught while she is young" (Rousseau 1974, 321). There was no place for a woman in the public sphere. Nor was there a need for female education beyond learning how to be a good wife and mother.

Rousseau, in fact, was pleased that there were no schools for girls: "There are no colleges for girls; so much the better for them" (Rousseau 1974, 327). He assumed that woman, once married, would either be pregnant or looking after her offspring, and even if this were not the case, could this lifestyle of childcare be changed overnight? He thought not: "Even if there were these long intervals, which you assume, between the periods of pregnancy, can a woman suddenly change her way of life without danger? Can she be a nursing mother today and a soldier tomorrow?" (Rousseau 1974, 325). The occupations for women, other than taking care of men and children, included household tasks, singing, and especially needlework: "Needlework is what Sophie likes best. . . . There is nothing that she cannot do without a needle . . . ; but lace making is her favorite occupation. . . . She has also studied all the details of housekeeping; she understands cooking and cleaning; she knows the prices of food and how to choose it; she can keep accounts accurately, she is her mother's housekeeper" (Rousseau 1974, 357).

And what of abstract thought and science? Are women even capable of such endeavors? Rousseau explained himself very clearly on this matter:

The search for abstract and speculative truths, for principles and axioms in science, for all that tends to wide generalization, is beyond a woman's grasp; their studies should be thoroughly practical. It is their business to apply the principles discovered by men, it is their place to make the observations which lead men to discover those principles. . . . The works of genius are beyond her reach, and she has neither the accuracy nor the attention for success in the exact sciences; as for the physical sciences, to divide the relations between living creatures and the laws of nature is the task of that sex which is more active and enterprising, which sees more things, that sex which is possessed of greater strength and is more accustomed to the exercise of that strength. Woman, weak as she is and limited in her range of observation, perceives and judges the forces at her disposal to supplement her weakness, and those forces are the passions of man." (Rousseau 1974, 349–350)

Rousseau believed not only that women were weak in intellect, but that to even attempt to educate them as one does a man is doing them a disservice: "Do not try to make your daughter a good man in defiance of nature." This does not mean that they cannot learn: "They should learn many things, but only such things as are suitable" (Rousseau 1974, 327).

In his *Lettre à d'Alembert* (1758), Rousseau expressed views similar to those found in *Emile*. Based on the natural order of things, woman's role was to be a modest, nurturing mother, to spend her life in the private sphere. Denis Diderot's (1713–1784) views were rather traditional when compared with some of his contemporaries. He took an active interest in medical science throughout his life, and the knowledge that he learned about women through medicine colored his views about women. Although he did not attend medical school, he read widely and learned medicine through discussions with physician friends, many of whom were the most prominent of their day (Fleder 1978, 23–24), men he met as chief editor of the famous *Encyclopédie*. He was especially interested in the physiology of the female sex.

There were two contemporary views of women from a physiological perspective. Some medical men still adhered to the view that woman was a deficient male; however, most commentators supported an analysis based on comparative anatomy. See for example, the views of Paul-Joseph Barthez, a prominent physician at Montpellier and author of the article entitled "Femme" (Woman). Anatomists no longer clung to the view of the "passive" uterus as an appropriate

Eighteenth-century French philosopher and author Denis Diderot (Helen Clergue, The Salon: A Study of French Society and Personalities in the Eighteenth Century, *1907)*

counterpart to the male member, which was active. Rather, the female was an equal counterpart of the male, an alternative sex, not an organism too weak to develop into a "more perfect" male stage, as Aristotle had it (Fleder 1978, 33). Diderot held very traditional views of women. According to Diderot, the primary role of the female was reproduction, and in reproduction lay her significance to society. Only through reproduction could the female serve the good of society; she did not have a public role (Fleder 1978, 56). Diderot's work focused on the biological or physiological aspects of the female. The functioning of the female body was more problematical and precarious than that of the male. In his essay "Sur les Femmes" (On Women), Diderot outlined the specifically female functions, which he interpreted as a series of physical burdens: menstruation, reproduction, and menopause. The female sex was not made for "serious study" (Diderot, cited in Fleder 1978, 43–44). The nature of woman according to Diderot can be summarized as follows: Woman is a "naturally weak and sick animal who must be kept away from functions which require reflection, good health and strength" (Diderot 1951, 169).

The eighteenth-century medical doctor Pierre Roussel set out a physiologically based theory, which provided support for Rousseau's more sociologically oriented views about women. His work entitled *Système physique et moral de la femme* (Moral and Physical System of Woman, 1775) was printed five times before 1809, and the information it expounded was considered sound well into the next century (McMillan 2000, 5–6).

Roussel supported Rousseau's hypothesis that there were great differences between the male and the female. These differences were not merely limited to the sexual organs (Roussel 1775, 2). He wrote, "We believe . . . that the difference between the sexes can be seen in their characters because different instruments must produce different effects" (Roussel 1775, 22). First, he pointed out that in terms of physical characteristics, the female was "delicate and tender and remained as a child." The texture of her organs never lost its original softness (Roussel 1775, 6, 16). This softness meant that women were designed for "a passive state" (Roussel 1775, 31). Second, he used the physical characteristics of women to justify his conviction that women were limited in their intelligence. Roussel was not entirely negative in his examination of women; he believed that women's strengths were in the realm of intuition rather than reason, and that her thoughts were spontaneous (Roussel 1775, 29). He also believed that women were superior to men in terms of courage and aptitude (Roussel 1775, 22). Women should be admired for their patience in carrying out the most painful tasks, such as carrying and bearing babies. But women should know their place in society, and "the woman who protests against her condition and destiny is depraved" (Roussel 1775, 48).

Immanuel Kant, eighteenth-century German philosopher (Library of Congress)

The German idealist philosopher Immanuel Kant (1742–1804) was one author greatly influenced by Rousseau's *Emile*. Key concepts in Kant with respect to male and female are the sublime (male) and the beautiful (female). The beautiful is charming, attractive, natural, and gladdening, while the sublime is noble. Kant wrote a pamphlet called *Observations of the Feeling of the Beautiful and the Sublime* in 1764, two years after Rousseau published his *Emile*. Kant identified two types of human beings, male and female: Females were characterized by beauty, males by nobility. Females were charming, attractive, and pretty, while males were sublime, or noble. "Woman is the beautiful sex." Kant generalized: "Her figure is finer, her features more delicate and gentler, and her mien more engaging and more expressive of friendliness, pleasantry, and kindness than in the male." He believed that "certain specific traits lie especially in the personality of this sex which distinguish it clearly from ours." Further, "the fair sex has just as much understanding; but it is a beautiful understanding, whereas ours should be a deep understanding" (Kant 1960, 78).

In terms of education, women should not receive any instruction in science—no history, geography, mathematics, or philosophy. From Kant's point of view, "laborious learning or painful pondering, even if a woman should greatly succeed in it, destroys the merits that are proper to her sex. . . . At the same time, they will weaken the charms with which she exercises her great power over the other sex." He saw it as a mistake to allow women to compete with men on intellectual grounds: "We must leave abstract speculation, useful knowledge to the laborious and solid mind of man. . . . Thus women should not learn geometry" (Kant 1764, 78).

Arguments in Favor of Women: D'Alembert, Helvétius, and Condorcet

Jean Le Rond d'Alembert (1751–1772), a philosophe like Rousseau and one of the editors of the famous *Encyclopédie,* took a more liberal stance in his view of women. D'Alembert attacked the education system of eighteenth-century France and recommended several reforms. He criticized Rousseau's dismal view of women, suggesting that perhaps it was related to Rousseau's unsuccessful personal relationships with women, such as Madame d'Epinay and his sister-in-law Madame d'Houdetot (Brooks in Williams 1975, 216). Another philosophe, Claude-Adrien Helvétius (1715–1771), took a similar view, also quarrelling with Rousseau over the question of female aptitude and education in his work, *De l'homme* (A Treatise on Man, 1772). Unlike Rousseau, Helvétius believed in an equality of mind in all individuals from birth. He believed males and females to be different: "The organization of the two sexes, is without a doubt, in some respects different." However, he did not see that this difference had to be seen as "the cause of the inferiority of the minds of women" (Helvétius 1969, 1: 156). He proved his point of lack of female intellectual inferiority by using examples of intelligent and powerful women from the past, including Sappho, Hypatia, Elizabeth of England, and Catherine II of Russia. He asked whether these women could be considered inferior to men. In common with Condorcet, Helvétius seemed to blame female inferiority on the poor education that females continued to receive (Helvétius 1969, 1: 156).

The Marquis de Condorcet (1743–1794) was one of the few Enlightenment thinkers who argued in favor of equality of rights for men and women. He recognized that women were first and foremost human beings before they were wives and mothers. As human beings, they possessed the same natural rights men did. Following from this principle, it was necessary that they "obtain the same facilities for acquiring knowledge that permit them to exercise these rights" (Condorcet 1847–1849, 7: 217).

Condorcet criticized contemporaries such as Rousseau who focused on the physical differences between male and female. He thought that these philosophers exaggerated these differences and on that unsound basis assigned "to each sex their roles, their prerogatives, their occupations, their duties and almost their desires, pleasures and feelings" (Condorcet 1847–1849, 9: 630).

Condorcet did acknowledge that women were physically weaker and emotionally different, but stated that this should not be seen as meaning they were unequal. In a speech to the French Academy (of which he was secretary before the French Revolution) on 21 February 1782, he inquired, "Has nature set some differences between men and women? Doubtless, women are weaker. . . ." However, he added, "The physical force depends on the muscles, upon which it is very doubtful that the force of mind and spirit depends." The other differences between male and female were all a result of education, or a lack of it: "As for intellectual qualities, it appears that in everything pertaining to subtlety of ideas or sentiments, to memory, to soundness of mind, to patience and assiduity in work, there are no differences other than those deriving from education. The only quality that no woman has ever demonstrated is genius, or the gift of discovery" (Condorcet 1976, 25–26). Condorcet provided some believable explanations for the lack of genius and great discoveries by women. He posited that very few women had devoted themselves to study and "none of the few women destined for genius has been in a position to display it." Female education at the time was seriously lacking in terms of the development of the thinking faculties. Finally, he wrote: "The gift of discovery pertains to one thing: the force of attention. Women's attention span is weaker than a small number of men and equal to the rest." Women's minds are not put to the most "enlightened use" when they are developing and this is "an obstacle to the advance of women in the arts and sciences" (Condorcet 1976, 26).

Women, he alleged, were endowed with reason. Again, when he made this remark, he was refuting what other writers of his age had alleged: "It has been said that women, in spite of much ability . . . are never governed by what is called reason. This observation is not correct. . . . They are governed by their own reason. Their interests not being the same as those of men through the fault of the laws, the same thing not having the same importance for them as us, they can (without lacking reason) govern themselves by different principles and seek a different goal" (Condorcet 1976, 99).

It is not surprising, then, that Condorcet put great stress upon education. He denounced the inequality in the education of men and women as the principal source of the moral and legal inferiority of women. In the tradition of Poulain de la Barre, the Cartesian feminist of the seventeenth century, Condorcet argued that each individual should be instructed well enough to exercise his or her civil rights. The issue of the role of education in determining the development of the human mind had been at the heart of feminist thought since Poulain de la Barre. Condorcet, however, went further than Poulain in declaring that the achievement of intellectual equality between male and female was an aspect of the perfectibility of thinking, reflection, memory, and attention. Condorcet stressed culture as a factor in equality. He wrote, "Thought creates a function of thinking. Knowledge is not merely the accumulation of facts, but a process of acquisition, an education of the organs themselves." Condorcet proposed a common education for both boys and girls in mixed schools (Condorcet 1847–1849, 7: 221–222).

Condorcet's plan for the instruction of females was not based simply on a desire to promote egalitarianism. His purpose was the perfection of humanity. He believed that this aim could be achieved through education and transmitted through the female. In other words, characteristics of physical and intellectual perfection that could be acquired through education would lead to the perfection of the species. Thus the female's right to learning, to knowledge, was not only a moral imperative but also an anthropological necessity. The female transmits to her children their potential according to the way she has developed her own faculties (Condorcet 1847–1849, 6: 275).

Condorcet specifically addressed the question of female scientists. Women could make a unique contribution to science and scientific discoveries, and might even be better suited than men to this discipline. For one thing, women had traditionally been more sedentary and were not usually engaged in paid employment; thus they could meditate and concentrate (Condorcet 1847–1849, 16: 333). But if women could make a useful contribution to the sciences, whether in terms of making observations or writing books, the question arose of why there had not been any great women scientists. Condorcet suggested, as mentioned above, that women were indeed inferior to a small group of male geniuses, though not to the average man: "Since it would be completely absurd to restrict to this superior class the rights of citizenship and eligibility for public functions, why should women be excluded from them any more than those men who are inferior to a great number of men?" (Condorcet 1847–1849, 16: 98).

Montesquieu: A Complex View of Women

The aim of Montesquieu's writings was to discuss the distinctively human means of achieving happiness, based on intelligence and the kind of knowledge animals cannot acquire. He stressed the relationship between man and society. According to Montesquieu, all men were born equal, and slavery went against nature. Montesquieu's view of mankind was a positive one (Rosso 1977). Scholars disagree about Montesquieu's views on women. Léon Abensour considered him to be a feminist; Jeannette Geffriaud Rosso thought of him as a misogynist, while Robert F. O'Reilly characterized him as an antifeminist (Absensour 1923; Rosso 1977; O'Reilly 1973). In many ways, he was none of the above. Montesquieu did not accept the view that women were naturally inferior to men, as did Rousseau. He attempted to explain how differing climates, geography, and political regimes affected their lives. In this sense, he was outside the debate about women. However, the vast majority of his comments and analyses concerning women "gave empirical support to the feminist ideas and to the demands for the improvement of the status of women" of his time (Kra in Spencer 1984, 272)

Montesquieu's views on women at first glance appear to be contradictory. In his article entitled "Femme" in the *Encyclopédie* (both Barthez and Montesquieu contributed an article titled "Woman"), he argued that woman was nothing greater than a deformed man. Yet in his *Spirit of the Laws,* he argued that women should be allowed to have political power, though not power in the home. In a section entitled "Of Female Administration" he wrote, "It is contrary to reason and nature that women should reign in families, as was customary among the Egyptians, but not that they should govern an empire." He reasoned: "In the former case the state of their natural weakness does not permit them to have pre-eminence; in the latter their very weakness generally gives them more lenity and moderation, qualifications fitter for a good administration than roughness and severity." Here Montesquieu argued that women's very moderation would make them better rulers than the more severe male (Montesquieu 1952, 17, 50). He referred to female rulers in Africa and, closer to home, in England (Elizabeth I) and Russia (Catherine the Great) as evidence to prove his statement. Thus Montesquieu was not a feminist in the same way as

Condorcet was. Women ought to be subordinate to men in the home, but they could play an important role in the world of politics.

Where Montesquieu differed from other writers of the Enlightenment was that he provided a sociological interpretation of political systems and laws, analyzing both women and men on the basis of the climate and the political, religious, economic, and social structures of their societies. Women's status depended significantly upon the politics of the society in which they lived, specifically on whether it was a monarchy, a republic, or a despotic regime. In a monarchy, women were freer than in either a republic or a despotic regime. In a monarchy, "the distinction of ranks calls them to court, there they assume a spirit of liberty" (Montesquieu 1952, 47). In a despotic regime, women are "an object of luxury. In this regime, where little freedom exists, women are in a state of the most rigorous servitude." In a despotic regime, "Usually women are shut away, and exercise no influence whatsoever." However, "in other countries [which are also monarchies], where women associate more with men," the lines between the genders are less clearly drawn. "What was once absolute is made to depend upon personal inclination, and *manières* [customs] change every day" (Montesquieu 1952, 211). In the last type of regime Montesquieu examined, republics, "women are free by the laws and restrained by manners" (Montesquieu 1952, 48). Montesquieu preferred monarchy as the ideal form of government.

In the same way, Montesquieu examined female nature in the light of climate and the surrounding society. Here Montesquieu resembled Diderot, in the sense that he believed that the differences between male and female physiology meant that their characters differed. The menstrual cycle did make an impact on mood and fibers, which were more delicate and flexible in women than in men. However, he did not believe that women's capabilities were inferior to those of men. Women were not lacking in reason (cited in Samia 1984, 278).

In his *Persian Letters,* which one commentator described as a "feminist manifesto" (Spencer 1984, 272), Montesquieu discussed the role and position of women in various societies. He saw them in a state of subordination and tried to figure out how they could emerge from this state. He considered to what extent freedom should be granted to women in Oriental and European societies and concluded that men possess a natural authority over women, but at the same time female talents have been repressed by a lack of education (Montesquieu 1973, 92–93, 247–254).

Emilie du Châtelet provides us with the most renowned example of an eighteenth-century woman of science, who, notwithstanding the dominant contemporary view of women and the role they actually played in society, was able to work as a mathematician and physicist. She was Voltaire's intellectual companion and mistress, and according to the experts, she had a tremendous impact on Voltaire's thought. Voltaire expressed his recognition of Emilie's expertise when he wrote a poem to her at the start of the 1738 edition of his *Eléments de la philosophie de Newton* (Elements of the Philosophy of Newton): "Immortal Emily, vast, pow'rful mind. . . . The pupil, friend, of Newton, and of Truth. . . . Thy fires transpierce me and thy charms control" (Voltaire 1967, iii). In the 1748 edition, Voltaire wrote a preface praising her efforts in these terms: "The sound study which you have done concerning many truths and the fruit of your respectable labor are what I offer to the public for your glory, for that of your sex, and for the usefulness of anyone wanting to cultivate his reason and to enjoy without effort the fruits of your research" (Voltaire 1877–1885, 22: 400). Although she assisted Voltaire with the translation of Newton into French, she did not receive credit for it at the time except from Voltaire.

Until recently, Madame du Châtelet has been relatively forgotten by both historians of the eighteenth century in general and those interested in the history of science in particular. In the past, those who have written about her tended to be either those who had an interest in Voltaire or those interested in her love affairs. (See Nancy Mitford, *Voltaire in Love* [1957]; Marguerite Claude Ferval, *Madame du Châtelet, une maîtresse de Voltaire* [1948]; Theodore Besterman, *Voltaire* [1969]; Ira Wade, *Studies on Voltaire with Some Unpublished Papers of Madame du Châtelet* [1947]; Ira Wade, *Voltaire and Madame du Châtelet: An Essay on the Intellectual Activity at Cirey* [1969].) As historian Judith Zinsser has correctly pointed out, Madame du Châtelet was the "principal woman physicien [physicist] and géomètre [mathematician] of the first half of the eighteenth century." Yet she is often "known more for her affair with Voltaire and connection with Voltaire than her own work" (Smith 1998, 1). Over the past few years, historians of science have treated aspects of her works on Leibniz's *vis viva* principle and other aspects of her *Institutions de physique* (Institutions of Physics, 1740) (Iltis 1977; Janik 1982). Esther Ehrman has published a short but informative biography, *Mme du Châtelet, Scientist, Philosopher, and Feminist of the Enlightenment* (1986). Ehrman maintained that although we have a number of

Emilie du Châtelet
(Bettmann / Corbis)

biographies, "all have focused on her life with Voltaire" (Ehrman 1986, 4).

Interestingly, Emilie was recognized in her day in the intellectual world. She was elected to the Bologna Academy of Sciences—the Italians tended to be far more open in their attitude toward women academics—and her *Institutions de physique* was translated into Italian. The Germans included her in a biographical dictionary. Kant gave her work on the nature of force a positive review (Spencer 1984, 184).

Gabrielle-Emilie le Tonnelier de Breteuil certainly came from a privileged background. She was born in Paris in 1706 and was the daughter of the baron Louis-Nicolas de Breteuil, a member of the minor nobility, and Alexandra-Elisabeth de Froulay. Her parents' home provided the venue for a lively salon every Thursday during

Emilie's youth. Her father, who taught her at home, provided her with an education superior to that of the majority of females at this time. By the age of twelve, she was trained in foreign languages, reading English, Latin, German, Spanish, and Italian. She translated Greek and Latin classical works such as Aristotle's *Politics*. As Voltaire stated, "Her father . . . made her learn Latin, which she knew as well as mme. Dacier; she knew by heart the finest passages of Horace, Virgil and Lucretius; all the philosophic works of Cicero were familiar to her. Her dominant taste was for mathematics and physics" (cited in Besterman 1958, 1: 178–179). Theodore Besterman, in his edition of her letters, commented that her education was "unique in the eighteenth century" (Besterman 1958, 1: 179).

In 1725, at the age of nineteen, Emilie married Florent-Claude, Marquis du Châtelet and count of Lomont. This was an arranged marriage, but a convenient one for Emilie; her husband, as a colonel in the French army, was rarely at home. Both partners had a series of lovers, which was not unusual for people of their class at this time. The marriage produced three children, two boys and a girl. Emilie and her husband remained on a friendly basis throughout their lives. While her husband was away, Emilie pursued her love of learning, especially mathematics, in her husband's Paris residence (Rose, Grinstein, and Rafailovich 1993, 101–102). Here she hosted a brilliant salon, attended by many of the leading mathematicians and scientists of the day. One of these was the astronomer and mathematician Pierre Louis Moreau de Maupertuis, a member of the French Academy of Sciences and author of a *Discourse on the Different Shapes of Stars* (1732). This work introduced the French to Newtonian theories (Sutton 1995, 245).

Madame du Châtelet soon became his student, and he taught her the latest scientific and mathematical discoveries. Her letters written to Maupertuis in the early 1730s clearly portray her keen interest in mathematics and their teacher-student relationship. She wrote of "an extreme desire to study" and her interest in becoming a geometrician (du Châtelet 1958, 1: 36–38). Other tutors were mathematician Alex-Claude Clairaut, Jean Bernouilli (fils), and the Swiss mathematician Samuel de Koenig. Through their teaching, she came to an understanding of the theories of Leibniz and Newton.

Yet for all of her erudition, Emilie du Châtelet was not entirely confident as a female scientist, and she certainly felt that she experienced much prejudice as a female scientist throughout her life. She aired these "feminist views" in her translation of Bertrand Mandeville's morality treatise entitled *Fable of the Bees*. Her translation of this work includes a preface written in 1735, in which she reveals her feelings of inferiority as a woman and her complaints about the existing social system, which did not allow women equal rights with men. First, she felt that women were systematically excluded from science: "I feel the complete weight of prejudice which universally excludes us from the sciences; it is one of the contradictions in life that has always amazed me, seeing that the law allows us to determine the fate of great nations, but that there is no place where we are trained to think" (cited in Wade 1947, 135). Working with some of the great minds of the age only reinforced her sense of inferiority. Although she obviously had received a unique education for her day and even for any period, her education was still inferior to that of her teachers. They had received the advantage of institutional education, from which she was excluded. She did not benefit from the intellectual stimuli of a university and the relationships that were forged there. She also realized that she would never be able to play an important public role because of her sex.

Second, she believed, like so many people, that women were lacking in education and that they had the right to a good one, like men. Most women, she argued, ignore their talents because of their terrible education, prejudice, and lack of courage. She was convinced of this because of her own experience. Like Mary Wollstonecraft and Olympe de Gouges who followed her, she felt that equal education was the key in allowing women to participate in all endeavors including science: "If I were king . . . I would redress an abuse which cuts back, as it were, one half of mankind. I would have women participate in all human rights, especially those of the mind. . . . The new education would greatly benefit the human race. Women would be worth more and men would gain something new to emulate" (cited in Wade 1947, 136).

She concluded her preface with the powerful statement "Men's injustice in excluding us from the sciences should at least serve to prevent us from writing bad books. Let us try to have this advantage over them, that their tyranny turns into a fortunate necessity for us and that in our works only our names are found fault with" (cited in Wade 1947, 136). Although she was well aware of her own limitations, she nevertheless wanted to make a contribution to knowledge in whatever capacity she could. Since she was barred from the French Academy and, as she believed, from original scientific research, she decided that she would become a translator of and commentator on the works of great men such as Newton.

Emilie du Châtelet's major contribution to science was her *Insti-*

tutions de physique (Institutions of Physics), a textbook published in 1740, which she dedicated to her son. It was composed during the most significant period of her life, the years spent at Cirey-sur-Blaise, the du Châtelet estate, with Voltaire. Historians believe that she met Voltaire in the spring of 1733 when she was twenty-seven years old and he was thirty-nine (Besterman 1958, 1: 12). They soon set up a household together. They had many interests in common, from a love of everything English to Newtonian science. Voltaire helped her with her studies, and they set up a common laboratory to pursue their scientific experiments. On her *Institutions*, Voltaire recalled: "We long employed all our attention and powers upon Leibniz and Newton; Madame du Châtelet attached herself first to Leibniz, and explained one part of his system in a book exceedingly well-written entitled, *Institutions de Physique*" (cited in Osen 1974, 56).

Voltaire's attitude toward women and science is ambiguous. On the one hand, he celebrated female intellectual capabilities. This is clear in his Epistle to Madame la Marquise du Châtelet at the start of his tragedy *Alzire,* performed in 1736. At the same time, he wrote that "it is not good for a woman to abandon her duty to cultivate sciences" (cited in Maité 1977, 191). In his eulogy of her, given when she died in 1749, he seemed amazed that the female brain could possibly grasp mathematics: "It is much for a woman to know simple geometry. . . . We have seen two miracles; one that Newton wrote this work; the other, that a lady has translated and explained it" (cited in Ehrman, 84).

Some controversy surrounded the *Institutions* at the time. Samuel Koenig, one of Emilie's tutors, claimed that she had plagiarized his lecture notes. She denied this, writing in a letter to her tutor Bernouilli, "During my leisure time at Cirey, I wrote the Eléments de physique which I intended for my son." She explained that she had written the work in 1738, a year before she had met Koenig (cited in Badinter 1983). Her statements are corroborated by a letter she wrote to Maupertuis in 1738, containing many of the same ideas contained in her *Institutions* (Badinter 1985, 323). One possible explanation for Koenig's accusations was that he was angry that Emilie had replaced his tutelage with that of Bernouilli in September 1739 (Showalter 1975, 218–220). Emilie protested to the secretary general of the French Academy of Sciences, Jean-Jacques d'Ortous de Mairan, believing (incorrectly) that he would come to her defense (Ogilvie 1986, 77). Mairan's letter to her underscores the argument that women scientists could not be taken seriously at this time. He pointed out that she had no original ideas and was dependent upon

Koenig for her interpretation of *vis viva*. With frequent references to her gender and class, Mairan described her as a "misguided woman who had brazenly abandoned the role of aristocratic philosophical spectator" (cited in Terrall 1995, 297).

Her *Institutions* was unquestionably influenced by the work carried out by her tutors Koenig, Clairaut, and Maupertuis, but she published her findings first. Abbé Nollet, an experimental physicist, cited her *Institutions* as "the best source for the Leibnizian position on collisions" in his work *Leçons de physique* (Lessons in Physics, 1759). However, he failed to mention the author's name (Nollet 1749, 2: 202).

Madame du Châtelet also wrote and later published a *Dissertation sur la nature et propagation de feu* (Dissertation on the Nature and Propagation of Fire), an essay for an Académie Royale des Sciences prize in 1736. This work on the subject of the nature of fire was not based upon experimentation, but on Lockean empiricism (Sutton 1995, 254). Once again, we can see how her gender affected her behavior in doing science. Emilie went through all sorts of schemes to keep Voltaire, who also submitted an essay, ignorant of her intentions. She felt that he would be upset—she did not want him to see her, a woman, as a competitor in science. Thus, she put in long nights, working in stealth, forgoing sleep. She had her husband submit her paper anonymously (Sutton 1995, 253). She described herself as "being bold" in writing a memoir for the Academy, and concerning Voltaire, she wrote, "I did not tell M. Voltaire because I did not wish to have to blush about an undertaking that might have displeased him." Further, she asserted that she had disagreed with his ideas! (cited in Ehrman 1986, 30). In the end, she did not win the prize, but neither did Voltaire. On the other hand, the distinguished astronomer and physicist Arago, her contemporary, praised Emilie's essay as "an elegant piece of work, embracing all the facts relating to the subject then known to science and containing among the experiments suggested one which proved so fecund in the hands of Herschel." The *Dissertation* was printed in the Academy's collections (cited in Mozans 1991, 201).

Some of her works were unpublished in her time. Ira O. Wade published her translation of Mandeville's *Fable of the Bees* in 1947. Her "Refléxions sur le bonheur" was published in 1796 in *Opscules philosophiques et littéraires,* edited by Suard. Her translation of and commentary on Newton's *Principia mathematica* was published in 1759, ten years after her death. It was the first translation of Newton's work into French and remains the standard translation; it was standard for years to accept this translation as Voltaire's rather than Emilie's (Spencer 1984, 184). In the preface to it, Voltaire commented: "Never was a woman so learned as she, and never did anyone more deserve that people should say of her, 'She is a learned woman.'" He spoke of her as a "woman who has translated and explained Newton, in one word a very great man" (cited in Mozans 1991, 152).

Other Women of Science

The French astronomer Joseph-Jérôme Lalande, who corrected the planetary tables for Halley's comet, greatly encouraged the participation of one woman of science, Nicole-Reine Hortense Etable de Brière, a French mathematician and astronomer, who became Madame Lepaute. Born in the Luxembourg Palace and the daughter of an employee of Elizabeth of Orléans, Lepaute made several contributions to astronomy during the second half of the eighteenth century. She was able to do this through the support of men such as her father, who provided her with an education (she was especially talented in mathematics), her husband, and Lalande. Lepaute married the royal clockmaker Jean-André Lepaute in 1748. She collaborated with both her husband and Lalande. With her husband, she worked on the oscillations of pendulums of various lengths. The table they created was published in his work *Traité de l'horlogerie* (Treatise on the Clock Industry) in 1755. With Lalande she worked on predictions of the return of Halley's comet.

Lepaute was also a friend of French mathematician and member of the Academy Alexis-Claude Clairaut, to whom she sent her studies. Lalande and Clairaut held divergent attitudes of Lepaute's work. Whereas Lalande was very supportive, Clairaut refused to acknowledge Lepaute's talents or give her credit for her work, to which his own was in debt. Clairaut took the credit for her work, which was subsequently praised in the press throughout France (Gillespie 1973, 7: 580). On the other hand, Lalande wrote that he was indebted to Lepaute for her work on the calculations of comets. She assisted with calculations on the return of Halley's comet by calculating the amount of attraction Jupiter and Saturn exerted on the comet. Lalande wrote that the male astronomers investigating Halley's return would never have undertaken this enormous task without her: "It would be difficult to realize the courage which this enterprise required, if one did not know that for more than six months we calculated from morning until night, sometimes even at meals" (cited in Rebière 1897, 181).

Lepaute also worked on the eclipse of the sun that occurred on 1 April 1764. She calculated the path of this eclipse for the European continent, and two years previous to the time when the eclipse was predicted, she published a chart for it. Her chart or map demonstrated the progress the eclipse would make every twenty-four hours. This map was published in the French Academy's publication *Connaissance des temps* (Knowledge of Time) in 1763. At the time, Lalande was the editor of this almanac. In addition to publishing her map in this almanac, she assisted Lalande with the publication of the almanac between 1759 and 1774, writing "Observations" in the *Connaissance.* Her "Observations" concerned the timing of the eclipse of the sun that was predicted for the year 1764 (Millar 1996, 199–200; Hoeffer 1811–1878, 30: 822). She also worked on the seventh and eighth volumes of the *Ephemeris,* an almanac of primarily mathematical calculations to predict the positions of the sun, moon, and planets during the 1780s and up to 1792. Lepaute was one of the astronomers who assisted Lalande in publishing *Ephémérides des mouvements célestes* (Ephemeris of Celestial Movements) between 1775 and 1784 (Lalande 1803/1970, 539).

She wrote many memoirs for the Academy (yet, of course, was never made a member). Lepaute remained childless; perhaps this was the reason for her ability to concentrate on her science without interruption throughout her life. However, she managed to help with the education of two male relatives on her husband's side. She published under both her own name and that of her husband.

In his eulogy of her written after her death in 1788, Lalande wrote: "Mme Lepaute merits to be cited here among the small number of women who have provided an example to their sex by the emulation of the exact sciences" (Lalande 1803, 676). He called her "the most distinguished female astronomer France had ever produced and the only woman in France who had acquired veritable knowledge of astronomy" (Lalande 1803/1970, 676–677). Her successor was Madame du Pierry.

Very little has been written about Louise Elisabeth Félicité Pourra de la Madeleine du Pierry, who was celebrated for her work as an astronomer and mathematician. She was born in 1746. Like Lepaute, she was involved professionally with Lalande. He owed a great deal to both women. Du Pierry was responsible for calculating the precise movements of the moon that Lalande used in his exploration of lunar motion. It is not surprising, then, that he dedicated his *Astronomie des dames* to her and applauded her "talent, good taste and courage" (cited in Rebière 1897, 188, 194). According to Lalande, she was the first professor of astronomy in Paris (Mozans 1981, 178). She composed the *Tables des dix tomes des connaissances chimiques* (Tables of the Ten Volumes of Chemical Knowledge), the *Tables de la durée du jour et de la nuit* (Tables of the Duration of the Day and the Night), and the *Tables de l'effet des réfractions* (Tables of the Effect of Refractions). She delivered a successful course in astronomy in 1789, the first such course open to women. Lalande explained the extent to which the course was useful to those who feared his own course to be too difficult (Lalande 1803, 687).

One can compare the experience of French women of science with the experience of those in Italy. Lalande recognized the problems of French women trying to be scientists and stated that the "example of Mlle. Agnesi of Milan and Laura Bassi should be followed in France" (Lalande 1803/1970, 687). In particular, the case of the Italian physicist Laura Maria Caterina Bassi (1711–1778) is illustrative of the contrasting attitude found in Italy toward women and science. Bassi, who was trained in mathematics and philosophy, was fully accepted in the community of male scientists. Not only did she receive a Ph.D. from the University of Bologna, she also held a chair of experimental physics from 1776 to 1778. She was also made a member of the Italian Academy of the Institute of Sciences—unthinkable in France. She was actually given a chair by the Institute of Experimental Physics when she was sixty-five. However, long before that, Bassi became the world's first female professor when she received a chair from the University of Bologna in 1732 (Wertheim 1995, 138). She often taught and conducted her experiments in her home because of family obligations. Married to a physicist named Giovanni Giuseppe Veratti, she had eight children in total.

Lalande, who attended her lectures and experiments in Newtonian physics, commented that Bassi indeed had "filled her professorial position with distinction" (cited in Ogilvie 1993, 28). She was one of the first Italians to champion Newton. Although Bassi was a great deal more accepted into the male community of scientists in Italy than Emilie du Châtelet in France, who also worked in the field of Newtonian physics, Bassi was always the woman physicist, whose every move was a topic of discussion and debate. She was never a "regular academic," but one whose role at the academy was largely "ceremonial" (Wertheim 1995, 139). No female was allowed to follow immediately in her footsteps.

The Age of Reason was clearly not an Age of Enlightenment for women in science. The debate over whether women could and should do science took place principally between those who followed Rousseau's lead—and these men were in the majority—and those who thought like Condorcet. This did not completely eliminate women from practicing science and participating in some of the scientific debates, as did Emilie du Châtelet, but they were viewed as amateurs, rather than professionals. They lacked the same education as men and they were barred from the scientific academies. In the nineteenth century, the debate would focus on the "new science" of craniology and evolution and what this new science meant for women.

8

The "New Science" and the Debate about Women

During the nineteenth century, many women and a few men campaigned for greater liberation for women. The most obvious and well-known areas in which women sought equality with men were at the ballot box and in education. Women were also looking for better-paid jobs and more parity with men in wages and access to the professions, including the scientific professions. A great number of eminent men, usually scientists, sought to fight against any furthering of female equality. One scholar working in the history of science asked and answered a key question: "Why did scientists, and men in general, feel compelled to respond to 'the woman question' at just that period? The drive for female emancipation was only one of a number of forces that, in the latter part of the nineteenth century, seemed to threaten social stability" (Mosedale 1978, 2). Scientists, sociologists, and others believed that all contemporary problems, including the female problem, could be solved by scrutinizing them under the microscope. In other words, sociological problems could be understood and solved by applying the laws of science to society.

The term "science" took on a new meaning in the nineteenth century when philosophers, scientists, epistemologists, and philosophers of science "stressed the progressive and cumulative nature of scientific knowledge." They no longer emphasized the metaphysical aspects of science, but now began to focus on "the experimental and anti-philosophical approach to nature." In other words, science became devoid of its philosophical and theological concepts (Corsi and Weindling 1983, 4–5). This new science may be attributed to the development of positivism, a philosophical movement that emphasized science and scientific method as the only sources of knowledge. Positivism made a sharp distinction between the realms of fact and value and held a strong hostility toward religion and traditional philosophy, especially metaphysics. An outgrowth of the empirical tradition, positivism was first introduced into the philosophical vocabulary in the early nineteenth century by the Comte de Saint-Simon. As developed by Auguste Comte, Ernst Mach, and others, the movement had great influence in philosophy well into the twentieth century (Gildea 1991). This new science would be used as a tool to improve mankind and his world.

Science in the nineteenth century also became increasingly specialized with the growth of subdivisions in disciplines such as chemistry, biology, and physics. Perhaps the greatest development in science at this time was the theory of evolution put forth by Charles Darwin and other evolutionary biologists. The nineteenth century also saw the rise of the social sciences, such as sociology, anthropology, and psychology, in addition to the now discredited branches of science such as craniology and phrenology.

The Size and Capacity of the Brain and Female Inferiority

The influence of the pseudoscience of craniometry, or craniology, meaning the measurement of the skull and its contents, was profound during the nineteenth century. Predating craniology, but related to it, was phrenology. The inventor and leader of the phrenology craze was a man by the name of Franz Joseph Gall, who died in 1828. Apparently, "Gall's impact in the early nineteenth century is paralleled only by that made in the twentieth by another Viennese doctor who first shocked, then shaped contemporary thought about mental mechanisms and was placed in the most exclusive section of the thinkers' pantheon: Freud" (Schiller 1992, 169). According to the *American Heritage Dictionary,* phrenology may be defined as "the practice of studying character and mental capacity from the conformation of the skull." Although it was discredited as a pseudoscience by the middle of the nineteenth century, its legacy remained important; it influenced the thought of serious medical researchers and scientists such as Paul Broca. Perhaps the most important contribution of phrenology to craniology was the belief that "brain size indicated mental ability," and following from this the view that intelligence, or rational ability, could be measured by measuring the size of the brain (Fee 1979, 421).

Paul Broca, professor of clinical pathology and founder of physical anthropology in France, was one of the more influential men who worked in the field of craniology. Broca's views were taken seriously, for he was a highly respected surgeon and anthropologist, credited with discovering the primary organ of the brain responsible for speech, known as Broca's area. In addition, he was the founder of the

Anthropological Society of Paris in 1859 (Schiller 1992, 5; Gould 1996, 114–115).

Broca used brains from contemporary dead people to prove his theories of male superiority. He felt that society had merely accepted female inferiority as a matter of faith in the past; it was now time to scientifically prove it. However, he based some of his theories about sexual differences between male and female on his examination of female skulls from the Stone Age found in a burial cave called Homme-Mort in mountains located in southeastern France. He found that the female skulls from the Homme-Mort series had a large capacity when measured in comparison with the male skulls. He concluded, "No other race shows such small sexual difference." This difference was much smaller than that found

Phrenology head with regions of human capacities (Bettmann/Corbis)

between modern male and female skulls. He also found that the constitution of the ancient female was much closer to the male's than in modern times. Why? Broca concluded that in barbaric societies, men and women "share in labor, the struggle, and the dangers of the tribe. Almost equally with man, they submit to the laws of natural selection. They go hunting, fishing, even into combat" (Broca 1873, 45–46). These findings of Broca were published in the *Revue d'Anthropologie* in 1873.

Broca's modern brains revealed something quite different from those ancient skulls from the Stone Age. He found that the weight of the average contemporary female brain was 14 percent less than that of the male brain, leading him to conclude: "We must not forget that women are, on the average, a little less intelligent than men, a difference, which we should not exaggerate, but which is, nonetheless, real. We are therefore permitted to suppose that the relatively small size of the female brain depends in part upon her physical inferiority, and in part upon her intellectual inferiority" (Broca 1861, 153).

Further, he argued that "in general, the brain is larger in mature adults than in the elderly, in men than in women, in eminent men than in men of mediocre talent, in superior races than in inferior races" (Broca 1861, 304). As Stephen Gould remarked in his study of craniology, at this time in history most agreed that the "human race could be ranked in a linear scale of mental worth" (Gould 1996, 118). Women were not very high in this ranking.

In a similar vein, German anatomist Carl Vogt, a professor at the University of Geneva, held that the brains of women, children, and blacks bore a strong resemblance. All three were less developed than the white male brain. He wrote: "By its rounded apex and less developed posterior lobe the Negro brain resembles that of our children, and by the protuberance of the parietal lobe, that of our females. . . . The grown-up Negro partakes, as regards his intellectual faculties, of the nature of the child, the female and the senile white" (Vogt 1864, 192).

The equation of the female adult with the child was also stated by Gustave Le Bon, probably best remembered for his book about crowd psychology, *La Psychologie des foules* (The Psychology of Crowds), published in 1895. As the founder of social psychology, Le Bon was well respected in his time. He was responsible for what Gould called probably the "most vicious attack on women in modern scientific literature" (Gould 1996, 136). His views fit with those discussed above, for he analyzed the weight of brains and their capacity for intelligence. He also published in the anthropological journal founded by Broca in 1872. He argued that female brains were "closer in size to those of gorillas than to the most developed male brains. This inferiority is so obvious that no one can contest it for a moment." Le Bon sounded very similar to Darwin when he wrote about the inferiority of female creativity, comparing female poets and novelists to their male counterparts. He was convinced that women "represent the most inferior forms of human evolution and that they are closer to children and savages than to an adult, civilized man." He concluded with a remark similar to Spencer's concerning reason, although Spencer was not quite as harsh: "They excel in fickleness, inconstancy, absence of thought and logic and incapacity to reason" (Le Bon 1879, 60–61). Small wonder that women were hindered from the serious practice of science when the major thinkers, many of whom were scientists themselves, were putting forth such views.

Even a practicing woman scientist, who set an example for many, held a low opinion of female intelligence. Mary Somerville (1780–1872) was known as the queen of science during the nineteenth century. When she died in 1872, the obituary in the London newspaper *The Morning Post* stated, "Whatever difficulty we might experience in the middle of the nineteenth century in choosing a king of science, there could be no question whatever as to the queen of science" (2 December 1872). Her story is quite amazing, given that her mother saw no need for females to be educated and that she could barely read until she was ten. She was sent by her father, an officer in the British navy, to boarding school for one year (Grinstein, Rose, and Rafailavich 1993, 538). She was mostly self-taught, reading algebra in women's magazines (Somerville 1873, 30).

Mary Somerville (Perry-Castaneda Library)

In spite of her achievements in astronomy, geography, and microbiology, Somerville herself considered female intellectual capacity as limited. She wrote, "We are women of the earth, earthy. . . . That part from heaven [original scientific] genius is not granted to the sex" (cited in Helsinger, Sheets, and Veeder 1983, 2: 78). Yet, at the same time, she advocated the teaching of the sciences to girls: "I can only say from experience, that the higher branches of mathematical science as well as natural history have been inestimable blessings to me throughout the whole course of my life. . . . As a source of happiness as well as of intellectual strength, mathematical science and classical learning ought to be essential branches of study in the higher and middle classes of women." She refuted the allegation that "the constitution of girls would be weakened by a classical and scientific education" (cited in Helsinger, Sheets and Veeder 1983, 2: 80).

The Evolution of the Female Species

Charles Darwin, the English naturalist, is most commonly known as the father of evolution, and his most famous work is *On the Origin of Species by Means of Natural Selection; or the Survival of the Fittest in the Struggle for Life* (1859). Darwin's other major work, *The Descent of Man*, *and Selection in Relation to Sex,* published in 1871, contained important and influential statements concerning the nature of both men and women.

In *Descent of Man,* Darwin delineated his theory of sexual selection, which was shaped by the struggle of the male to possess the female. The fact that males had to conquer other males to win females meant that males over time developed and evolved differently from females. The male was required to work harder than the female; therefore "their greater strength would have been kept up" (Darwin 1981, 325). Man was "more courageous, pugnacious and energetic than woman, and has more inventive genius. His brain is absolutely larger" (Darwin 1981, 316–317). Darwin also noted physical as well as mental differences between the sexes. The female was "rounder" and less hairy than the male. He implied that women were underdeveloped men. Children of both sexes tended to resemble the adult female rather than the male (Darwin 1981, 317).

In a section entitled "Difference in the Mental Powers of the Two Sexes," Darwin expanded on his belief in female inferiority and in intellectual and emotional differences between the sexes. Here Darwin argued that sex selection has been very important in making women more tender and less selfish than men; they have more maternal instincts and are more intuitive (Darwin 1981, 326). Because of the various factors in evolution, such as natural selection and sexual selection, man's reason had evolved more than woman's. Darwin organized mental functions into a hierarchy with reason at the top and emotion at the bottom. Because the female brain was not as highly developed as that of the male, it was more compatible with the lower functions of the brain. How then could women possibly be capable of doing science with such an inferior and underdeveloped mental capacity? He wrote that "the higher powers of imagination and reason have developed more fully in men than in women . . . due to a) sexual selection contest of rival males for females and b) natural selection (success in the general struggle for life). These 'struggles' will take place in maturity therefore the characters gained will have been transmitted more

Charles Darwin
(Library of Congress)

fully to the male than to the female. This makes man superior to woman" (Darwin 1981, 328).

Darwin supported his point that women were inferior to men by pointing out that women had not achieved an equal level of accomplishment in the arts and the sciences. He asserted:

> The chief distinction in the intellectual powers of the two sexes is shown by man attaining to a higher eminence, in whatever he takes up, than woman can attain—whether requiring deep thought, reason or imagination, or merely the use of the senses and hands. If two lists were made of the most eminent men and women in poetry, painting, sculpture and music—comprising composition and performance, history, science and philosophy, with half-a-dozen names under each subject, the two lists would not bear comparison. From the law of averages, it follows that because of man's greater achievement over woman in so many subjects, that the average standard of mental power in man must be above that of woman. (Darwin 1981, 327)

Was there any chance for women to reach the same level of intellectual achievement as men? Here, Darwin was not entirely negative, for he thought that if women were educated and their minds exercised as much as men's minds were, then acquired characteristics such as intelligence could be transmitted. Therefore women's mental powers were capable of improvement. He wrote: "In order that woman should reach the same standard as man, she ought when nearly adult, to be trained in energy and perseverance, and to have her reason and imagination exercised to the highest point; and then she would transmit these qualities chiefly to her adult daughters." This was only possible if many generations of women "who excelled in the above robust virtues were married, and produced offspring in larger numbers than other women" (Darwin 1981, 329).

Darwin was very much a man of his times, in the sense that his ideas were greatly influenced by the craniologists such as Carl Vogt, whom he cited in his *Descent of Man* on the subject of the "cranial cavity." Darwin not only believed that the white female brain was inferior to that of the white male, but he also held that there was a hierarchy of "races," and that the "male European excels much more the female than the Negro the negress." Darwin claimed this to be true on the basis of the work of E. Huschke, a nineteenth-century craniologist, who measured Negro and German skulls (Darwin 1981, 329–330, n. 24). In short, the white European male was superior to all others. The use of evolutionary theory, skull measurement, and brain weight to justify white male superiority over others, including the white female, was very much de rigueur in the mid- to late nineteenth century.

The British philosopher and sociologist Herbert Spencer, a contemporary of Darwin, also applied the theories of evolution to the intelligence and role of women. Spencer, perhaps less well-known to a modern audience than Darwin, was the most influential thinker of his day. It was Spencer, not Darwin, who coined the term "survival of the fittest," and he is remembered today for this term and also for being a social Darwinist, meaning that he applied Darwin's evolutionary theories to society. Spencer had an enormous impact on the increasingly important middle class in England.

Spencer, who began his career as a civil engineer, wrote extensively on race, class, and sex. Like Darwin, Spencer believed that the female brain was less developed than that of the male and thus there were differences "between the modes of thought of men and women; for women are more quick to draw conclusions, and retain more pertinaciously to the beliefs once formed" (Spencer 1900, 1: 581). In short, female mental faculties were not as powerful as male. According to Spencer, the reason for the inferiority of female brainpower was that female evolution had stopped at a "stage before man's to preserve vital organs for reproduction." Women's primary function in society was to reproduce, and it was to this purpose that her capacities were devoted. In short, she had not evolved to the same level as a man (Spencer 1897, 342–343). Her ability to survive as a species had been credited to her "sentimental qualities" (cited in Kennedy 1978, 93).

The intellectual sophistication necessary to become a scientist was simply not present in the female brain. Women's thoughts were characterized by "special and mainly personal experiences, but with few general truths and no truths of high generality." Women tended to make hasty judgments, and "such a thing as framing a hypothesis and reasoning upon it as an hypothesis, is incomprehensible to them; and that thus it is impossible for them deliberately to suspend judgment, and to balance evidence" (Spencer 1900, 2: 537–538).

Spencer was strictly against any change in the order of things in society and in the role of women. He argued that "it must be concluded that no considerable alteration in the careers of women in general, can be, or should be produced; and further, that any extensive change in the education of women, made with the view of fitting them for business and professions, would be mischievous" (Spencer 1893, 2: 757–758). Spencer extended this exclusion of women from the professions to the franchise. He was writing at a time when many were campaigning in favor of female enfranchisement. He argued that "the comparative impulsiveness of women is a trait which would make increase of their influence an injurious factor in legislation. . . . Women are carried away by the feelings of the moment still more than men. This characteristic is at variance with that judicial-mindedness which should guide the making of laws" (Spencer 1892–1893, 2: 194).

Patrick Geddes (1854–1932), a Scottish biologist, physiologist, sociologist, town planner, and pioneer ecologist, was influenced by both Darwin and Spencer. Geddes had studied under Thomas Huxley (1825–1895), a zoologist and advocate of Darwin's theories, and became a professor of botany and zoology at Dundee University in 1882. (See "The Papers of Sir Patrick Geddes" at Strathclyde University Archives, http://www.strath.ac.uk.) Although many have forgotten Geddes today, he was a very significant scientist in his day.

Many of the ideas Geddes expressed concerning women and science and women and evolution are very similar to those of Darwin and Spencer. Geddes, however, felt that the differences between the sexes had more to do with dissimilarity in cell metabolism than with reason as stated by Darwin (Vicinus 1972, 144–145). Geddes coauthored a book with J. Arthur Thomson entitled *Evolution of Sex* (1889). This work categorized male and female traits in animals in a manner reminiscent of Darwin: Female animals are "more passive, vegetative and conservative," while males are "more active, of higher body temperature, and short-lived" (cited in Mosedale 1978, 33). These characteristics were also present in human males and females. The lethargic nature of the female human meant that she was more "altruistic" and "intuitive" than the male and had a "constancy of affection" and "sympathy and continuous patience." In contrast, the male possessed "greater independence, and courage" and was "more active," and therefore his experiences were wider in scope. To sum up, the male "thinks more" and the woman "feels more" (Geddes 1889, 270–271). Applying his views of the female brain to society, Geddes opposed allowing women a more public role in society. He was writing at a time when women were agitating for the vote, and Geddes opposed this: "What was decided among the prehistoric *Protozoa* can not be annulled by an act of Parliament" (Geddes 1889, 247). Once again, biology was used to explain male dominance and superiority and female subjection and inferiority (Conway 1982).

Another rather forgotten figure, but a very influential physiologist in the nineteenth century, was George John Romanes (1848–1894), born in Kingston, Ontario. He was "one of the most brilliant of the second generation of British Darwinists" (Gillespie 1970–1980, 11: 517). Romanes was the son of a classical scholar and theologian at

Queen's University in Kingston. The family moved to London, England, where Romanes attended a preparatory school; from 1867 to 1873 he attended Gonville and Caius Colleges at Cambridge, where he read mathematics (Gillespie 1970–1980, 11: 517).

Romanes was influential both in Europe and in America. His works were translated into German and French. A correspondent of Darwin, he was an expert on animal intelligence. In 1887, Romanes published an influential article entitled "Mental Differences between Men and Women" in the British magazine *Nineteenth Century*. The influence on Romanes of Darwin, Vogt, and others writing about the inadequate mental capacity of the female brain is clear here. He cited Darwin's *Descent of Man* concerning secondary sexual characters (Mosedale 1978, 13). Because the brain weight of the female is five ounces lighter than the male's, there is "a marked inferiority of intellectual power." The inferiority of the female brain "displays itself most conspicuously in a comparative absence of originality, and this more especially in the higher levels of intellectual work." The more fully developed male brain has more power in "amassing knowledge" (Romanes 1887, 115–116).

Like Darwin, Romanes compared the achievement of the female to the male in various fields and concluded, "in the matter of original work . . . the disparity is most conspicuous." What could account for this apparent discrepancy? The female's level of judgment falls below that of the male, the female is more "superficial, emotional, in short, the weaker vessel" (Romanes 1887, 117). Following Vogt, he wrote, the "sexes are diverging more and more in their mental characteristics with continued evolution" (cited in Mosedale 1978, 19). The female is superior in terms of affection, devotion, self-denial, modesty, long suffering, and religious feeling. As a result of these traits, "feminine taste is proverbially good in regard to the smaller matters of everyday life, although it becomes, as a rule, untrustworthy in proportion to the necessity for intellectual judgment." For example, he thought that women were good at furnishing rooms, arranging flowers, and so on; however, "in matters of artistic or literary criticism, we turn instinctively to the judgement of men" (Romanes 1887, 121).

Romanes based his explanations for female weakness or "delicacy" on Darwin's principles of natural and sexual selection. He cited both Darwin and Darwin's cousin, the eugenicist Francis Galton, to substantiate his views. Natural and sexual selection, he argued, determined the greater strength in both body and mind of the male part of the species (Romanes 1887, 129). A second explanation for female "delicacy" of body and mind was education. Romanes conceded that education had played a role in the differences between men and women. He admitted that in the previous century, the goal of education had been to "make women good housekeepers" and that in his day it was to "make women artists—to provide them with skills in drawing, dancing and music." He was obviously writing about the education of the upper classes, which he declared had been a form of "mental decoration." The purpose of education, according to Romanes, was for women to complement men. He believed that "no amount of female education will overcome the natural and fundamental distinction of sex" and that it was not desirable to try to overcome the differences between the sexes: "If we attempt to disregard them, or try artificially to make of woman an unnatural copy of man, we are certain to fail, and to turn out as our result a sorry and disappointed creature who is neither one thing nor the other" (Romanes 1887, 149). His final conclusion was that women should be educated to be better wives and mothers (Mosedale 1978, 22–23).

The French View: Comte, Michelet, and Proudhon: The Subordination of Women to Men

The father of positivism, Auguste Comte (1798–1857), was also an important contributor to the debate about women during the nineteenth century. Modern scholars have tended to neglect Comte's importance until recently. According to his latest biographer, Mary Pickering, Comte was "the founder of sociology, positivism, and the history of science." For these reasons, she argues that he was "the most important nineteenth century French philosopher" and "among the dozen most important intellectual figures in modern Europe" (Pickering 1993, 1).

Comte's views on women can be divided into two distinct periods: When he was a young man, he was greatly influenced by feminist writers such as Mary Wollstonecraft, the Marquis du Condorcet, and John Stuart Mill, all of whom spoke in favor of women, with Condorcet, in particular, advocating a role for women in the sciences. In 1819 Comte wrote such positive things as "Women in general and collectively have suffered so much from the male species, that I believe that I am particularly obliged to compensate as much as I can for the general offences of my sex." He claimed that his goal was to "liberate women from men's domination and improve their economic independence" (cited in Pickering 1993, 146). In a letter to Pierre Vallat in 1819, he criticized men for taking the best professions and leaving "women only the very smallest number of professions and the least lucrative ones" (cited in Pickering 1993, 145).

As he grew older, his opinion became more traditional, mainly because of an unhappy marriage to a powerful woman. His ideas came to resemble those of Rousseau rather than Condorcet, in the sense that he adopted the view of woman as a complement to man. He was particularly vitriolic toward those women seeking independence in any fashion from men, whether sexual, economic, or any other form (Pickering 1993, 326–328).

In the 1850s, Comte was still writing that the female was superior to the male, but only in the moral sense. According to Comte, the principal reason women needed to be kept subordinate to men was to enable women to achieve a certain superiority over men. Woman was the "moral providence" and "keeper of manners and morality," and in this respect she was above the man. Woman's role was to preserve the purity and superiority necessary to accomplish her mission as moral arbiter. The ideal woman was tender; perhaps in reference to his own domestic situation, he wrote that "any woman without tenderness constitutes a social monstrosity even more than a man without courage" (Comte 1851, 1: 210). Although women were "never to leave the family," Comte argued that his "positive regime" offered women both "a public and a private role which conformed to their true nature." He saw them as participating in power by being "moderators between the philosophers and the proletarians. . . . They constitute, in a word, spontaneous priestesses of Humanity. . . . Their office, most of all, consists in directly cultivating the affective principle of the unity of humanity" (Comte 1851, 1: 227).

In the final analysis, Comte perceived the female to be the complement of the male, and he believed that this was a positive feature: "In effect, the natural differences between the two sexes, happily completed by their social diversity, make each one indispensable to the moral perfection of the other. Man is clearly dominant by the qualities proper to his active life, with his speculative ability. On the contrary, woman is most of all dedicated to her emotional life. One is superior in tenderness, while the other in all matters of strength" (Comte 1851, 1: 234–235). Women's reason was weak and imperfect. She was unable to think in the abstract, but she was superior in the social and emotional sense. There was no room for her in the rational world of science (Comte 1851, 2: 186–187).

The analysis of Jules Michelet, French historian, archivist, and revolutionary, in many ways resembled and echoed that of Comte. Michelet articulated his views on women and the family in his works *La Famille* (Family, 1845), *L'Amour* (Love, 1858), and *La Femme* (Woman, 1860). Michelet's *Love* was published seven years after Comte's major work entitled *Système de politique positive ou traité de sociologie* (System of Positive Politics or Treatise on Sociology, 1851). Although Michelet is primarily remembered as a poet and a historian, he had a strong knowledge of medical science, and his views about women were molded by his readings of medical writers such as Louis René Villermé and Achille Chéreau. Michelet paid particular attention to the discoveries made by French doctors during the 1840s about the female reproductive system. Chéreau stressed the importance of the ovaries and menstruation and the power of menstrual blood in female fertility (McMillan 2000, 102).

In *Family,* Michelet stressed the importance of woman as wife and mother based on these medical theories. He covered the subjects of woman's maternal instincts and her physiological makeup as a woman. He argued that although it was the male who nourished the female "both spiritually and materially," the female nourished the male with "her love, with her milk and with her blood." The woman was far more important than the man in the family, as he explained: "She who carries the baby for nine months does a great deal more for him than the father." Michelet praised this role for women, saying that men "are all and will always be eternally indebted to woman." However, the female role did not extend beyond the family: "They are all mothers . . . that suffices. . . . We are the ones who must work. To be loved, to give birth, then to give moral birth, to raise man up . . . this is the business of woman" (cited in Bell and Offen 1983, 1:172–173).

In *Love,* Michelet described the female character as ethical, sensitive, and emotional. The two sexes complement each other. Women's emotions make men's ideas possible: "Man's power is in abstracting, in dividing; but woman's power is in not knowing how to abstract; it is in preserving everything, every idea entire and living, so to be able to render it alive and to fructify it." He continued by contrasting the male with the female brain. The male "brain, an arsenal of the finest steel blades, contains scalpels which will cut through everything. Anatomy, war, critical philosophy: behold the head of man. But the organ of woman is another thing. That sweet organ, which is a second brain to her, dreams only dreams of love" (cited in Kaplan 1977, 123–124). As one Michelet expert has commented, "Like virtually all of his contemporaries Michelet is a 'male chauvinist,' he subordinates woman to man" (Kaplan 1977, 116).

In *Woman,* Michelet described the female as a secular goddess and a figure remaining under man's authority in mind as well as body. He made plain his views on the differences between the education of girls and boys: "The education of the boy, in the modern sense, aims to organize a force, an effective and productive force, to create a creator, which is the modern man. The education of a girl is to produce harmony, to harmonize a religion." In other words, he romanticized, even idolized, the woman, who, he wrote, "is a religion" (cited in Bell and Offen 1983, 340–341). Michelet made significant contributions to the debate through his writings on women, love, and the family. He romanticized women, yet he did not praise their intellectual qualities. In the tradition of Rousseau, Michelet saw the female as the emotional, rather than the rational, half of humankind.

The nineteenth-century French anarchist Pierre-Joseph Proudhon is primarily remembered for his statement "property is theft" and for his philosophical debates with Karl Marx over the nature of socialism. Less well-known are Proudhon's misogynistic commentaries about women and their role. Proudhon's views are contained within his *De la justice dans la révolution et dans l'église* (Justice in the Revolution and the Church, 1858). He began his pamphlet by bringing up the questions of complementarism, equality between male and female, and the role of the female. His conclusion, which he claimed to have based on fact, was that women were physically, intellectually, and morally inferior to men (cited in Bell and Offen 1983, 326). Unlike his contemporaries who thought women were morally superior to man, Proudhon did not grant even that to women. Women were not adults, not even defective males, as Aristotle had argued: "The woman is a diminutive of man, and lacks an organ necessary to become anything other than a potential adult" (cited in Bell and Offen 1983, 327).

Proudhon was indebted to Aristotle for his view of woman as "a receptacle. Just as she receives the embryo from man, so she receives her intellect and her sense of duty from him" (cited in Bell and Offen 1981, 329). Because she is "by nature unproductive, inert, lacking industry or understanding, lacking a Sense of Justice or modesty, she requires a father, a brother, a lover, a husband, a master, a man of some sort to give her . . . the wherewithal that will render her capable of the virile virtues, and of social and intellectual faculties" (cited in Bell and Offen 1983, 329–330). Proudhon disputed the views of feminist authors such as George Sand and Daniel Stern (pseudonym for Marie d'Agoult), who argued that equality of education would lessen the differences between men and women (cited in Bell and Offen 1983, 328). His conclusion, which he believed to be proved by his own calculations, was that men were superior to women by a ratio of two to three in moral, intellectual, and physical attributes (cited in Bell and Offen 1981, 330).

There was another side to the nineteenth-century debate: the writers who put forth articulate and forceful arguments on the side of women. These voices on the side of women included both men and women, and they presented a number of arguments based on ethics, economics, and law that supported equality for women.

WILLIAM THOMPSON

The nineteenth-century writer William Thompson (1785–1833), based his treatise in support of women on economics and social justice. In a recent publication about him, he was called the "forgotten man of the woman's movement," and the author pointed out that in his tract, *Appeal of One Half of the Human Race* (1825), he anticipated the arguments of more well-known feminists such as John Stuart Mill. In fact, Thompson's tract was a reply to a pamphlet by James Mill (father of John Stuart), *Article on Government,* in which he maintained that women should not be entitled to political rights because their interests are tied to those of either their fathers or their husbands (cited in Helsinger, Sheets, and Veeder 1983, 1: 22). Thompson came from Ireland and was an estate owner in Glenore. He was committed to both educational and social reform—which he began on his own estate where he set up schools (Helsinger, Sheets, and Veeder 1983, 21).

Although Thompson did not focus specifically on science in his writings, he stressed the importance of learning, education, and the cultivation of the female brain in all fields of knowledge. Rather than blaming female inferiority and lack of achievement on cranial capacity, Thompson focused on social causes. He singled out marriage as it was practiced in England during the nineteenth century as the single most important barrier to female emancipation and, in particular, as playing a key role in preventing women from using their minds. He wrote that "as soon as adult daughters become wives," they became "idiots." Their minds, which had previously been rational, were completely altered. Female brains became "stunted by disuse and want of education. . . . From want of education, of early culture, *equal to that of men,* in every branch of useful knowledge, women lose the immense accession to their happiness which intellectual culture could afford them" (cited in Helsinger, Sheets, and Veeder 1983, 30).

JOHN STUART MILL

One cannot discuss the voices defending and promoting women without examining the ideas of John Stuart Mill (1806–1873), perhaps the most well-known feminist of the nineteenth century. Mill wrote extensively on the rights of women, sometimes in collaboration with his wife Harriet Taylor and her daughter, Helen Taylor, whom he adopted. His most famous work is the classic *On the Subjection of Women,* published in 1869. In this work, Mill articulated the premise that formed the basis of all of his works: "the principle which regulates the existing social relations between the sexes, the legal subordination of one sex to the other is wrong in itself, and . . . it ought to be replaced by the principle of perfect equality" (Mill 1984 21: 261). Although Mill did not specifically discuss science, he wrote extensively about female education and the role of women in society. He argued passionately for equal opportunity for women and for equal access to all types of education because he believed that society as a whole would benefit (Mill 1984 21: 327). He even went so far as to posit that, given an equal education, "women . . . would be brought up equally capable of understanding business, public affairs, and the higher matters of speculation, with men of the same class in society . . ." (Mill 1984, 21: 327).

Mill made such suggestions for the improvement of both the opportunities and education for women because he was convinced that "there is no natural inequality between the sexes; except perhaps in bodily strength; even that admits of doubt: and if bodily strength is to be a measure of superiority, mankind are no better than savages," (Mill 1984, 21: 42), a position in stark contrast to what many of his contemporaries wrote.

Antoinette Brown Blackwell: A Reply to the British Evolutionists

Antoinette Brown Blackwell (1825–1921), America's first ordained woman minister, led the debate in criticizing views put forward by Darwin and his followers, particularly Herbert Spencer. In her work entitled *The Sexes throughout Nature* (1875), she argued that scientists were at a disadvantage when dealing with the "normal powers and functions of woman" (Blackwell 1875, 7). She held that female intuition was not inferior to male reason and that it provided an important mental faculty necessary for society's progress. Women and men were equal: "It may be found, process for process, in detail totality, that the average woman is equal to the average man" (Blackwell 1875, 111). Women, she asserted, "may have invented less cleverly . . . but it is entirely certain that, if impelled to do so, they would have gone to work with much less indirection (Blackwell 1875, 121). Women had not received the same opportunities as men to do science, but this did not mean they could not do it:

The female is not incapable of appreciating the most highly complex fact or the most abstract principle. . . . That she is not his
peer in all intellectual and moral capabilities at least cannot be
very well proved until she is allowed an equally untrammelled
opportunity to test her own strength. It would be possible to
carry on running comparison in detail; to laud her untested
powers, prophesying her future success in executive ability, in
abstract thinking, or in physical and moral science. (Blackwell
1875, 134–135)

HAVELOCK ELLIS: A REPLY TO THE CRANIOLOGISTS

The English doctor Henry Havelock Ellis (1859–1939), in his work
Man and Woman: A Study of Human and Secondary Sexual Characteristics,
published in 1894, challenged some of the views put forth by men
such as Broca concerning the relationship between brain weight and
size and intelligence. In a section entitled "Cranial Capacity," he
wrote, "A considerable amount of attention has been given to the
question of sexual differences in cranial capacity, but the results have

been small. . . . At the best, cranial capacity is not an exact indication of brain size" (Ellis 1926, 113). He commented upon how many scientists distorted or simply discounted scientific data to support their own personal views of female inferiority. He tried to refute those who wrote that the frontal regions of the skull were "the nobler regions" and "more developed in men than in women." To the contrary, Ellis argued that there was "no reason for supposing that the frontal region is higher or more characteristically human than any other cranial region; and there is just as little reason for supposing that the frontal region is more highly developed in men" (Ellis 1926, 116–117).

Ellis stressed the complementary nature of the sexes, but in a different manner from Rousseau, since Ellis saw the sexes as equal. "The sexes are perfectly poised; men and women are at every point different and at all points equivalent. There is no reason why men should be anxious to do everything that women do, or women be anxious to do everything that men do; but there is likewise no reason why each sex should not be absolutely free to develop all the possibilities within its own proper nature, even when the development is along exceptional lines" (Ellis 1926, x). Further, he stated:

> I am among those who would concede no privileges to one sex which should not be conceded to the other and would put no artificial limits to the activities of one sex which must not restrain the other, believing that while the aptitudes of the sexes differ, yet in the end the sexual balance will always be found true, and neither show any pre-eminence over the other. (Ellis 1926, vii)

On the subject of the brain itself, Ellis was seriously at odds with his European counterparts. He wrote that "men possess no relative superiority of brain-mass; the superiority in brain-mass, so far as it exists, is on women's side." He did not state that this meant that women were more intelligent than men (Ellis 1926, 142–143). Taking issue with Broca, he asserted, "From the present standpoint of brain anatomy, there is no ground for attributing any superiority to one sex over another." He continued by positing that Broca himself in later life "became inclined to think that it was merely a matter of education—of muscular . . . not merely mental, education," and he thought that if left to their spontaneous impulses, men and women would tend to resemble each other as happens in the savage condition. Ellis cited a paper by Broca from 1879 and added that this later view of Broca was not nearly as well publicized as his earlier ones from the 1860s (Ellis 1926, 143).

In France, followers of the French utopian socialist Saint-Simon, known as the Saint-Simonians, also put forth favorable views of women, even arguing that a female messiah would free humanity (Moses 1982, 240–267). Although they did not specifically write about women in science, they influenced thinkers who did. One of these was Ernest Legouvé, a professor at the prestigious Collège de France, who lectured on the moral history of women during 1848. This series of lectures, sponsored by the French government's minister of education, Hippolyte Carnot, advocated several improvements in the education of women. Legouvé felt that women should be allowed to pursue careers in science and medicine as well as in literature and the arts. He indicted the current educational and professional system, which was closed to women:

> They are deprived of pursuing professional or liberal careers. The Sorbonne prevents them from not only obtaining chairs, but also from its courses; a woman cannot even audit science courses. . . . The medical school, with the exception of one speciality, prevents them from performing this art. . . . Paris has five Academies and there is not one place for women. France has more than three hundred colleges, and there is not one woman occupying a professorial chair. (Legouvé 1849, 318)

A government system of higher education open to both sexes was clearly needed in order for women to be on the same footing as men in society:

> The state maintains a university for men, a polytechnic school for men, academies of arts and trades for men, agricultural schools for men—for women, what has it established? Primary schools! And even these were not founded by state, but by municipalities. No inequality could be more humiliating. There are courts and prisons for women, there should be public education for women; you have no right to punish those whom you do not instruct. (Legouvé 1849, 66–67)

But even Legouvé, who was on the side of the feminists, placed limits on women, relegating them to careers in "art, literature, instruction, administration and medicine." They should stay out of the government for they had no ability for politics (cited in Moses 1982, 138–139).

Jules Michelet's views that women should only be mothers did not go unchallenged in his lifetime. A mostly forgotten French writer by the name of Jenny P. d'Héricout replied not only to Michelet but to a number of other thinkers, including Comte and Proudhon. D'Héricourt had studied medicine privately in Paris—women were not allowed to attend medical school at this time—and had worked as a midwife in both Paris and Chicago. Her treatise, *A Woman's Philosophy of Woman,* argued with Michelet and the other writers on the woman question. D'Héricourt took issue with Michelet's views that women were created to serve men, that they were continually unwell and thus unfit for labor. She made the point that Michelet, in contending that women were sickly because of their "monthly crisis," "has not only erred in erecting a physiological law into a morbid condition, he has also sinned against rational method by making general rules of a few exceptions and proceeding from this generalization, contradicted by the vast majority of facts, to construct a system of subjection" (cited in Bell and Offen 1983, 1: 342–344). She disputed that woman was "destitute of high intellectual faculties, that she is unsuited for science, that she has no comprehension of method" (cited in Bell and Offen 1983, 1: 345), and concluded that she had in common with her male counterparts "an intellect and a free will." D'Héricourt was even so bold as to suggest that women might be superior to men, claiming that it was an absolute necessity that women join the public sphere for the problems of civilization "can only be resolved by the cooperation of woman delivered from her fetters and left free in her genius." She thus demanded woman's place at the side of man, not as his domestic companion, but in fields such as science, philosophy, justice, and politics, which women were equally competent to pursue (cited in Bell and Offen 1983, 346). In order to propagate her views and improve the lot of women, d'Héricourt suggested the founding of a newspaper and the writing of treatises to defend women's rights. Finally, she advocated the establishment of a female Polytechnic Institute for women to study subjects such as science (Bell and Offen 1983, 349).

D'Héricourt's views were echoed by those of Juliette Lambert, although Lambert restricted her assault to the views of Proudhon. Lambert, married at age eighteen to a government official from whom she later separated, became influenced by and involved with the Saint-Simonians. She published her riposte to Proudhon at her own expense in August 1858. She refuted a number of his theories, including his declaration that women were physically weaker than men, but the major thrust of her treatise was her demand for equity and for the opportunity for women to prove themselves in the public sphere. She wrote, "They must become productive. Work alone has emancipated men; work alone can emancipate women" (cited in Bell and Offen 1983, 333). She chastised men "like Proudhon, who want to return us to patriarchy by imprisoning women in the family" (cited in Bell and Offen 1983, 332). Like many other feminists, she stressed the education of women.

The nineteenth-century debate was dominated by men of one form of science or another: evolutionists, biologists, physiologists, social scientists, and positivists. The new science was not progressive in terms of its thinking about women, and proponents of it used their "scientific evidence" to keep women in a subordinate position, denying them access to education and a career outside the home. They put a great deal of emphasis on the reproductive role of the female. The debate was weighted heavily against women. Most who participated believed that, as Spencer stated, the intellectual sophistication necessary to become a scientist was simply not present in the female brain. There were, however, more positive voices, which supported female intelligence and women's right to pursue science, in this century than there had been in the eighteenth. The first feminist movements of the nineteenth century had an impact on the right of women to obtain an education and to participate in professions such as science. There would be a growing demand, even among men, for women to participate equally in the world of work, but this would not come until the feminist movement of the 1960s.

9

"Doctoring Only for Men": Women and Medicine

Intense debates raged from medieval times to the late nineteenth century over the question of women midwives and physicians, both as practitioners of medicine and as writers. During the nineteenth century, the debate was focused in Great Britain and continental Europe. In some ways, this debate about women as healers has persisted into the twentieth century. Medical schools accept women without hesitation—indeed many medical schools are composed of at least 50 percent female students—but as recently as the 1960s, it was a different story. Women who were accepted into medicine were often marginalized by their teachers and by male students.

Concerning midwives, in many parts of the United States, the debate continues with doctors hotly resisting their presence at births and the practice of home birthing with only a midwife present.

Trotula and the School of Salerno

Women were excluded from most traditional medical schools in the Middle Ages. This exclusion obviously meant that they could not attain the level of knowledge and expertise to write medical treatises. One school, however, did accept women, the School of Salerno, which dates from the ninth century (Walton, Beeson, and Scott 1986, 2: 1457). Salerno, which is located 35 miles southeast of Naples, became a health resort because of its location. The school itself, which has been called "the unquestioned fountain and archetype of orthodox medicine," had a difficult course of study (Mozans 1991, 283–284). Students were required to complete three years of philosophy and literature before pursuing medical studies, and the medical course itself took five years. Two hundred and eighty-four women were admitted to the school; they were known as the *mulieres Salernitanae* (the Ladies of Salerno), physicians and professors of medicine (Mozans 1991, 283–284).

The controversy that surrounds the School of Salerno concerns the female figure of Trotula. As one writer has commented, "No other woman physician has aroused such debate or such high feeling. Male physicians are convinced she was a man, or else fictitious" (Brooke 1995, 29). Some experts claim that there is no documentary evidence of her professional status, family, or even historical existence. The eminent historian of medieval medicine, Charles Singer, wrote that "a lady of Salerno, known as 'Trotula,' is said to have been the author of the only two books by Salernitan women that the ages have left to us. Yet these treatises of the so-called Trotula are in fact compilations from sources far more ancient than the Middle or even Dark Ages." He went on to say that Trotula had no real historical existence (Singer and Sigerist 1924, 128). Others have seen her as a significant female doctor of the Middle Ages. Kate Campbell Hurd-Mead, who was a gynecologist and a former president of the American Medical Women's Association, called her the "most noted woman doctor of the Middle Ages" (Kristeller 1945; Hurd-Mead 1930, 349–367). Both Kate Campbell Hurd-Mead and Elizabeth Perl-Hohl, who made the first English translation of Trotula's *Passionibus Mulierum Curandum,* have provided convincing evidence of Trotula's historical existence and authorship of many texts on gynecology (Trotula 1940).

What do we know about the supposed Trotula? Apparently Trotula was born circa 1050 and died around 1097 at Salerno. She was the wife of Johannes Platearius, a doctor and a medical writer. There are extant manuscripts of her work in the libraries of France, Germany, Belgium, Austria, and England. The Bibliothèque Nationale in France has a large collection, including the oldest complete manuscript, dating from the thirteenth century, Fonds Latin, no. 7056. Fragments of manuscripts actually signed by her are in Breslau, in addition to those in Leipzig and Florence (Lipinska 1930, 28–30). She wrote a number of works concerning women's diseases, including *De Passionibus Mulierum,* also known as *Trotula Major.* This treatise, composed of sixty-three chapters, was copied many times. Topics discussed in this work include menstruation, conception, pregnancy, childbirth, and general disease. Historian H. P. Bayon argued that in spite of the controversy over authorship, this work was the first major treatise on gynecology in history (Underwood 1953, 1: 203–219). Trotula's other work was entitled *Ornatu Mulierum,* or *Trotula Minor.* Paul O. Kristeller claimed that Italy continued the Greco-Roman tradition, which accepted female doctors (Kristeller 1945). Italian historians, proud of their heritage of women doctors, have continued to praise Trotula's contributions (Alic 1986, 55).

The authors of a recent biographical dictionary of women in science argued that a good part of the reason for the controversy over Trotula as a medical doctor stems from the prejudices surrounding women in medicine. Women were simply not considered capable of practicing medicine. They claimed that Trotula was indeed a historical person who taught medicine at the University of Salerno and authored a number of treatises: *Practica Brevis* (Brief Handbook) and *De Compositione Medicamentorum* (On the Preparation of Medicines) in addition to the two cited above (Shearer and Shearer 1996, 382–385). Examples of the impact of this prejudicial attitude on the controversy about Trotula can be traced back to Kaspar Wolff of Basle in the sixteenth century, who denied that a woman was capable of producing a medical treatise. He attributed Trotula's work to a man by the name of Eros Juliae (a physician to Julia, daughter of the first-century Roman emperor Augustus). Wolff published an edition of *De Passionibus Mulierum* in 1566 (Wolff in Benton 1985, 36, and Alic 1986, 54). The twentieth-century German medical historian Karl Sudoff argued that Trotula and the Ladies of Salerno were not physicians but midwives and nurses. Since they were not doctors, they could not possibly have possessed the medical knowledge to produce a textbook on gynecology. Sudoff's students carried on this tradition.

Even today, the controversy over Trotula continues. Josette Dall'ava-Santucci stated in the 1980s that "the medical world accepts the conclusions of John F. Benton that a medical woman named Trotula existed but she was not the author of the famous treatise on female illnesses" (Dall'ava-Santucci 1989, 45). Benton, in his article, concluded that "the professionalization of medicine in the twelfth and thirteenth centuries, combined with the virtual exclusion of women from university education, prevented them from entering the best paid and most respected positions. . . . Though the treatises of 'Trotula' bear a woman's name, they were the central texts of the gynaecological medicine practiced and taught by men" (Benton 1985, 53). On the other hand, the authors of the recent *Oxford Companion to Medicine* wrote that the earliest medical school was indeed at Salerno and that Trotula was its "most famous teacher and practitioner." They gave her credit for classifying diseases as "inherited, contagious and 'other'" (Walton, Beeson, and Scott 1986, 2: 1458).

Historian of medicine Monica H. Green has carried out considerable research on the problem of "The Trotula" and has very recently provided a modern translation of the compendium of works. The historical person and the texts, she maintained, are linked. "The Trotula" was originally the title given to the "most popular assembly of materials on women's medicine from the late 12th to the 15th centuries." They were written in Latin, and their intended audience was the educated elite. Green posited that the Trotula comprised three separate texts, each authored by a different person: "Conditions of Women," "On Women's Cosmetics," and "On Treatments of Women." The first two texts, she claimed, were written by men and the last one by a woman from Salerno named Trota (Green 2001, xi, 17, 48–51). Green's translation and conclusions seem to have been accepted by scholars and experts as "the definitive Trotula."

Female Midwives and the Medical Profession

Throughout history, women have been in charge of the birthing process. Midwifery has traditionally involved prenatal and postnatal care as well as attending to the actual birth. Midwives can be found in the Bible in a number of books in the Old Testament. One example is that of two Hebrew midwives who refused to kill male infants in defiance of the king of Egypt (Exodus 1:15–22). Other verses in the Bible also make passing references to midwifery attendance at birth, implying that the practice was ubiquitous (Genesis 35:17; 38:28). The tradition of midwifery continued into Greek and Roman times and into the early modern period, particularly on the European continent. Until the twentieth century, childbirth was a female affair, and male doctors intervened only when there was a problem with the birth (Wiesner 1993, 66–67).

In most cases, early midwives received no formal training—the only training available was through an apprenticeship. In England, midwives were not under any official control until 1512, when they came under control of the church (Moscucci 1993, 43). Most midwives were illiterate and could not read the first midwives' manual published in English, *The Byrth of Mankynde,* a translation by Thomas Raynalde published in 1545. As Raynalde wrote in his preface, most midwives learned their craft "by haunting women in their labours" (cited in Clark 1968, 269).

The controversy around midwives was centered in the British Isles, primarily in England. On the Continent, midwives were accepted and even praised. In Germany, there was a tradition of midwifery, and there midwives were and are generally accepted. Midwife Justine Dittrich Siegemund (1636–1705) made midwifery a profession through her work and writings. In the early nineteenth century, Prussia passed a law that made it a requirement for midwives to attain a certain level of education, and established schools of midwifery to realize this goal.

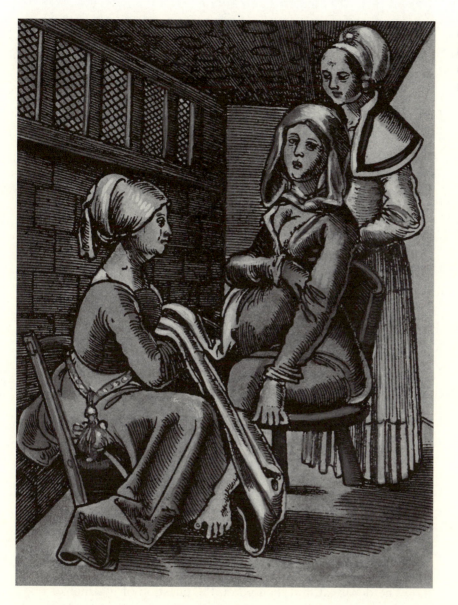

Standards were high, and one school was even affiliated with the University of Berlin (Smith in Carroll 1976). In France, there were several famous midwives who set standards for the profession, including Louise Bourgeois (1563–1636), the midwife to Queen Marie de Médicis and author of several treatises and texts on childbirth. She became the authority on the matter and founded a school for midwives (Gélis 1988, 28–31). The traveling midwife and instructor Marguerite Le Boursier Du Coudray (1712–1794) invented the first life-size obstetrical mannequin for the simulation of live births and published a popular how-to book on delivery techniques. At the explicit and unprecedented behest of King Louis XV, she spent more than thirty years training country women in the art of childbirth (Gelbart 1998).

In the late eighteenth and early nineteenth centuries, Marie Anne Victoire Boivin (1783–1841) published, in collaboration with Antoine Louis Dugès (1797–1841), an important work on women's ailments, *Traité pratique des malades de l'utérus et de ses annexes* (A Practical Treatise on the Diseases of the Uterus and Its Appendages). Her work included several significant medical texts, such as those on the improvement of the speculum, internal pelvimetry, and uterine hemorrhages, to name a few. The University of Marburg in Germany awarded her an honorary M.D. in 1827 (Uglow 1999, 76).

In England, midwifery or obstetrics was one aspect of medicine that had been exclusively female until the sixteenth century. The changes that took place in midwifery and the debate over the exclusion of women from this profession originated in the seventeenth century. The debate that took place between the midwives and the male surgeons was really an attempt to bar women from practicing any sort of medicine. The debate over midwifery occurred at this time because of the increasing professionalization of medicine and the secularization of society. At the heart of the issue was the application of monopolistic privileges in order to exclude women. Examples of the attitude come from prominent men of science. The physician and scientist William Harvey, in his 1651 pamphlet, condemned midwives for their ignorance. The medical doctor James McNath, in his *The Expert Midwife* from the mid-seventeenth century, argued that midwives were in league with the devil. He believed they were a necessary evil whose role was limited to easy births. The midwives themselves petitioned King Charles I in 1634 to grant them a charter for their incorporation into a society to control the standards of their practice, but the granting of such a charter was opposed by the physicians of the time.

The debate at first focused on the question of whether or not a male midwife or doctor should be employed rather than a female midwife in cases of difficult delivery. As McNath commented, "Natural labour, where all goes right and naturally, is the proper work of the Midwife, and which she alone most easily performs aright, being only to sit and attend Nature's pace and progress . . . and perform some other things of smaller moment, which Physicians gave midwives to do, as unnecessary and indecent for them" (cited in Clark 1968, 281).

The Chamberlen family attempted to keep women from practicing as midwives. William and his two sons were members of the Barber-Surgeon's Company and practicing obstetricians. Peter was the queen's surgeon. What made them unusual and ahead of their time was their use of forceps, which they tried to keep secret. They attempted to dominate the profession of midwifery by having it incorporated in the College of Physicians, which the college opposed in 1616 and the House of Lords did in 1634 (Smith 1976, 109–110). This plan had originated with a group of midwives who wanted the king to grant them a charter that would allow for the secular control of their profession. In England, midwives were still under the control of the church, which was not the case in continental Europe, where municipal councils granted licenses. A charter would allow for a general standard of practice and regulations for their trade. The Chamberlens did not support the midwives' cause per se, but only wanted to further their own position as the men who would control the distribution of licenses (Donnison 1979, 13). The 1634 petition to the House of Lords originated with William Chamberlen's nephew, Peter, and was opposed by a number of midwives, led by a Mrs. Shaw and Mrs. Whipp, who did not trust the Chamberlens and saw that they wanted to control them (Donnison 1979, 15).

Support for female midwives came from physician and herbalist Nicholas Culpeper (1616–1654) who wrote *A Directory for Midwives* in 1651, which he dedicated to midwives. He opposed men becoming midwives because of the elitism and exclusiveness of the medical profession. Culpeper wrote books designed for midwives, to teach them how to upgrade their skills so that they could deal with difficult births. He complained about the seriousness of not allowing the proper education of midwives: "What an insufferable injury it is, that men and women should be trained up in such ignorance." He stated that he would write his book in English so that all could understand it. And he promised the book would be short and simple: "If you please to make experience of my Rules, they are very plain and easy enough; neither are they so many, that they will burden your brain, nor so few that they will be insufficient for your necessity. If you make use of them, you need not call for the help of a man-midwife, which is a disparagement not only to yourselves but also to your profession." He closed with the words: "All the perfections that can be in a woman, ought to be in a midwife; the first step which is, You know your ignorance in that part of Physick which is the basis of your Act. When you know what you want, then you know what to crave. . . . Grave Matrons, be diligent in your Office, and be as careful as diligent" (Culpeper 1671, introduction). The chapters in his book provide the details of subjects of which he felt the midwives were ignorant: female anatomy, the conception of a child and its "furthering," miscarriage, labor, the lying in, and the nursing of children.

Jane Sharp and Elizabeth Cellier, both midwives of the seventeenth century, also worked to defend and organize female midwives.

Sharp of London was the author of the first educational textbook on midwifery by a woman, *The Midwives Book, or the Whole Art of Midwifery* (1671). She feared the threat by men, who had an educational advantage, to female midwives:

> Some perhaps think, that then it is not proper for women to be of this profession, because they cannot attain so rarely to the knowledge of things as men may, who are bred up in Universities, Schools of Learning or serve their Apprenticeship for that end and purpose, where Anatomy Lectures being frequently read the situation of the parts both of men and women . . . are often made plain to them. But that objection is easily answered, by the former example of the Midwives amongst the Israelites, for, though we women cannot deny that men in some things may come to a greater perfection of knowledge than women ordinarily can, by reason of the former helps that women want; yet the Holy Scriptures hath recorded Midwives to the perpetual honour of the female sex. . . . It is commendable for men to employ their spare time in some things of deeper Speculation than is required of the female sex; but the art of Midwifery chiefly concerns us. (Cited in Clark 1968, 281)

The lack of education and of language skills required to read the many medical texts still in Latin was not the only disadvantage of female midwives, as is demonstrated in the career of midwife Elizabeth Cellier, who worked to improve the lot of midwives. She tried to unite midwives into a corporation and got the government to establish one, but that was as far as it was taken. She was arrested on a number of occasions for her activities. Cellier also wrote a treatise entitled *A Scheme for the Foundation of a Royal Hospital* (1687), in which she envisioned a school for midwives. She proposed that only one thousand midwives should be admitted in the first instance and that they should pay a fee of five pounds sterling upon being admitted and each year in attendance. The money from the fees would be employed for the purpose of building "one good, large and convenient House, or Hospital." There would be "twelve lesser convenient houses, in twelve of the great parishes, each to be governed by one of the twelve Matrons, Assistants to the Corporation of Midwives, which Houses may be for the taking in, delivery and month's Maintenance, at a price certain of any woman . . ." (cited in Clark 1968, 273). James II welcomed her plan and did promise to incorporate the midwives. Her pamphlet *To Dr.—— An Answer to his Queries, concerning the Colledg of Midwives,* written a year later, was a response to a critique of her plan for the school and incorporation of midwives. We do not know the author of the critique, but it was likely Dr. Hugh Chamberlen, a male midwife. Cellier defended midwives by stating that women were the first physicians, going back to the ancients. This is not unlike what Shopia Louisa Jex-Blake, an English physician who founded the London School of Medicine for Women, argued in the nineteenth century when putting forth a case for women attending medical schools in the United Kingdom.

Throughout the next century, women midwives continued to lose ground. From 1720 to 1730 onward, the number of men midwives increased dramatically, and they began to take over routine cases. They became responsible for everything related to childbirth and children: pregnancy, delivery, postpartum care, and even childhood diseases. This is how Thomas Young (ca. 1726–1783), the first professor of midwifery at Edinburgh University, described the establishment of his chair of midwifery at the University of Edinburgh, which of course meant an education in midwifery intended only for men:

> Disturbed by the many fatal consequences that have happened to women in childbirth, and to their children, through the ignorance and unskillfulness of midwives in this country and city, who enter upon that difficult sphere at their own hand, without the knowledge of the principles upon which they are to practice that art, the town council added a chair of midwifery to those of anatomy, chemistry, institutes of medicine, practise of medicine and botany in the formation of its new medical faculty. (Edinburgh Town Council, "Council Records," 9 February 1726, cited in Hoolihan 1985, 327–345)

What was happening here was the replacement of female custom and tradition by supposedly modern, scientific, objective, and professionalized medical knowledge (Moscucci 1993). The female midwife became marginalized. This occurred for many reasons: the use of forceps by doctors, fashion, education, and secularization—the church no longer licensed midwives. The Industrial Revolution was also an important factor, as governments encouraged larger populations. Male midwives, it was thought, had the expertise females did not possess. The upper classes felt that it was more fashionable and socially acceptable to have a man deliver a baby. The old question of education appeared once again. Females were ill educated and unprofessional.

An intense debate arose over the use of forceps. Midwife Elizabeth Nihell (b. 1723) published at midcentury a pamphlet against the use of forceps and other instruments and against the incursion of the male midwife into the female practice. Her pamphlet was entitled *A treatise on the art of midwifery. Setting forth various instruments: the whole serving to put all rational inquirers in a fair way of very safely forming their own judgment upon the question; which it is best to employ, in cases of pregnancy and lying-in, a man-midwife or, a midwife,* and was published in London in 1760. She claimed, in her preface, not to be attacking any individual, rather addressing her pamphlet to the male practitioners in general, "who in these later times have . . . added new and worse errors of their own to those bequeathed to us by the ancients" (Nihell 1760, iv–v). What particularly angered her was the arrogance of the male midwife, whose "subtleties of theory . . . when reduced to practice, are infinitely worse than any deficiency in some particular female practitioners" (Nihell 1760, vi). Men midwives were no better at the practice of their craft than women. In fact, she argued, "the surgeons, in form of men midwives, have been the death of more children with their speculum matrices, their crotchets, their extractors or forceps, their tire-têtes, than they have preserved" (Nihell 1760, xii, 54). She directed her attack specifically against the obstetrician William Smellie (1697–1763). Smellie was the inventor of a type of forceps; he led the movement against midwives and for their replacement by male doctors. She specifically referred to how Smellie "intended to improve on forceps"; however, she maintained that these practitioners would soon be forced to admit that their instruments were "prejudicial and dangerous" (Nihell 1760, 414, 417).

In the end, these women were fighting a losing battle. Men had taken over the birthing process. In the nineteenth century, Walter Channing wrote in his pamphlet *Females as Physicians* that "women may be neither physicians nor midwives, because the science of bringing healthy babies into the world is better left to trained male obstetricians." He argued that women have "finer sensibilities and tend toward more delicate feelings; there is no place in medicine for the display and indulgence of such feelings; therefore, women ought not to be midwives" (Channing 1820, 5).

Women and Access to Medical School: The Debate

The key players in the debate over female access to a proper medical education were Emily Davies (1830–1921), Elizabeth Garrett Anderson (1836–1917), and Sophia Jex-Blake (1840–1912). Although not a medical doctor, Davies was an English feminist and educational reformer and a friend of Elizabeth Garrett Anderson, the first female physician in England. Davies fought hard for women's equality, especially in the realm of higher education. In 1864, she convinced the

Schools Inquiry Commission to investigate inequalities between the sexes in the schools. A year later, she was successful in her campaign to allow girls to take the Cambridge senior and junior local examinations. Davies founded Girton College, Cambridge, as a college for women (Uglow 1999, 150). Jex-Blake eventually became a licensed M.D., but only through a great controversy. Unlike her contemporary, Elizabeth Garrett Anderson, who gained her license through the Society of Apothecaries, Jex-Blake refused to accept the status quo in British universities. Jex-Blake led what became known as the Battle of Edinburgh (Roberts 1993).

EMILY DAVIES AND WOMEN IN MEDICINE

Davies wrote several letters and delivered a number of speeches on the subject of women and higher education. Her writings and speeches were grouped together and published by Cambridge University as *Thoughts on Some Questions Relating to Women* (1910). Davies challenged contemporary attitudes toward women in her works. In "Letters to a Daily Paper, Newcastle-on-Tyne" (1860), she argued that medicine was a profession that could be practiced by both men and women. She felt that female medical practitioners would be beneficial to women and children, for women preferred female doctors. The obstacles that women faced were the prejudices of the medical authorities (Davies, 1971, 9–10).

In a speech delivered to the Annual Meeting of the National Association for the Promotion of Social Science in 1862, Davies made a case for what she called "a re-adjustment" of labor between the sexes (Davies 1971, 34). She attempted to refute the arguments put forth against women becoming doctors: One was that it would involve the admission of women to male schools of medicine. She suggested separate classes for women, with both taking the same examination (Davies 1971, 38–39). In addition, she advocated beginning the medical course at a young age.

Davies took up the question of women in medicine in more detail a year later in her article "Female Physicians," which appeared in the *Englishwoman's Journal*. Here we are presented with a debate between Davies and a contemporary male physician of "twenty-one years' standing" who put forth many arguments against females entering medical school, which Davies refuted. She opened by taking up the question that women lacked proper training for medical studies. The physician claimed that the previous training male medical students had received as boys was such that it was impossible for girls to receive the same. Their primary education was simply insufficient, and therefore they should be barred on that premise alone. Davies did not deny that women were at a disadvantage here: "LADY students entering upon the course without preliminary training, do so at an immense disadvantage. . . . It is perhaps the strongest point in our case, as regards mere power, both physical and intellectual, that women have been able to do so much while debarred from the advantages of early education open to most men" (Davies 1971, 19).

Nor did Davies deny that women were of lesser physical strength than men, the second reason asserted by the physician for keeping women from attending medical school. "Yes, men are stronger, but does that justify us in assuming that every individual man is stronger than every individual woman?" No, according to Davies, who claimed that many women were stronger than many men. "We learn from our observation, though not from your correspondent, that in various parts of the country, women of the lower classes go through an amount of labour under which a gentleman would break down." She argued "that while women are showing themselves to be capable of such an amount of physical exertion, the comparatively far easier career of a physician should not be closed to us on the ground of physical weakness" (Davies 1971, 22).

The next issue Davies and the physician addressed was whether or not there would be employment for women when they had completed their course of study; Davies put forward the case for women as caregivers and healers for other women and children. Women would have their own bailiwick and would not take patients away from men: "All diseases to which women and children are liable would naturally come within the province of the female physician, and surely that domain is wide enough, without encroaching upon the sphere of men." She admitted that although the physician of twenty-one years did not believe that women would consult female physicians, for females were "shallow, superficially taught," and really a kind of "superior nurse," Davies countered by stating that the "sympathy and tenderness of a woman would be absolutely more curative than the possibly superior skill of a man." She acknowledged that men, at this time, were more skilled than women (Davies 1971, 23–24).

The final question of dissension between Davies and the physician concerned an issue that remains with us to this day. This is the question of a professional career versus marriage and family. Given his low opinion of the female's physical and mental capabilities, the male physician did not think that a woman could possibly do both. Here Davies came up with an interesting and clever response. The female doctor, she asserted, "might indeed exercise a more independent choice, because she would not be driven into marriage by the mere longing for some satisfying occupation; but if suitable marriage came in her way, her profession need be no hindrance." She added that study could be a preparation for marriage and work and that the two need not be incompatible (Davies 1971, 25). Further, medicine could open new doors and new career pathways for women. Degrees in medicine would be "valuable as opening the way for useful and remunerative employment to those ladies who do not wish to be governesses, or to engage in ordinary trade; and as affording to all women the alternative of being attended by physicians of their own sex." She added that women were already awarded medical degrees by universities on the Continent in countries such as Italy and France. It was time for the English to catch up (Davies 1971, 61–62).

ARGUMENTS AGAINST WOMEN IN MEDICINE

Medical practitioners themselves, particularly those in gynecology and obstetrics, were the greatest opponents to women in medicine. The major reason was competition. These medical men feared a loss of patients. In addition, they argued that the mental stress that the practice of medicine would put on women would harm their reproductive systems and affect their ability to have children. Among those who joined in the debate were John Thorburn, professor of obstetrics at Owens College, Manchester; Robert Lawson Tait, president of the British Gynecological Society; and William Withers Moore, president of the British Medical Association.

These views were fully developed by one of the leading contributors to the debate, Henry Maudsley, a professor of medical jurisprudence at University College, London, and fellow of the Royal College of Physicians. He published an article entitled "Sex and Mind in Education" in the *Fortnightly Review* in 1874. In it, he wrote about the seriousness of the question of women in higher education. Believing that the current system of education had been "framed and adapted for men," he thought that the first consideration must be whether or not this kind of education would be harmful to a woman's "health and strength" (Maudsley 1874, 466). The real issue at hand was whether or not the stress of education would harm a woman's ability to bear children (Maudsley 1874, 467). This idea had already been put forth by an American doctor, Edward H. Clarke (1820–1877) of Harvard College. Maudsley drew rather heavily upon Clarke's book, *Sex in Education, or a Fair Chance for the Girls*, for evidence to prove that "the number of female graduates of schools and colleges who have been permanently disabled to a greater or lesser degree by improper methods of study, and by a disregard of the reproductive apparatus and its functions is so great as to excite the greatest alarm, and to demand the serious attention of the community" (Maudsley 1874, 474).

Clarke's book, published in 1873, incited much debate. At this time, British doctors drew heavily on research being produced in the United States to demonstrate their theories that women should not receive a higher education. The problem was that the U.S. and British educational systems were quite different: The Americans had admitted women to coeducational institutions since the 1830s and the English had not. The English were trying to apply evidence from the United States that women could not keep up in these institutions to the situation in British institutions. The Americans insisted upon daily attendance at classes, daily recitations, and daily grading. In England, examinations occurred only on an occasional basis. These differences did not stop British doctors from drawing upon studies from the United States to prove that women were "physiologically unfit for strenuous intellectual work" (Burstyn 1973, 79–89).

In terms of mental ability, Maudsley's views were very different from those of the Cartesian writer Poulain de la Barre, discussed in Chapter 5, who wrote extensively on the subject of women and education in the 1670s, and argued that females were equal to males in mental capacity but they had been held back in society because of their inferior education. Maudsley saw gender as playing a strong role in determining the nature of the mind.

> It is sometimes said . . . that sexual differences ought not to have any place in the culture of the mind, and one hears it affirmed with an air of triumphant satisfaction that there is no sex in mental culture. This is a rash statement, which argues want of thought or insincerity of thought in those who make it. There is sex in mind as distinctly as there is sex in body; and if the mind is to receive the best culture of which its nature is capable, regard must be had to the mental qualities which correlate with differences of sex.

Education was incapable of assimilating the "female to the male mind." This was as "fruitless and unwise labour as it would be to strive to assimilate the female to the male body by means of the same kind of physical training and by the adoption of the same pursuits" (Maudsley 1874, 468). The different mental characteristics of the sexes became apparent at puberty, when sexual maturity began: "To attribute to the influence of education the mental differences of sex which declare themselves so distinctly at puberty, would be hardly less absurd than to attribute to education bodily differences which then declare themselves" (Maudsley 1874, 470).

Maudsley thus denied women entry to higher education on physiological grounds. Women were simply physiologically unfit for strenuous mental work. Women's bodies were designed for different functions than those of men. Men were designed to do heavy work, women light work. Men's minds were made for concentrated thought, women's for general subjects, and with plenty of rest periods. Women were not designed to do men's work, and the education of women "should manifestly be the perfect development, not of manhood but of womanhood" (Maudsley 1874, 481).

A CHALLENGE TO MAUDSLEY: ELIZABETH GARRETT ANDERSON

Among the women who challenged the views put forth by Maudsley and Clarke was Elizabeth Garrett Anderson. Garrett Anderson took up her pen only after Emily Davies and Frances Mary Buss (1827–1894), an English educational pioneer who founded the North London Collegiate, had requested her to do so (Uglow 1999, 98). Garrett Anderson was the first Englishwoman to obtain a medical certificate, which she did through the London Society of Apothecaries after passing a licensing examination in 1865. She received her M.D. from the Sorbonne in Paris in 1870 (Shearer and Shearer 1996, 11).

Elizabeth Garrett Anderson replied directly to Maudsley in *Fortnightly Review* later the same year. She argued that Maudsley reproduced Clarke's lecture with additions to suit an English audience "as an excuse for placing medical and physiological views before the readers of a literary periodical" (Garrett Anderson 1874, 582). Maudsley's paper, she wrote, "consists mainly of a protest against the assimilation of the higher education of men and women, and against the admission of women to new careers; and this protest is founded upon a consideration of the physiological peculiarities of women" (Garrett Anderson 1874, 583). She disputed Maudsley's view that "the physiological difference between men and women seriously interferes with the chances of success a woman would otherwise possess," providing examples of domestic servants and others who performed much physical labor and suffered no ill effects. As for the question of examining girls, she wrote that Maudsley "has not attempted to show how the adoption of a common standard of examination for boys and girls, allowing each a considerable range in the choice of subjects, is likely to interfere more with a girl's health than passing an inferior examination" (Garrett Anderson 1874, 584–585). She continued by refuting Maudsley's arguments that "the cases that Dr. Clarke brings forward in support of his opinion against

continuous mental work during the period of development could be outnumbered many times over even in our own limited experience, by those in which the break-down of nervous and physical health seems . . . to be distinctly traceable to want of adequate mental interest and occupation in the years immediately succeeding school life." Girls became depressed and feeble because they lacked solid intellectual work and thought (Garrett Anderson 1874, 590–591).

Maudsley wrote of the weakness of the female going through puberty and claimed that she was incapable of hard work and intellectual challenges during these physiological changes. Garrett Anderson pointed out that the period of stress for girls was before they reached the age of eighteen, and before eighteen, girls were not admitted to women's colleges such as Girton College, Cambridge. They were required to be eighteen and then sit their exams two to three years later.

The American system that Clarke had studied was much different, in that girls' education was over by the time they were eighteen. In this British case, it was just beginning (Garrett Anderson 1874, 593).

Garrett Anderson's ideas were in turn refuted by Robert Lawson Tait in *Diseases of the Ovaries* (1883) and John Thornburn in *Female Education from a Physician's Point of View* (1884). Tait wrote about the destructive nature of higher education to both women and men. He spoke of the "mischief women will do to themselves and the race generally if they avail themselves too fully of these rights [meaning higher education] when conceded" (cited in Thornburn 1884, 11). He reiterated the view that women should not be educated, for that would harm both women and society.

Sophia Jex-Blake and the Admission of Women to Medical School

Sophia Jex-Blake led the crusade to allow women to study medicine in Great Britain. She was born in Hastings and educated at Queen's College for women in London. She taught mathematics for three years at Queen's. Jex-Blake studied under Dr. Elizabeth Blackwell (1821–1910) in New York State. Blackwell, although of English birth, was the first American woman to qualify as a doctor in the United States, graduating from Geneva University in 1849 (Finkelstein 1995, 334).

In 1869, Jex-Blake and six other women were allowed to matriculate in the medical program at the University of Edinburgh. Women were authorized to attend separate classes, and whether they could or could not attend a specific class was the decision of the individual professor (Jex-Blake 1886, 693). In 1873 the University Council nullified the women's original admission; the battle to complete their studies took four years. Their opponents argued that a female presence in all-male classes would disrupt discipline, and that the discussion of sensitive subjects, such as various parts of the anatomy, would not be permissible, thus compromising the education of future doctors. When Jex-Blake applied to the Royal Infirmary to study medicine, one of the professors declared that they were "obliged to consider the interests of the male students whose feelings of delicacies were violated by the idea of the presence of women" (Pratt 1867, 111–113).

Religious and biological reasons were also pressed into service to keep women out. The following excerpt from an article written in 1870 by a Dr. Henry Bennett for the British medical journal the *Lancet* is representative of the mentality of the times: "I believe most conscientiously and thoroughly that women as a body are sexually, constitutionally and mentally unfitted for the hard and incessant toil required for the heavy responsibilities of general medical and surgical practice." Bennett believed that white males were superior to people of all other races, as well as, of course, the female sex:

> The principal feature which appears to me to characterize the Caucasian race, to raise it immeasurably above all other races, is the power that many of its male members have of advancing the horizon of science, of penetrating beyond the existing limits of knowledge—in a word, the power of scientific discovery. I am not aware that the female members of our race participate in this power, in this supreme development of the human mind; at least I know of no great discovery changing the surface of science that owes its existence to a woman or of any race. What right then have women to claim mental equality with men? (Bennett 1870)

Jex-Blake refuted Bennett's arguments in a reply published in the *Lancet*. She argued that one could not fairly compare male and female abilities in science, since women had not been given the same access to education as men. Women had not received the same training, nor had they been able to take the same examinations as men (Jex-Blake 1870).

Jex-Blake's case was widely discussed by contemporaries, particularly in Parliament, where views on both sides of the debate were expressed. One member of Parliament delineated woman's work and man's work in the traditional fashion: "God sent women to be ministering angels, to soothe the pillow, administer the palliative, whisper words of comfort to the tossing sufferer. Let that continue to be woman's work. Leave the physician's function, the scientific lore, the iron wrist and iron will to men" (cited in Lutzker 1959, 43, 59). Others, however, were sympathetic, notably Sir William Cowper-Temple, James Stansfeld, and Russell Gurney. James Stansfeld wrote an article entitled "Medical Women" in support of female doctors in the July 1877 edition of *Nineteenth Century* magazine. The efforts of these three members of Parliament resulted in ending the restrictions on granting medical degrees to women in May and June 1876 (Lutzker 1959, 59). The Irish College of Physicians was the first medical establishment to allow women to qualify under the new law; Jex-Blake received a medical degree from it in 1877.

Jex-Blake published widely on the subject of women in medicine. In one of her earlier writings, *Medical Women,* she published two essays, "Medicine as a Profession for Women" and "Medical Education of Women." They were published in 1872 during her attempt to gain full status at the University of Edinburgh. In supporting her case that women should be educated in medicine, Jex-Blake quoted the contemporary feminist Harriet Taylor, Mrs. John Stuart Mill. "We deny the right of any portion of the species to decide for another portion, or any individual for another individual, what is, and what is not, their 'proper sphere.' The proper sphere of all human beings is the largest and highest which they are able to attain to. What this is cannot be ascertained without complete liberty of choice" (Jex-Blake 1872).

In this treatise, Jex-Blake surveyed the long history of women in medicine and sketched the reasons why women are currently kept out of the profession. She argued that women once held a "recognized place in the profession." To demonstrate her argument, she cited examples of medical women from antiquity and the Middle Ages. Why, then, was there so much prejudice against women entering the medical profession in Jex-Blake's day? She cited custom as one reason, since "it is only custom and habit which blind society" (Jex-Blake 1872, 10–16). The next reason she repeated is that "women do not require, and are not fitted to receive, the scientific education needful for a first-rate Physician, and that 'for their own sakes' it is not desirable that they should pursue some of the studies indispensably necessary." In response to this argument, she quoted the maxim "that each human being must be a law unto himself" and has the right to be and do what is best for him. Boldly, she asserted: "If women claim that they do need and can appreciate instruction in any or all sciences, I do not know who has the right to deny the assertion" (Jex-Blake 1872, 34). She also refuted the argument that the study of "science may injure a woman's character," stating, "if a woman's womanliness is not deep enough in her nature to bear the brunt of any needful education, it is not worth guarding" (Jex-Blake 1872, 35).

Responding to the view that there is no need for women medical practitioners and that women would rather be looked after by a male doctor, Jex-Blake declared that because women have not been allowed to receive a decent medical education, there is little reason to have confidence in them:

> It is probably a fact, that until lately there has been "no demand" for women doctors, because it does not occur to most people to demand what does not exist; but that very many women have wished that they could be medically attended by those of their own sex I am very sure, and I know of more than one case where ladies have habitually gone through one confinement after another without proper attendance, because the idea of

employing a man was so extremely repugnant to them. (Jex-Blake 1872, 38)

She concluded that "far from there being no demand for female physicians," the contrary is true and "that a tremendous amount of work is awaiting them" (Jex-Blake 1874, 42).

Jex-Blake was not the only person to suggest that women would prefer to be treated by their own. In 1871 a Dr. Mackenzie of Inverness wrote to the local newspaper that women refused to consult with male doctors: "Having been a physician and surgeon for nearly fifty years, I state as a thoroughly well-known, undeniable fact that great numbers of women are sickly for life and die, simply because they shrink from speaking of their ailments to men" (Mackenzie 1871).

Fourteen years later, Jex-Blake was still writing about the most significant obstacles to women in medicine; she found three: (1) jealousy, (2) continued exclusion of women from medical schools, and (3) finances. The "jealousy and ill will on the part of some of the medical profession toward medical women" she saw as a major hindrance. She pointed specifically at the practitioners who specialized in women's diseases, obstetricians and gynecologists. She referred to both her own experience and that of Garrett Anderson with their professional organizations. The Obstetrical Society had excluded Garrett Anderson from its membership in 1874, and the Soho Square Hospital for women in London had refused Jex-Blake admission (Jex-Blake 1886, 704). Both were excluded simply on the basis of their sex. She reported what she called an almost comical incident of jealousy involving the prestigious medical journal *The Lancet*:

> For instance, I received for two successive years a lithographed circular inviting me by name to send to the Lancet the reports of interesting cases that might occur in my dispensary practice; but when I wrote in response to this supposed offer of professional fellowship, I received by next post a hurried assurance from the editor that it was all a mistake, and that in fact the Lancet could not stoop to record medical experiences, however interesting, if they occurred in the practice of the inferior sex! Probably it will not require many more years to make this sort of thing ridiculous even in the eyes of those who are now capable of such puerilities. (Jex-Blake 1886, 705)

She viewed the continued exclusion of most women from access to higher education or universities and to prestigious professional bodies such as the English College of Physicians and Surgeons as a further obstacle in the face of women wanting to become professional medical practitioners. She suggested to Parliament that it "should refuse supplies to those bodies whose sense of justice cannot be otherwise awakened." Going even further, she recommended that the government refused to grant charters to universities unless male and female were treated equally (Jex-Blake 1886, 705).

Jex-Blake also discussed the quandary of inadequate finances. Since women were barred from attending state-funded schools, they were forced to make their own arrangements at much additional expense. She advocated that public money should be set aside for the education of women. Women tended to have less money than men anyway, and fathers were much less likely to spend money on a daughter's education than a son's. "Surely public money should not be altogether denied to them." She also stressed the importance of private funding for female students (Jex-Blake 1886, 705).

The debate over women medical practitioners, particularly female midwives and doctors, has been intense since medieval times. The exclusion of women from the universities established during the Middle Ages kept them from studying medicine. Midwifery, which had been an exclusively female practice until relatively recently in history, saw the age-old customs and healing arts of women being dismissed by British men in the seventeenth century. The professionalization of the medical profession, which took place around the same time as the Scientific Revolution, was a direct attempt by male medical practitioners to exclude women from the healing arts.

The medical profession is one place where women have won the right to study and practice as equals with men. It is because of the pioneering acts of courage and determination by women like Jex-Blake and Garrett Anderson that women have won this victory.

10

The Feminist Critique of Science

The most recent debate concerning women and science has taken the form of more a critique than a debate; the most vocal and prolific voices discussing women and science during the twentieth century and at the opening of the twenty-first century have been those of feminists. Feminist criticism of science has taken many forms since it emerged in the 1960s, and the critics are not a unified group—they have debated among themselves. The feminist critique of science arose out of a more general debate surrounding the philosophy and methodology of science. Science was long accepted as "value free." This meant that scientific knowledge was acquired through logical reasoning applied to experiments conducted in a laboratory, and that this scientific method was not influenced by the values held by the scientist or those of the wider society. A number of philosophers and historians of science, most prominently Thomas S. Kuhn, Paul Feyerabend, and Norwood Russell Hanson, contested the neutrality of science. Kuhn, a Harvard-trained physicist, wrote one of the most influential works on the philosophy of science during the twentieth century, *The Structure of Scientific Revolutions* (1962). Feyerabend, who was a philosopher of science at Berkeley and author of *Farewell to Reason* (1987), *Science in a Free Society* (1978), and *Against Method* (1975), claimed that scientists had no objective standards by which to establish truth, that scientific theories were subjective, and that there was no logic to science. He waged war against what he called the "tyranny of truth" (Feyerabend 1993, 36). Hanson, also a philosopher of science, questioned the validity of accepted truths in science. All observations, he claimed, were theory laden. One of his well-known statements is "There is more to seeing than meets the eyeball" (Hanson 1958, 7).

Their theories were highly controversial and influential. Feminists agreed with Kuhn and his colleagues that science is neither objective nor value free. Science, in common with any other form of knowledge about the world that surrounds us, is influenced by society and culture.

Although the feminist critique is international in scope, it has been strongest in the United States. With the explosion of work in this field of feminism and science, it is impossible to offer conclusive coverage in such a brief chapter—this chapter serves as an introduction to the theories, methodologies, and contributions of those who have provided us with a new and important way of examining science.

The Prefeminist Debate: The Early Twentieth Century

Throughout the twentieth century, men continued to justify excluding women; women's ability to do science remained in question and women were still considered biologically inferior. Women's access to the scientific professions was very limited before the 1980s. Psychologist Anne Roe conducted a study of U.S. scientists in the 1950s titled *The Making of a Scientist* (1953). The sixty-four scientists she examined included no women because science was still a white male profession (Roe 1953).

During the early years of the twentieth century, men continued to justify the exclusion of women from the sciences on the same basis as in previous centuries. The ability of women to do science remained in question. Women were stereotyped according to their sex. This meant that certain jobs were reserved for women—clerical work and nursery school teachers—jobs that emphasized the traditional female role of wife and mother. Journalist Walter Lippmann (1889–1974) popularized this viewpoint, which was widely accepted in the 1920s. His book *Public Opinion,* which supported this view, was published in 1922 (Rossiter 1982, 100).

Women were still considered to be biologically inferior to men. The new method of proving their inferiority was through various quantitative theories. James McKeen Cattell (1860–1944), a psychology professor at Columbia University and editor of the influential journal *Science,* was a major proponent of this view during the early years of the twentieth century. He produced a "Statistical Study of Eminent Men" in 1903, studying the eminent people in history. Only thirty-two women appeared in his top one thousand eminent people (Rossiter 1982, 103). Rossiter's eminent people were individuals who had distinguished themselves in a particular field, whether literature, the arts, or science. He wrote, "I have spoken throughout of eminent men as we lack in English words including both men and women, but as a matter of fact women do not have an important place on the list. . . . Belles lettres and fiction—the only department in which women have accomplished much—give ten names. . . . Women have not excelled in poetry or art. Yet these are the departments . . . in which the environment has been, perhaps, as favorable for women as for men. Women depart less from the normal than men—a fact that usually holds throughout the animal series. . . . The distribution of women is represented by a narrower, bell-shaped curve" (Cattell 1903, 526).

In 1910, he published *American Men of Science,* a biographical dictionary of eminent men of science. He included only eighteen women, or 1.8 percent in the top one thousand scientists, and concluded that these statistics proved the genetic inferiority of women (cited in Rossiter 1982, 107).

Cattell's conclusions were refuted by mathematics professor and champion of women's rights Ellen Hayes (1851–1930), who taught at the all-female Wellesley College. Hayes attributed the low number of women scientists to socialization. Girls, she argued, were taught to value their appearance rather than their minds. Moreover, she wrote that discriminatory hiring and promotional practices in corporations further explained why there were so few women scientists of note. Once again, the argument of sex typing came into play: Women were more likely to be assigned the jobs of cleaning the implements of science, the test tubes, the bottles, etc., than to be given the opportunity to conduct experiments. Hayes published her findings in *Science* in 1910 (cited in Rossiter 1982, 108).

Around the same time that Hayes was disputing the alleged inferiority of the female brain, the influential educational theorist and philosopher John Dewey (1859–1952) became involved in the debate. In 1911, he wrote that there was virtually no scientific evidence for the theories positing the inferiority of the female brain. Rather, he asserted that "any mental differences between male and female are those of arrangement, proportion and emphasis, rather than kind or quality" (Dewey 1978, 6: 160). He also conjectured that there were more differences between individuals of the same sex, for example differences between men, than differences between men and women (Dewey 1978, 6: 160). Although Dewey defended women in terms of their equal intelligence to men, he believed that women's role was that of homemaker. He believed that the female role of wife, mother, and household manager required a college preparation. Thus, he thought that women should attend college to study domestic science and hygiene, a "scientific preparation for the responsibilities of par-

John Dewey (Library of Congress)

enthood and household management" (Dewey 1978, 6: 164).

During World Wars I and II, middle-class women in Western countries had the opportunity to work outside the home. Their contribution to the war effort was primarily on the home front, although some women did serve abroad in the social services, such as nursing. At home, women worked in the social services, home economics, and as the war dragged on, in munition factories. After the war, the situation returned to "normal," and women were expected to return to their homes and reproduce (Ambrose et al. 1997, 20).

Barriers to science remained. The pressures facing women were more subtle than in previous centuries, with the cultural pressures to marry and have children most prominent. These pressures were very strong during the 1950s, as Betty Friedan argued in her classic work of feminism, *The Feminine Mystique* (1963). Women's role was considered to be in the kitchen and the home. World War II had been disruptive for the family and for society as large numbers of women worked outside of the home, and there were tremendous pressures for women and society to return to prewar status. Following this period, the twentieth-century debate of women in science began in earnest during the 1960s.

The Background to the Feminist Critique

The 1960s brought much social change in Western culture, in particular in the United States. The women's movement, or the second wave of feminism, the increased activity in the late 1960s by women in the United Kingdom, Europe, and the United States in the realm of political rights, grew out of the Civil Rights movement. Middle-class women were no longer content to stay at home and raise children. *The Feminine Mystique* and the classic text by Simone de Beauvoir, *The*

Second Sex (published in French in 1949 as *Le Deuxième sexe* but not read widely until the 1960s), led middle-class women to question their views of themselves and their roles in society. Friedan went so far as to compare the situation of the American housewife with that of the prisoner in a concentration camp. What defined the "feminine mystique" was the depersonalization of women, their passivity and dependence on being married and having children (Friedan 1963). De Beauvoir argued much the same point: "Shut up in her flesh, her home, she sees herself as passive before these gods [men] with human faces who set goals and establish values. . . . The lot of woman is respectful obedience" (de Beauvoir 1974, 664–665). The image of woman as a mere appendage to man, a baby machine, and a homemaker had a great impact on women and their opportunities to do science.

The Soviet launch of Sputnik I on 4 October 1957 had a tremendous effect on science education in the United States. Before Sputnik, Americans did not consider science and scientific education as a weapon in the cold war. They soon discovered with Sputnik that they were technologically inferior to the Soviets, and this inferiority stemmed from inadequate science education. The U.S. government poured millions of dollars into scientific education at all levels. The impact for women, however, was not positive as Margaret Rossiter, the Marie Underhill Noll Professor of History of Science at Cornell University, demonstrated. She argued that after World War II, women's participation in science and technology declined precipitously. Modernization after the war and the response to Sputnik in the educational institutions, from schools to universities, meant "masculinzation." In an effort to "catch up" to the Russians, special emphasis in the schools was placed on science, mathematics, and foreign languages (Van Til 1978, 172). For the first time, the U.S. government passed legislation supporting education, including higher education (Brown 1984, 15, 26). However, the expanding colleges and universities hired men rather than women to increase faculty. This was true even at all-women colleges such as Smith College where the percentage of men on the faculty increased from 39.9 percent in 1947 to 64.8 percent in 1965 (Rossiter 1995, 224).

During the 1960s, debate began over the low participation rate of women in science. An exemplary piece of literature from this period was the fruit of the Symposium on American Women in Science and Engineering held at Massachusetts Institute of Technology in October 1964. The conference proceedings were published in book form a year later, *Women and the Scientific Professions.* Many of the concerns contained in this volume foreshadowed the later topics of debate, including barriers to women who desire a career in science, the low representation of women in the scientific professions, the problems of juggling motherhood and career, negative perceptions of women scientists, and the different methods of male and female socialization. The conference became much more important than its organizers had imagined. As stated in the preface to *Women and the Scientific Professions,* "What began as a local meeting to consider only career possibilities and problems for MIT's women students quickly expanded into a national conference which was attended by 260 student delegates from 140 colleges. . . . What began as a modest informational effort resulted in a fascinating exchange of ideas by distinguished and enthusiastic participants." Also in attendance were college deans, women employed professionally in science, and employers (Mattfield and Van Aken 1965, v–vi).

This work and others like it could be considered pioneers in the field of issues facing women and science in the later twentieth century. It is interesting to note, as Alice Rossi explains in her contribution, that female students in the early 1960s, although clad in blue jeans and checked shirts, had similar life expectations to their grandmothers. They expected to live their lives in the shadow of their husband's and children's achievements. They would be the nurturers of both (cited in Mattfield and Van Aken 1965, 51–127).

Toward a Definition of the Feminist Critique of Science

The feminist model of science defines science as a product of the culture and society in which we live, dominated by white males (Tuana 1988, 2). It rejects the view that started with the ancient Greeks that science is objective, based on reason, and value free. Nancy Tuana, professor of philosophy at the University of Oregon, Eugene, and others argued that scientists work within the value system and worldview of their society (Tuana 1988, 35).

Feminists in science have principally focused on the current methods employed in science. Some have inquired as to whether or not the practice of science by women differs from that of men. Those who write in this specialized branch of knowledge generally share certain views: (1) They would like to eliminate research that leads to any kind of exploitation and oppression; (2) they are antiauthoritarian and anti-elitist—they would like to make science accessible to anyone who expresses an interest; (3) they stress not only gender in their writings, but also cultural diversity; and (4) they see science as it has been practiced in the West as having excluded women. Questions addressed by these critics include: "Are we asking for a feminist science? Is there a feminist science? Is there a feminist method? Why should feminist values take precedence over others? Do women do science differently from men? and Is sexist science bad science?" (Tuana 1989, vii).

Evolution of the Feminist Critique

As Elizabeth Fee maintained, it took a long time for science and technology to be scrutinized under the feminist microscope. Unlike other disciplines, such as those in the humanities, the arts, and the social sciences, the "hard" sciences during the early years of the twentieth century kept a distance from feminism. The feminism of the 1960s did not reach science until the late 1970s and early 1980s (cited in Bleier 1986, 42–56).

The feminist critique of science of which Elizabeth Fee wrote has passed through several stages since it began in the late 1970s. Many of the contributors to the debate have been scientists, such as Evelyn Fox Keller and Ruth Bleier, who experienced isolation and discrimination as female scientists firsthand. Others are philosophers, sociologists, and historians of science. The feminist critique of science began with research into the forgotten women of science from the past. Several biographies of female scientists were written, the most notable of which were Anne Sayre's biography *Rosalind Franklin and DNA* (1975) and Evelyn Fox Keller's *Feeling and Organism: The Life and Work of Barbara McClintock* (1983). Margaret Alic's *Hypatia's Heritage* (1986) attempted to recover the forgotten female practitioners of science from prehistory to the nineteenth century. It was an attempt to fill in the blanks and to write the wrongs in the history of science.

One of the most recent examples of this genre of work is Sharon Bertsch McGrayne's study of female Nobel Prize winners. Written in biographical format, this study of the lives of fifteen women who have been awarded the Nobel Prize makes clear to the reader the widespread discrimination against women who were serious about contributing to science, starting with Marie Curie, who won the prize for physics in 1903 and chemistry in 1911. To quote the author, These "lives . . . illustrate the changing patterns of discrimination against women in science, starting with legal bars to academic high schools and universities in Europe, and continuing in the United States with laws against working wives in universities" (McGrayne 1998, x). Rather than asking why there have been so few winners among women, McGrayne inquired as to why there have been so many, given the extreme obstacles they were forced to confront. These women were exceptional, in the sense that they were able to succeed in male-dominated science.

Fox Keller's study of geneticist Barbara McClintock, who was a Nobel Prize winner in medicine and physiology (1983), was an important contribution to the biography as a form of feminist critique, in the sense that the book is both a biography and a demonstration of a different view of science from the traditional one, which considers science to be objective, neutral, value free, and rational. In her work, Fox Keller explained as part of her discussion of McClintock that "good science cannot proceed without a deep emotional investment on the part of the scientist" (Fox Keller 1983, 198). In other words, scientists must feel passionately about their subjects. In subsequent works, Fox Keller has expanded upon this different view of science. In *Reflections on Gender and Science* (1985), she took an historical and linguistic approach to science, arguing that the language of science has excluded women since the scientific revolution of the seventeenth century. In terms of language, Fox Keller believes that the issue of women and science goes beyond the mere exclusion of women from practicing science. She has said that she wished "it were that simple" (Fox Keller 1994). She claimed that the problem involves "the deep penetration between our cultural construction of gendering and our naming of science." She pointed to the writings of Francis Bacon, who used terms such as "male," "masculine," and "rational" to describe science and "female" to characterize nature. The language of Bacon has lasted until today. And anything that is female, or feminine, is excluded from the realm of science (Fox Keller 1994, 47).

Carolyn Merchant, a professor of environmental history, philosophy, and ethics, is similar to Fox Keller in stating that the traditional view of nature is that it is something that must be tamed, "bound into service," made a "slave" (Merchant 1980, 169). Both critics of modern science and its methods understand that females are excluded from science. Added to this reality, Merchant argues that Bacon's "new man of science" was a "harbinger of many modern research scientists" (Merchant 1980, 181–182). Science was mysterious, secretive, and only understood after years of training. Scientists thus had a power that the ordinary citizen lacked. This viewpoint, which began with Bacon, remains to the present day.

Does Fox Keller believe that women do science differently from men? In 1993, she wrote that the question was almost impossible to

*Genetic researcher
Barbara McClintock
receives the 1983
Nobel Prize for
medicine from
King Carl Gustaf
of Sweden
(Bettmann / Corbis)*

answer and perhaps irrelevant, as she believed women cannot be separated from "the cultural messages" that inundate them. These "messages" are conflicting, for on the one hand they tell her how to be feminine, and on the other, they inform her how to be masculine as a
scientist (cited in Jackson 1993).

Fox Keller has also argued that women are equal to men in their
capacity to do science and that women, to be good scientists, must be
feminists as well. She urges female scientists to be open to feminist
thought in their science. In 1982, Fox Keller demanded what she
called a "radical critique of feminism in science" (Fox Keller 1982).
She believes that "gender specific assumptions" have a tremendous impact on women's research (Fox Keller 1993).

Fox Keller wants to move on from the "natural commonality" of feminists, or the "entrenched opposition between women scientists and feminist analysts of science and to seek to situate the women, science and gender question" (Fox Keller 1997, 17). She used the example of the German female Nobel Prize winner for physiology in 1995, Christiane Nusslein-Volhard, to demonstrate that one does not need to be a feminist to succeed in science. Nusslein-Volhard has an "ambivalent" attitude to "feminism," yet she has succeeded in a very male-dominated sphere of molecular biology. She has been the only female director of the Max Planck Institute. Germany has one of the lowest rates of female professors in biology, at less than 3 percent (Fox Keller 1997, 25). The key point, according to Fox Keller, is Nusslein-Volhard's ambivalence about feminism: "She has not needed to be an unequivocal supporter either of feminism or of women in order to make an intervention of immense value to women in science." She pointed out, however, that gender is important to this example of a successful women in science because of the scientist's "situatedness, as a woman, in a field in which gender has mattered for a very long time." Nusslein-Volhard has been successful because she was able to take advantage of "local alliances," meaning the "strains in feminism that accord with and those women who share her goals." Fox Keller urged feminist critics of science to try the same method to get their message across (Fox Keller 1997, 28).

Another strategy of feminist critics of science has been to include an analysis of the participation, or lack thereof, of women in science and the reasons for women's underparticipation and underrepresentation. The issues addressed have included the structural barriers to women and the socialization of girls and boys, involving the different expectations of each gender. Suggestions as to how to address the gender imbalance have also been put forth, such as better access to science education for girls and jobs in science for women. Ruth Bleier is one of the contributors to this aspect of the discussion. She was a medical doctor—she died in 1988 of cancer—educated at the Women's Medical College of Pennsylvania and Johns Hopkins University, where she studied neurophysiology. Her research dealt with the "structure and organization of the hypothalamus" (Bleier 1988, 189). During the 1970s, she joined the women's movement. She wrote extensively on the issue of women and science, beginning with *Science and Gender: A Critique of Biology and Its Theory on Women* in 1984. This book was the first work in this genre, and it was followed by the works of other scientists, sociologists, and others.

Bleier stated that when she began to examine the position of women in science, there had been no critique of the discipline from a gender perspective, with the exception of Ruth Herschberger's *Adam's Rib,* written in 1948. Some of the questions addressed by Bleier were: (1) Why is women's voice absent in the natural sciences? (2) How would science be different if women did have a voice? (3) How can women change both science and society to make science more accessible to women? (Bleier 1986, 1). Bleier opened the discussion dealing with the fundamental structure and thinking processes behind the way in which Western science has been carried out since the seventeenth century. She, along with those who followed her, challenged the commonly held perception that science is objective, value free, male, rigorous, tough, and not an appropriate field for women.

Later, Bleier also inquired as to why there has been so much resistance by men to a feminist critique of traditional science and why so few women scientists learn feminist theory or know about the feminist critiques of science (Bleier 1988, 193). On the latter question, Bleier suggested that women scientists, unlike women doctors, do not identify themselves as female but see themselves only as scientists. They are not engaged in the debate, for the most part. Interestingly, science, which by its nature and definition should be critical, has been seriously "lacking in a tradition of self-scrutiny and self-criticism" (Bleier 1988, 193). Moreover, she wrote that although government agencies are finally waking up to the lack of female participation in science, the scientific profession itself has ignored the feminist critique of its profession (Bleier 1988, 194).

Writing in the early 1980s, Sheila M. Pfafflin sketched explanations for the lower participation of women than men in the fields of science and technology in both developing and developed nations. She found that the kind of education women received was geared toward traditional occupations and not science or technology (Pfafflin 1982, 180). Subtle practices have been employed to keep women out of science. For example, women may be admitted at the lower echelons of universities, as part-time or full-time lecturers or assistant professors, but very few are full professors. Women were allowed in, but denied promotion: Between 1971–1972 and 1977–1978 the percentage of women at the assistant professor level in physics increased from 3.3 to 4.5. At the full professor level, the percentage during this period actually decreased from 2.4 to 1.4. Her findings were similar in other fields of science (Pfafflin 1982, 184). She also cited the old-boy network as an important barrier preventing women from gaining access to employment and research funds.

Another important barrier often overlooked by the more philosophical feminist critics of science is domestic responsibilities. Women have done and continue to do the majority of housework and childcare. With the demanding nature of scientific research, Pfafflin argued that it is almost impossible for women to carry out intensive scientific research and take care of the home. She wrote: "If women are to enter the sciences on an equal basis, not only must the formal barriers be removed, but the cultural environment must cease to burden them with responsibilities that do not burden their male colleagues" (Pfafflin 1982, 185). Better provision for childcare and more sharing of the household responsibilities would improve this situation.

Marion Namenwirth, who holds a Ph.D. in developmental genetics from Indiana University, echoed many of Bleier's concerns and arguments. She put forth the view that Western society encourages boys who show talent for science and math, but treats girls in the opposite way. Our entire method of socialization works against instilling in girls the attributes necessary to survive as professional scientists: Girls are socialized to be sensitive, emotional, obedient, kind, dependent, shy, lacking in confidence, and self-sacrificing. Because of these values instilled in girls from birth, they are "gently discouraged" from doing science, and "only a minority" of determined women continue. Girls are made to feel unfeminine and thus socially unacceptable if they challenge the status quo. She wrote: "Our society presumes that because of the personal qualities required, science is an essentially masculine enterprise" (cited in Bleier 1986, 20). Thus the majority of women who might otherwise consider science as a career never move in that direction at all. Even the few who make it in science are not promoted, praised, and encouraged as much as men. Women tend to work as research assistants rather than the chief researcher of a project. Namenwirth points to the example of Rosalind Franklin, whose work on the structure of the DNA molecule was "pirated and appropriated by Wilkins, Watson and Crick." They gave her credit only for taking photographs of the molecule, not for interpreting them (cited in Bleier 1986, 21). Namenwirth concluded that science, as practiced in the West, is patriarchal and works against rather than for women. Much of the career path in university science is intrinsically connected to an old-boy network (cited in Bleier 1986, 24).

In a similar vein, historian Margaret Rossiter wrote a study of women scientists in the United States to 1940. She explored the biographies of women scientists; studied employment patterns in business, government, and academia; and examined the education of girls. She questioned the conventional beliefs concerning female capabilities in science. Rossiter argued that the few women who had made it as scientists did so through the adaptation of strategies. Women scientists often remained single (they did not have family responsibilities) or they worked under the auspices of their husbands, who were scientists. Women would work at home, while their husbands had access to the laboratories, research funding, and a career through a university or corporation (Rossiter 1982).

Another issue concerning the debate deals with the old belief that women are biologically best suited to domestic responsibilities at home. Ruth Hubbard took issue with sociobiological research, pointing out that since the 1970s there had been a renaissance in research in sex differences. This research, based upon hormone testing of rats, attempted to prove that women were biologically suited to the home and private sphere and men to the public sphere. She pointed to the work done by sociobiologists such as E. O. Wilson in his 1975 book *Sociobiology: The New Synthesis* (Hubbard 1988, 9). Hubbard is especially concerned with the lack of recognition of women scientists of the past who were sisters, wives, or daughters of male scientists. Without them, the work of the male scientist could not have been carried out. She proposed a model for a new kind of science, "a domestic science project." Further, she proclaimed, "If feminists are to make a difference in the ways science is done and understood, we must not try to become scientists who occupy the traditional structures, follow established patterns of behavior and accept prevailing systems of explanation; we must understand and describe accurately the roles women have played all along in the process of making science" (Hubbard 1988, 14).

There is much diversity of viewpoints among the feminist critics of science. Philosopher Sandra Harding, for example, has criticized women scientists who do not question the profession and practice of science itself but are primarily concerned with greater access of women to the scientific professions as they currently exist. Harding approached the problem from an epistemological standpoint. She proposed something far more radical: She questioned the system of science itself and what she called the masculinization of women. In other words, the profession of science does not allow women to be women. Its structure has no place or makes no accommodation for women who are mothers and caregivers for their families. Harding concluded that the structural framework of science explained why there are so few women in science. Thus, rather than stopping at tinkering with the current system to allow better treatment for women, Harding asked "how a science apparently so deeply involved in distinctively masculine projects can be possibly used for emancipatory ends" (Harding 1986, 29).

Such models of female epistemology have been criticized by feminist E. Anne Kerr, who believes that theories such as these are not particularly relevant to working women of science. She is particularly critical of Harding's view of women's "unique and privileged standpoint" because it "alienates" women scientists who do not see their gender as important to their work (Kerr 2001, 386–387).

Harding invented a concept called "strong objectivity" in science, which she defined as "extending the notion of scientific research to include systematic examination of cultural influences in science" (Harding 1991, 149). In other words, scientists should come to their discipline from the position of the socially disadvantaged "as a source of critical questions about received belief." If they do not, these questions will remain unasked (cited in Longino and Fox Keller 1996, 240). What she asked was that ways of thinking and belief systems other than those of white males should be considered important, calling attention to the worldviews of outsiders to science: women, people of color, and people from lower socioeconomic backgrounds.

Helen E. Longino, philosopher and director of the women's studies program at the University of Minnesota, advocated social and ethnic diversity in the scientific community. She contended that "as long as representatives of alternative points of view are not included in the community, shared values will not be identified as shaping observations or reasoning" (Longino 1989, 272). Feminist Donna Haraway, trained in biology, English, and philosophy, suggested a doctrine of "situated knowledge," by which she meant a "doctrine and practice of objectivity that privileges contestation, deconstruction, passionate construction, webbed connections and hope for transformation of systems of knowledge and ways of seeing" (Haraway 1988, 575–599). Further, she contends that she "would like a doctrine of embodied objectivity that accommodates paradoxical and critical feminist science projects: feminist objectivity means quite simply '*situated knowledge*'" (cited in Lederman and Bartsch 2001, 173). She pointed out that people have many angles or perspectives and that these are based not only upon gender, but also class, race, and so on. Dorothy Smith, a feminist sociologist, put forth the view that the genders do not possess or come from the same epistemological perspectives because of the "gendered division of labor" (cited in Longino and Fox Keller 1996).

Evelyn Fox Keller appealed to object relations theory (a branch of psychoanalytic theory) in order to argue that a certain objectivist and domination-directed conception of science is the result of a distinctively masculine psychology.

Together, Fox Keller, Longino, Haraway, and Harding have developed what is called a feminist epistemology of science. What this has come to mean is that value-free science does not exist, that objective science is never without "the contextual values of our interpretive frameworks and these guide our observations" (Fox Keller 1987, 54). In other words, even the observations of scientists are determined by their cultural construct, their socialization, their worldview. Objectivity is a phenomenon that requires rethinking and redefinition. As Harding put it, "We cannot restrict ourselves simply to the elimination of bias, but must expand our scope to include the detection of limiting and interpretive frameworks and the findings or construction of more appropriate frameworks. We need not, indeed should not, want for such a framework to emerge from the data" (Harding and O'Barr 1987, 60). The goal, according to Harding, is to find better "conceptual filters" (Harding and O'Barr 1987, 111).

From the European Standpoint

Thus far, this chapter has focused on American women debaters, who were the most prominent and the most outspoken on the issue of women in science during the twentieth century. This is not to say that European women have been absent from the debate. British sociologist Hilary Rose, for example, offered a somewhat different perspective and framework from that of her American counterparts working in the field of feminist criticism of science. Rose united Marxism with feminism. In an article published in 1983, she contended that bourgeois science is a form of "alienated and abstract knowledge." Her examination focused on the impact of the gender division of labor on science. Women have traditionally received less remuneration than men and have been kept in the lower echelons of the profession. Science for women, she stated, has been a "shared experience" of "oppression." In common with Fox Keller, Rose called for a "re-unification of hand, brain and heart" as a method of creating a new type of science forging a harmony with nature (Rose 1983, 73–90).

Veronica Stolte-Heiskanen, who edited *Women in Science: Token Women or Gender Equality?* (1991), provided a significant contribution to the debate. This work consists of articles discussing the problems faced by women in science throughout twelve European countries. These studies all demonstrated that although attitudes toward women's capabilities of doing science are no longer what they were in the nineteenth century, many obstacles remain. Gender equality in science is not a reality; educational opportunities have greatly improved (undergraduate females are often 50 percent of biology classes, for instance), but career opportunities have not (Stolte-Heiskanen 1991, 1–4).

In Western European countries, as in the United States, the women's movement of the 1960s and 1970s had a profound impact on women in science. Women began to enter the workforce in greater numbers; policy makers began to take an interest in women, and academic theoreticians wrote studies focusing on the Marxist-Freudian analysis of patriarchy. These led to similar questions being raised in Europe and the United States about the barriers to women in science: Studies pointed to the lack of female role models, lack of confidence and encouragement, domestic responsibilities, and the conservative nature of the scientific community itself, resulting in resistance to women gaining powerful positions (Stolte-Heiskanen 1991, 5–8). Social stigma was also cited as a deterrent to women entering the sciences (Stolte-Heiskanen 1991, 179).

The problem of women's greater participation in science came to the attention of the United Nations during the 1980s. Studies were conducted, and the UNESCO Sector for Social and Human Sciences recommended that barriers confronting women be removed. Barriers to women's participation in science are now considered to be a violation of human rights (Stolte-Heiskanen 1991, 227).

As in the American debates, European women have disputed the pervasive notion that science is objective, value free, and an entity apart from the dominant culture. They have seen it as fundamentally linked to patriarchy. The Swedish scholar Elisabeth Hermodosson reflected this view in her comments concerning the patriarchal nature of Western science and technology: "The hypertechnocratic civilization can be seen as the ultimate consequence of patriarchy's desire to master what is nature, woman and life. Humanity defined as man, as aggressor, as conqueror, as the right of the stronger to rule the world. . . . Women who have been excluded from codetermination in political and cultural development have not been involved in creating this hypertechnocratic culture" (Stolte-Heiskanen 1991, 40).

Gender and Science from the Historian's Perspective:
Londa Schiebinger and Margaret Rossiter

Thus far, this chapter has examined the twentieth-century debates about women in science in terms of sociology, philosophy, linguistics, and science itself. The terminology and arguments put forth by these critics are often inaccessible to the general reader: They use language that the educated layperson cannot understand, and they publish their findings in scholarly journals not read by most people. Historian Londa Schiebinger, on the other hand, writes in accessible English free of the jargon that characterizes a great deal of academic scholarship today. Moreover, she provides the reader with a historical perspective on the position of women in science. Schiebinger is probably the most widely known and well-published historian studying gender and science. Her earlier works, including *The Mind Has No Sex? Women in the Origins of Modern Science* (1989) and *Nature's Body: Gender in the Making of Modern Science* (1993), were primarily historical, focusing on questions such as why women scientists throughout history have been so unusual. In *The Mind Has No Sex?* Schiebinger examined the rise of science in Western culture from the seventeenth century onward, concluding that both ideology and institutions shut women out of science. In *Nature's Body* she examined "how gender—both the real relations between the sexes and ideological renderings of those relations—shaped European science in the eighteenth century, and natural history in particular" (Schiebinger 1993, 2).

Schiebinger's latest book-length contribution to the debate, *Has Feminism Changed Science?* (1999), took into consideration much of the scholarship over the past thirty years and made it clear to readers from diverse backgrounds. The author stressed the importance of history for understanding the current state of play in the sciences. She devoted her first chapter, "Hypatia's Heritage," to a historical survey of women in science, dating from approximately the fifteenth century.

In later chapters, she provided her own unique contribution to the debate. In addressing the question as to whether or not women do science differently from men, she replied in the negative: "There is no 'feminist' or 'female style' ready to be plugged in at the laboratory bench or the clinical bedside" (Schiebinger 1999, 8). She did think that more stress needed to be put on taking into consideration people's race and class as well as gender when examining women in science. Often white women from single-sex colleges, for example, are better represented in the scientific professions than others.

Going against some of the views of feminist critics of science, she argued that the time had come to "move away from conceptions of feminist science as empathetic, nondominating, environmentalist or people-friendly" (Schiebinger 1999, 8). She argued that women should be treated the same as men, trained the same, and represented in equal numbers, which they are not in mathematics and physics (Schiebinger 1999, 9–10).

In providing a response to her own question, "Has feminism changed science?" Schiebinger answered in the affirmative, in terms of the numbers of women who work in the scientific profession today. She wrote that the "ascent has been remarkable when looking through the long run of history" (Schiebinger 1999, 181). There are many women primatologists, biologists, and health scientists today. She described her goal in practical terms: It is "not to create a feminist science, if that means (as it does for many critics) a special or separate science for women or feminists. . . . What we need is a healthy working relationship between scholars involved in developing gender critiques of science and those doing science." This kind of relationship has already developed in fields such as medicine, primatology, biology, and archaeology, the areas in which gender criticism has been most influential (Schiebinger 1999, 184–185). More gender analysis needs to be done in chemistry, mathematics, and physics. Schiebinger suggested such remedial methods as "site visits," which would allow students to actually visit workplaces of physics, the teaching of the history of gender and science in science programs, and even gender analysis in actual science courses (Schiebinger 1999, 187).

Margaret Rossiter, as mentioned above, has also analyzed women in science during the twentieth century from the perspective of an historian. Her work, *Women Scientists in America: Struggles and Strategies to 1940* (1982), questioned the conventional beliefs concerning female capabilities in science. The few women who made it in that period in science were successful because of strategies they adopted to survive. Female scientists were unusual people; they were not the norm of womankind.

Rossiter also saw a correlation between the income of a particular subfield of science and the number of women involved. Women tend to be clustered in the lower-paid and less prestigious scientific fields. They are rarely in engineering, agricultural sciences, and physics. Like Schiebinger, she pointed out that women are rarely to be found in the scientific fields (such as engineering) closely related to the military (Rossiter 1982, 181).

Rossiter perceived the most significant gauge of the quality of the female experience in the scientific disciplines as the proportion of women to men in that discipline. Some areas of science have more women than men. One of these areas is nutrition. This area of science, because it is dominated by women, has been "trivialized" and often not even considered to be a science (Rossiter 1982, 182). Rossiter found that the proportion of women to men within a discipline may change over time for many reasons. A good number of the subdisciplines that people have considered to be "soft" have made an effort to become "harder" by incorporating technically advanced instrumentation or more experimentation. Intensified analysis and tracking of the various scientific disciplines and subspecialties, she has recently said, would help in understanding the barriers to education, employment, and promotion of women in science (Rossiter 1997, 169–185).

The feminist critique is not without its own critics. For the most part, those who tend to dissent from some aspects of the feminist critics' perspective are practicing scientists themselves, such as E. Anne Kerr. Kerr is a physics graduate and a feminist. In a recent article, she wrote that the feminists critics tend to be uncomfortable with the natural sciences, for they are mostly social scientists and perhaps do not fully comprehend the experience of women in the natural or physical sciences. According to Kerr, the critics tend to put too much stress on "women's shared experience" and focus too much on the difference between men and women. She agreed with their point that masculine has meant science in the past and often continues to do so today, and that science is not any more neutral than history.

What was constructive about Kerr's article was that she investigated the subject of women in science from the perspective of a practicing scientist as well as a social scientist. She interviewed thirty female scientists—chemists, physicists, and biologists—in Canada, the United States, and the United Kingdom. All made concrete, tangible recommendations such as providing more funding and a more nurturing environment, making the natural sciences more accessible to a wider group of people, and removing preconceived ideas about women and science. The creation of an atmosphere of cooperation rather than competition (she found that women tend to share their research findings more than men do) and flexible career paths would also enhance science and allow more women to feel a part of the scientific community, which has been dominated by men. What was important about her findings was that the women in science wanted to change science from within science.

Reasons for Optimism? Still Room for Improvement

One of the demands currently being made is that we must change science, not women. There must be new ways of thinking about and experiencing the relationship between women and science. In 1993, Anne Fausto-Sterling, a professor of biology and women's studies at Brown University, wrote that we can no longer state that "wrong science is being done." That is, in the past, the questions posed and the evidence presented by scientists were dominated by political motivations. Today, however, scientists should make clear their politics and thus strive for "good science" (Fausto-Sterling 1992, 12). Echoing writers like Kuhn and Feyeraband, she maintains that science is not value free. Rather, it is influenced by the social and political context, and thus social change toward a more equal society is urgently needed (Fausto-Sterling 1992, 120, 270). Elizabeth Potter, director of the women's studies program at Mills College, thinking along the same lines, believes that one's culture should be included in the scientific method. And, according to Evelyn Fox Keller, we should "seek the best science," which should be a human science. She no longer seems to speak only of women in science, but of people in science. Feminist arguments must be heard by the mainstream, but they are to be incorporated into a truly human science (Jackson 1993).

Philosopher Sandra Harding is positive about the future of women in science. In a fairly recent article, she stated that thinking has definitely changed for women in science over the past thirty years, really since the feminist critique began. Women are moving into positions of importance, and this is significant for society as a whole. Younger women have been encouraged to enter the sciences. Women's ability to apply the scientific method is no longer questioned. And the very presence of these women has helped to change the nature of research being carried out. For example, women's health issues are now being taken seriously because of the presence of women in this field as researchers. Previously drug testing was only done on men. More women are needed here. She also urged the presence of more women on policy-making boards and councils, where they could make much more of a political contribution in the field of policy making. In her closing remarks she pointed to the importance of women's issues to science and society as a whole (Harding 1998, 1599–1600).

In 2001, female scientists continued to report that women were underrepresented in science, especially the natural sciences, at every level from school to the workplace. The lack of women in science continues to be part of a wider societal issue "associated with the norms and expectations of science." The typical scientist in our society remains a white male from an upper-middle-class background who has time to spend alone in his laboratory. It appears that our culture, in spite of all the progress we have made in women's rights and feminism, has progressed very little when it comes to women in science. We have only to read the words of two practicing scientists,

Muriel Lederman at Virginia Polytechnic Institute and Ingrid Bartsch at the University of South Florida: "The fact that our culture does not make it possible for us to assume that scientists can be women means that women scientists *are* an anomaly, that they are categorized as exceptions that deserve a special title" (Lederman and Bartsch 2001, 9). They argue that adding women to the existing culture of science does nothing to change the status quo. Instead, programs must be altered to take into consideration women's work, which remains undervalued and unrecognized (Lederman and Bartsch 2001). Women in science continue to occupy positions of lower employment, lower prestige, and lower pay, particularly in engineering. The climate of science remains hostile to women. The deeper issue here is that society regards the typical scientist as white, male, and upper-middle-class. Until that vision of the scientist changes, the avenues open to women in science will remain limited. Those women who have "made it" in science form a minority of survivors alongside other minorities, such as people of color. In their study of women in engineering, a field of science that has one of the lowest areas of female participation rates, Margaret A. Eisenhart at the University of Colorado, Boulder, and Elizabeth Finkel, coauthor with Eisenhart of *Women's Science: Learning and Succeeding from the Margins,* argue that women are "discouraged, barred, or chased from science" (cited in Lederman and Bartsch 2001, 19). Many girls do not go into engineering because of its white male "nerdy" reputation, the "chilly climate of science classrooms and degree programs," and the fact that women and minorities are considered to be people "who leave science and engineering programs" (cited in Lederman and Bartsch 2001, 19).

What can be done to change this rather depressing situation? Some argue in favor of a more inclusive science that takes into account race and class as well as gender. Others plead for an improvement in programs for women. In a recent article, historian of science Schiebinger maintained that we are entering a new era for women in science, but that there is a need to educate scientists in the debates on gender. The fundamental challenge from her point of view is women and physics. As Rossiter also observed earlier, physics has shunned women and women physicists for various reasons: its close ties with the military, its image as a "hard science," and its extensive use of mathematics. Schiebinger argued for something she called "sustainable science," meaning a science that is "socially responsible" and that includes collaboration with experts from the arts such as historians and philosophers (cited in Lederman and Bartsch 2001, 466).

A New Field of Scientific Inquiry

The debates concerning women and science that began some forty years ago have become institutionalized in a new field of study: "feminist studies of science." Multidisciplinary scholars, scientists, social scientists, and educational specialists have come together to pool their knowledge and resources to develop a new field that considers race, class, gender, science, and technology. They apply feminist theories to "scientific ideas and practices to explore the relationship between feminism and science and what each can learn from the other" (Lederman and Bartsch 2001). These women see themselves as going beyond the criticisms their foremothers made about women in science. They see themselves as part and parcel of a creative process making life and the academy more equitable.

The feminist debate about science has fundamentally changed the way in which science is understood, taught, and practiced. As stated earlier in this chapter, it really began with a re-interpretation of the scientific revolution of the seventeenth century with philosophers such as Thomas Kuhn who posited that science is not value-free, that science, like any other human endeavor, is full of prejudices and subjectivity, if not subliminal undercurrents. The prejudice against women in science is part and parcel of this argument.

The women who opened up the feminist debate some forty years ago have made possible works such as this one, for the issues surrounding the ability of women to do science would never have been raised had these women not asked the fundamental questions summarized in this chapter: Why have women been barred from science for so long? And why are there so few women scientists?

The questions of equal opportunity and equal access of women to science have not been resolved. For the most part, women are no longer considered, as they were in previous centuries, biologically inferior and incapable of reason, yet women have not achieved equity in terms of careers, funding, and leadership positions in science.

Further Reading

Preface

The works listed below will provide readers with a starting point for further reading on women in science throughout history. There are some excellent general biographical and bibliographical works about women and men of science, some of which have been published since I started work on this project. These works contain details about the lives and contributions of female scientists, which are not available elsewhere. These include Marilyn Bailey Ogilvie and Joy Harvey, *The Biographical Dictionary of Women in Science* (New York: Routledge, 2000); Roy Porter and Marilyn Bailey Ogilvie, *The Hutchinson Dictionary of Scientific Biography.* 2 vols. (Oxford: Helicon, 2000); as well as Roy Porter and Marilyn Bailey Ogilvie, *The Biographical Dictionary of Scientists* (New York: Oxford University Press, 2000). Ogilvie's earlier works—*Women in Science: Antiquity through the Nineteenth Century* (Cambridge: MIT Press, 1986) and with Kerry Lynne Meek, *Women and Science: An Annotated Bibliography* (New York: Garland, 1996)—are extremely useful compendia of biographical and bibliographical information about women in science from antiquity to the present. Particularly helpful is the historical essay discussing women's struggle to practice science throughout history. Other biographical sources include three bio-bibliographical sourcebooks edited by Louise S. Grinstein et al.: *Women of Mathematics: A Bibliographic Sourcebook* (Westport, CT: Greenwood, 1987), *Women in Chemistry and Physics: A Biographical Sourcebook* (Westport, CT: Greenwood, 1993), and *Women in the Biological Sciences: A Bibliographic Sourcebook* (Westport, CT: Greenwood, 1997).

For readers unfamiliar with women's history, Bonnie S. Anderson and Judith P. Zinsser, *A History of Their Own: Women in Europe from Prehistory to Present.* 2 vols. (Oxford: Oxford University Press, 2000) is a good introduction. A useful survey of women in science that serves as an excellent and readable introduction to the topic is Margaret Alic, *Hypatia's Heritage: A History of Women in Science from Antiquity through the Nineteenth Century* (Boston: Beacon, 1986). Lynn M. Osen, *Women in Mathematics* (Cambridge: MIT Press, 1974) does the same for women in mathematics.

Patricia Phillip's work on British women of science, *The Scientific Lady: A Social History of Women's Scientific Interests, 1520–1918* (London: Weidenfeld & Nicolson, 1990) focuses on female amateur scientists. It contains some very useful information about education and attitudes toward female roles during this period. The biographies of fifteen women scientists who either won the Nobel Prize for science or came to close to winning it are explored in Sharon Bertsch McGrayne, *Nobel Prize Women in Science* (Secaucus, NJ: Citadel, 1998).

Chapter 1

There exists a great deal of secondary literature on the topic of classical thinkers and their views of the female. For a general introduction to life in ancient Greece, see Thomas R. Martin, *Ancient Greece from Prehistoric to Hellenistic Times* (New Haven: Yale University Press, 1996). Bonnie Anderson and Judith Zinsser, *A History of Their Own: Women in Europe from Prehistory to the Present*, vol. 1 (Oxford: Oxford University Press, 2000) is particularly useful for an overview of the context of and attitudes toward women in the ancient world. Prudence Allen, *The Concept of Woman: The Aristotelian Revolution, 750 B.C.–A.D. 1250* (Grand Rapids: Eerdmans, 1997), the only work of its kind, is encyclopedic in its scope and information and is an important and comprehensive work on sex differentiation in Western thought from the pre-Socratics to the middle of the thirteenth century. Anne Carson, "Putting Her in Her Place: Woman, Dirt, and Desire" in David M. Halperin, John J. Winkler, and Froma I. Zeitlin, *Before Sexuality: The Construction of Erotic Experience in the Ancient Greek World* (Princeton: Princeton University Press, 1990) provides numerous examples of "wetness" from Homer, Aristophanes, Alkaios, and others. Helen King, *Hippocrate's Women: Reading the Female Body in Ancient Greece* (New York: Routledge, 1998) and Joan Cadden, *Meanings of Sex Difference in the Middle Ages: Medicine, Science, and Culture* (Cambridge: Cambridge University Press, 1993) are very useful for the medical (gynecological) history of this period.

There has been much written about Aristotle's view on woman as a defective male. Maryanne Cline Horowitz, "Aristotle and Women" from *Journal of the History of Biology* 9, no. 2 (Fall 1976): 183–213, Susan Moller Okin, *Women in Western Political Thought* (Princeton: Princeton University Press, 1979), and Lynda Lange, "Woman is Not a Rational Animal: On Aristotle's Biology of Reproduction" in Sandra Harding and Merrill B. Hintikka, *Discovering Reality* (Boston: D. Reidel, 1983) are all insightful and helpful here. The recent feminist scholarship on both Plato and Aristotle provides a useful corrective to some of the older literature that does not deal with women. Cynthia A. Freeland, *Feminist Interpretations of Aristotle* (University Park: Pennsylvania State University Press, 1998) and Susan Moller Okin's work are also useful for Plato's views, as is Dorothea Wender's essay titled "Plato: Misogynist, Paedophile and Feminist" in John Peradotto and J. P. Sullivan, *Women in the Ancient World: The Arethusa Papers* (Albany: State University of New York Press, 1984).

For information about Hypatia, I rely primarily on the most recent and accurate biography of Hypatia, which is based entirely on primary sources, Maria Dzielska, *Hypatia of Alexandria* (Cambridge: Harvard University Press, 1995). Pages 25–29 of Gilles Ménage, *The History of Women Philosophers* (Lanham, MD:

University Press of America, 1984) also provides useful information. See Mary Ellen Waithe, *A History of Women Philosophers*, volume 1 of *Ancient Women Philosophers 600 B.C.–A.D. 500* (Dordrecht: Kluwer Academic, 1987) for a biography and summary of Hypatia's contributions. Waithe provides a translation of Hypatia's commentaries on pages 178–180 and 182, as well as a lengthy discussion of these on pages 176–191.

Chapter 2

There is a great deal of literature concerning women and Christianity. Volume 1 of Bonnie S. Anderson and Judith P. Zinsser, *A History of Their Own: Women in Europe from Prehistory to the Present* (New York: Oxford University Press, 2000) provides a very valuable introduction to Christianity and women in chapter 5, part 1, "The Effects of Christianity" and in part 3, "Women in the Churches." *Daughters of the Church: Women and Ministry from New Testament Times to the Present* by Ruth A. Tucker and Walter L. Liefeld (Grand Rapids: Academie Books, 1987) is a well-documented work full of information pertinent to the early church from the time of Jesus on. See especially chapters 1 through 4, which cover Christianity to the end of the Middle Ages. The essays that focus on the early years of Christianity in Rosemary Radford Ruether and Eleanor McLaughlin, *Women of Spirit: Female Leadership in the Jewish and Christian Traditions* (New York: Simon & Schuster, 1979) provide enlightening information on women in the early church. Mary T. Malone, *Women and Christianity, Volume 1: The First Thousand Years* (Ottawa: Novalis, 2000) is a recent addition to the list of works exploring Christianity and women. Lina Eckenstein, *Women under Monasticism* (Cambridge: Cambridge University Press, 1896), although dated, remains a standard text.

For a discussion of Paul's views on women, see Margaret Y. MacDonald, "Rereading Paul: Early Interpreters of Paul on Women and Gender" in Ross Shepard Kraemer and Mary Rose D'Angelo, *Women's Christian Origins* (New York: Oxford University Press, 1999). For a summary of Roman views on women, see Vern L. Bullough, *The Subordinate Sex: A History of Attitudes toward Women* (Urbana: University of Illinois Press, 1973). Elizabeth A. Clark and Herbert Richardson, *Women and Religion: A Feminist Sourcebook of Christian Thought* (New York: Harper & Row, 1977) provides a selection of primary sources from ancient Greece to the 1970s. The introduction provides useful context and background information, and some of the excerpts are from the Church Fathers. The *New Advent Catholic Encyclopedia* online is an excellent source for biographical information on the Church Fathers. The online edition, by Kevin Knight, is located at http://www.newadvent.org/cathen and dates from 1999. The articles from the *Decretum Magistri Gratiani* (Canon Law) are summarized on pages 380–389 in René Metz, *La Femme et l'enfant dans le droit canonique medieval* (London: Variorum Reprints, 1985).

Barbara Newman wrote the first full-length study of Hildegard in *Sister of Wisdom: St. Hildegard's Theology of the Feminine* (Berkeley: University of California Press, 1987). Since her book, there have been many studies and translations of Hildegard's works into English; however, space permits mention of only a few of interest here. See Sabina Flanagan, *Hildegard of Bingen, 1098–1179* (New York: Routledge, 1998) for a scholarly biography. A good translation of Hildegard's *Scivias* is the 1990 edition by Mother Columba Hart and Jane Bishop, with an introduction by Barbara J. Newman and preface by Caroline Walker Bynum (New York: Paulist). An important collection of essays commemorating the nineteen-hundredth anniversary of Hildegard's birth was published in 1998. It provides information on a wide-ranging number of subjects from Hildegard as a zoologist to her music. The most recently published biography is *Hildegard of Bingen: The Woman of Her Age* (London: Headline, 2001) by Fiona Maddocks. A final source that may be of interest is Florence Eliza Glaze, "Medical Writer, 'Behold the Human Creature'" in Barbara Newman, *Voice of the Light: Hildegard of Bingen and Her World* (Berkeley: University of California Press, 1998).

Chapter 3

Lula McDowell Richardson, *The Forerunners of Feminism in French Literature of the Renaissance from Christine of Pisan to Marie de Gournay* (Baltimore: Johns Hopkins University Press, 1929) remains the most accessible English language work on the *querelle des femmes.* Joan Kelly, "Early Feminist Theory and the Querelle des Femmes, 1400–1789" in *Signs* 8 (1982): 4–28 covers the origins of the *querelle des femmes* to 1789. Maité Albistur and Daniel Armogathe, *Histoire du féminisme français* (Paris: Des Femmes, 1977) provides an excellent summary of French feminism.

Recently, work on Christine de Pizan as a feminist has blossomed. New editions of her works have appeared, such as Renate Blumenfeld-Kosinski, *The Selected Writings of Christine de Pizan* (New York: W. W. Norton, 1997). Most of it, however, does not deal with the issue of science. Susan Groag Bell, "Christine de Pizan (1364–1450): Humanism and the Problem of a Studious Woman" in *Feminist Studies* 3 (1976): 173–184 continues to be one of the most helpful works on Pizan as a woman of learning. Some of the best works are in French: Marie-Joseph Pinet, *Christine de Pisan, 1364–1430: Etude bibliographique et littéraire* (Paris: Champion, 1927) is the standard biography, and Rose Rigaud, *Les Idées féministes de Christine de Pisan* (Geneva: Slatkene Reprints, [1911] 1973) is very useful for her feminist ideas. Astrik L. Gabriel's article "The Educational Ideas of Christine de Pisan" in *Journal of the History of Ideas* 16 (January 1955): 3–21 is useful for Pizan's views on the education of women. Edith Yenal, *Christine de Pizan: A Bibliography of Writings by Her and about Her* (Metuchen, NY: Scarecrow, 1982) is a place to start when looking for works on Pizan, and it also provides a useful introduction to her life and works. For editions of Pizan's books in English, see *A Medieval Woman's Mirror of Honor: The Treasury of the City of Ladies* (New York: Persea, 1989) and *The Treasure of the City of Ladies, or, The Book of the Three Virtues* (New York: Penguin, 1985). There are several editions of *The Book of the City of Ladies.* A very readable one with a good foreword is the 1982 edition translated by Earl Jeffrey Richards and with a foreword by Marina Warner (New York: Persea). The most recent translation is by Rosalind Brown-Grant (New York: Penguin, 1999), in which she provides an introduction and notes along with her translation.

There are many sources for views of women and the Renaissance: Joan Kelly's classic work "Did Women Have a Renaissance?" in *Women, History and Theory: The Essays of Joan Kelly* (Chicago: University of Chicago Press, 1984); Ian Maclean, *The Renaissance Notion of Woman: A Study in the Fortunes of Scholasticism and Medical Science in European Intellectual Life* (Cambridge: Cambridge University Press, 1980); Merry Wiesner, *Women and Gender in Early Modern Europe* (Cambridge: Cambridge University Press, 1999); Margaret L. King, *Women of the Renaissance* (Chicago: University of Chicago Press, 1991); Margaret W. Ferguson, Maureen Quilligan, and Nancy J. Vickers, *Rewriting the Renaissance: The Discourses of Sexual Difference in Early Modern Europe* (Chicago: University of Chicago Press, 1986); Lorna Hutson, *Feminism and Renaissance Studies* (Oxford: Oxford University Press, 1999); and Marilyn Migiel and Juliana Schiesari, *Refiguring Women: Perspectives on Gender and the Italian Renaissance* (Ithaca: Cornell University Press, 1991). An older but comprehensive volume is Ruth Kelso, *Doctrine for the Lady of the Renaissance* (Urbana: University of Illinois Press, 1956).

Many of the works on the major contributors to the debate remain in French such as Gustave Reynier, *La Femme au XVIIe siècle: Ses ennemis et ses défenseurs* (Paris: J. Tallandier, 1929). For more specific works on individual female writers, see Diane S. Wood, *Hélisenne de Crenne: At the Crossroads of Renaissance Humanism and Feminism* (London: Associated University Presses, 2000) and Dorothy O'Connor, *Louise Labé: Sa vie et son oeuvre* (Paris: Les Presses Françaises, 1926).

Chapter 4

For an overview of education during the Renaissance, see Margaret L. King, *Women of the Renaissance* (Chicago: University of Chicago Press, 1991). Barbara J. Whitehead, *Women's Education in Early Modern Europe: A History, 1500–1800* (New York: Garland, 1999) covers the period as well. A classic work on the education of women from the Renaissance to the nineteenth century is Phyllis Stock, *Better than Rubies* (New York: G. P. Putnam, 1978).

The standard biography for Mary Astell is Ruth Perry, *The Celebrated Mary Astell: An Early English Feminist* (Chicago: University of Chicago Press, 1986), which contains Mary Astell's correspondence. For her writings on education, see Bridget Hill, *The First English Feminist: Reflections upon Marriage and Other Writings* (Aldershot, UK: Gower, 1986) and parts 1 and 2 of Patricia Springhouse, *A Serious Proposal to the Ladies* (London: Pickering & Chatto,1997).

Most of Johann Amos Comenius's works and studies about him remain in Czech. For English translations, see *Panorthosia, or Universal Reform* translated by A. M. O. Dobbie (Sheffield: Academic Press, 1995) and M. W. Keatinge, *The Great Didactic* (New York: Russell & Russell, [1923] 1967).

For an introduction to the debate in France, see M. Rowan, "Seventeenth-Century French Feminism: Two Opposing Attitudes" in *International Journal of Women's Studies* 3, no. 3 (1980): 273–291 and Wendy Gibson, *Women in Seventeenth-Century France* (Basingstoke, UK: Macmillan, 1989). Paul Rousselot, *La Pédagogie féminine* (Paris: Delgrave, 1881) and *Histoire de l'éducation des femmes* (Paris: Didier et Cie, 1883) contain several excerpts from primary sources.

Chapter 5

Wendy Gibson provides an overview of the lot of women in seventeenth-century France in *Women in Seventeenth-Century France* (Basingstoke, UK: Macmillan, 1989). For information on the *précieuses*, see Donna A. Stanton, "The Fiction of Pré-ciositeé and the Fear of Women" in *Yale French Studies* 62 (1981):107–134. David Shaw, "Les Femmes Savantes and Feminism" in *Journal of European Studies* 14 (1984): 24–38 is another useful study of these women. Erica Harth, *Cartesian Women* (Ithaca: Cornell University Press, 1992) remains the standard text for this subject and is particularly useful for information on the women of the salons.

On Descartes and women, see Susan Bordo, *Feminist Interpretations of Descartes* (University Park: Pennsylvania State University Press, 1999), her earlier study, *The Flight to Objectivity: Essays on Cartesianism and Culture* (Albany: State University of New York Press, 1987), and Margaret Atherton, "Cartesian Reason and Gendered Reason" in Louis M. Anthony and Charlotte Witt, *A Mind of One's Own: Feminist Essays on Reason and Objectivity* (Boulder: Westview, 1993).

For Poulain de la Barre, see Madeleine Alcover's *Poullain de La Barre : une aventure philosophique* (Paris Papers on French Seventeenth-Century Literature, 1981) and in English, Michael Seidel, "Poulain de la Barre's "*The Woman as Good as the Man*" in *Journal of the History of Ideas* 35 (1974): 499–508. There are two recent translations of Poulain de la Barre, *De l'égalité des deux sexes*: Gerald M. Maclean's translation, *The Woman as Good as the Man: Or, the Equality of Both Sexes* (Detroit: Wayne State University Press, 1988) and a British translation by Desmond Clarke, *The Equality of the Sexes* (Manchester: Manchester University Press, 1990), which also provides useful notes and an introduction.

See Julian Eugene White, *Nicolas Boileau* (New York: Twayne, 1969) for a modern study of Boileau's life and works. For biographical details on Fontenelle, see Nina Gelbart's introduction to *Conversations on the Plurality of Worlds*, translated by H. A. Hargreaves (Berkeley: University of California Press, 1990).

Chapter 6

For insights on women and science in the writings of Francis Bacon, see "Dominion over Nature" in Carolyn Merchant, *The Death of Nature: Women, Ecology and the Scientific Revolution* (New York: HarperCollins, 1980). Evelyn Fox Keller also covers this subject in "Baconian Science" in *Reflections on Gender and Science* (New Haven: Yale University Press, 1985).

A crucial work on the masculine nature of science during this period is David Noble, *A World without Women* (New York: Oxford University Press, 1992), which provides an insightful overview of the impact of the development of masculine institutions, such as scientific academies, on women and science and is also helpful in its commentary about Bacon's views of women in science. Although dated, see "The Royal Society" in Martha Ornstein, *The Role of Scientific Societies in the Seventeenth Century* (Chicago: University of Illinois Press, 1928) for details concerning the formation and role of the royal society. Lewis Pyenson and Susan

Sheets-Pyenson, *Servants of Nature* (New York: W. W. Norton, 1999) is an accessible contribution to literature on scientific societies.

For Anne Conway's writings see *The Principles of the Most Ancient and Modern Philosophy* (The Hague: Martinus Nijhoff, 1982). A selection from this edition is reprinted in Mary Warnock, *Women Philosopher* (London: J. M. Dent, 1996). Also see Alison P. Coudert and Taylor Corse, *The Principles of the Most Ancient and Modern Philosophy* (Cambridge: Cambridge University Press, 1996) as well as *The Conway Letters,* edited by Marjorie H. Nicolson (Oxford: Clarendon, 1992). For information about Conway and her contributions to science, see Jane Duran, "Anne Viscountess Conway: A Seventeenth-Century Rationalist" in *Hypatia* 40, no. 1 (1989): 64–79; Lois Frankel, "Anne Finch, Viscountess Conway" in Mary Ellen Waithe, *A History of Women Philosophers* (Dordrecht: Kluwer Academic, 1991); Sarah Hutton, "Of Physic and Philosophy: Anne Conway, F. M. van Helmont, and Seventeenth-Century Medicine" in A. Cunningham and O. P. Grell, *Religio Medici: Medicine and Religion in Seventeenth-Century England* (Menston, UK: Scolar, 1996); and Carolyn Merchant, "The Vitalism of Anne Conway: Its Impact on Leibniz's Concept of the Monad" in *Journal of the History of Philosophy* 17, no. 3 (July 1979): 255–269.

Most of the scholarship about Margaret Cavendish has been in article or book chapter form. Recently, she has become an industry with scholars in women's history, philosophy, and English. Jacqueline Broad, *Women Philosophers of the Seventeenth Century* (Cambridge: Cambridge University Press, 2002) provides a useful introductory chapter on Cavendish. New editions of her writing include Eileen O'Neill, *Observations upon Experimental Philosophy* (Cambridge: Cambridge University Press, 2001) and *Paper Bodies: A Margaret Cavendish Reader*, edited by Sylvia Bowerbank and Sara Mendelson (Calgary: Broadview, 1999).

Useful studies of Cavendish are Sophia B. Blaydes, "Nature Is a Women: The Duchess of Newcastle and Seventeenth-Century Philosophy" in *Man, God and Nature in the Enlightenment*, edited by Donald C. Mell Jr. et al. (East Lansing, MI: Colleagues, 1988) and Susan Mendelson, *The Mental World of Stuart Women: Three Studies.* (Brighton: Harvester, 1987). For her role as a scientist, the best introduction is Londa Schiebinger, "Margaret Cavendish: Natural Philosopher" in volume 3 of *A History of Women Philosophers: 1600–1900*, edited by Mary Ellen Waithe (Dordrecht: Kluwer Academic, 1991).

Chapter 7

See Londa Schiebinger, "Skeletons in the Closet: The First Illustrations of the Female Skeleton in Eighteenth-Century Anatomy" in *Representations* 14 (Spring 1986): 42–81 for an overview of the eighteenth-century debate concerning the nature of women. Geoffrey V. Sutton, *Science for a Polite Society: Gender, Culture, and the Demonstration of Enlightenment* (Boulder, CO: Westview, 1995), examines the growing interest in the science practiced by men and women in seventeenth- and eighteenth-century France. On the attitudes of individual philosophes toward women and science, see Samia Spencer, *French Women and the Age of Enlightenment* (Bloomington: Indiana University Press, 1984). The chapters examine major Enlightenment thinkers such as Montesquieu and Rousseau; includes a discussion of Emilie du Châtelet. Robert F. O'Reilly, "Montesquieu: Anti-Feminist" in *Studies on Voltaire and the Eighteenth Century* 102: 143–156 also deals with Montesquieu's attitude toward women's abilities. Keith Michael Baker, *Condorcet: Selected Writings* (Indianapolis: Bobbs-Merrill, 1976) contains useful writings by this philosophe with respect to women and their scientific potential. A full discussion of Diderot and women may be found in Laura W. Fleder's unpublished dissertation, "Female Physiology in the Works of Diderot and the Medical Writers of His Day" (New York: Columbia University, 1978).

There is no full-length biography of Emilie du Châtelet in English, although there are plenty of articles and shorter studies. Although brief, Esther Ehrman, *Mme du Châtelet: Scientist, Philosopher and Feminist of the Enlightenment* (Oxford: Berg, 1986) is the only English biography of Châtelet. For a recent discussion of Emilie du Châtelet as a woman attempting science in a man's world, see Mary Terrall, "Emilie du Châtelet and the Gendering of Science" in *History of Science* 33 (1995): 283–310. Other studies include Judith P. Zinsser, "Emilie Du Châtelet: Genius, Gender, and Intellectual Authority" in Hilda Smith, *Women Writers and the Early Modern British Political Tradition* (Cambridge: Cambridge University Press, 1998) and Ira O. Wade, *Voltaire and Madame du Châtelet: An Essay on the Intellectual Activity at Cirey* (New York: Octagon, 1969).

Chapter 8

Susan Sleeth Mosedale, "Science Corrupted: Victorian Biologists Consider 'The Woman Question'" in *Journal of the History of Biology* 11, no. 1 (spring 1978): 1–55 provides an overview of the debate about women and biology during the nineteenth century. See Jill Conway, "Stereotypes of Femininity in a Theory of Sexual Evolution" in Martha Vicinus, *Women in the Victorian Age: Suffer and Be Still* (Bloomington: Indiana University Press, 1972) for a discussion of the use of biology to explain male dominance and superiority and female subjection and inferiority. Elizabeth Fee, "Nineteenth-Century Craniology: The Study of the Female Skull" in *Bulletin of the History of Medicine* 53 (1979): 415–433 provides insight into the justification of female inferiority based on brain size. Sections of Stephen J. Gould, *The Mismeasure of Man* (New York: Norton, 1996) are excellent for analyzing French anthropologist Paul Broca's work with respect to the inferiority of female intelligence.

For other French contributors to the debate, see volume 1 of Mary Pickering, *Auguste Comte: An Intellectual Biography* (Cambridge: Cambridge University Press, 1993). For information on Comte, see pages 1750–1880 in Susan Groag Bell and Karen M. Offen, *Women, the Family, and Freedom: The Debate in Documents. Volume 1: 1780–1880* (Stanford, CA: Stanford University Press, 1983). James F. McMillan, *France and Women, 1789–1914* (New York: Routledge, 2000) discusses the ideas of medical men René Villermé and Achille Chéreau who influenced Jules Michelet, as well as Pierre-Joseph Proudhon. Edward K. Kaplan, *Michelet's Poetic Vision: A Romantic Philosophy of Nature, Man and Woman* (Amherst: University of Massachusetts Press, 1977) provides further insight into Michelet's ideas. Claire

Goldberg Moses, "Saint-Simonian Men/Saint-Simonian Women" in *Journal of Modern History* 54 (1982): 240–267 is a discussion of this group and their views on women. Information about William Thompson is available in Elizabeth K. Helsinger, Robin Lauterbach Sheets, and William Veeder, *The Woman Question: Defining Voices, 1837–1883* (New York: Garland, 1983).

For information on Mary Somerville, see Elizabeth Chambers Patterson, *Mary Somerville and the Cultivation of Science, 1815–1840* (The Hague: Martinus Nijhoff, 1983) and Geoffrey Sutton and Sung Kyu Kim, "Mary Fairfax Grieg Somerville (1780–1872)" in Louise S. Grinstein, Rose K. Rose, and Miriam H. Rafailavich, *Women in Chemistry and Physics: A Biographical Sourcebook* (Westport, CT: Greenwood, 1993).

Chapter 9

The debate concerning Trotula is well documented in the following sources: John F. Benton, "Trotula, Women's Problems, and the Professionalization of Medicine in the Middle Ages" in *Bulletin of the History of Medicine* 59, no. 1(1985): 30–53 and Paul Oskar Kristeller, "The School of Salerno: Its Development and Its Contribution to the History of Learning" in *Bulletin of the History of Medicine* 17 (1945): 138–194. See Monica H. Green, *The Trotula: A Medieval Compendium of Women's Medicine* (Philadelphia: University of Pennsylvania Press, 2001) for a recent and modern translation of the work. Francis R. Packard, *History of the School of Salernum* (London: Humphry Milford, 1922) is a study of the medical school here. Useful information on midwives in England, including primary sources, may be found in Alice Clark, *Working Life of Women in the Seventeenth Century* (New York: Routledge, [1918] 1968). The definitive study of the struggle of midwives in London is Jean Donnison, *Midwives and Medical Men* (London: Heinemann, 1979).

For the debate surrounding women's access to medical school, see Emily Davies, *Thoughts on Some Questions Relating to Women* (1910; reprint, Millwood, NY: Kraus, 1971) for a contemporary account. Joan N. Burstyn, "Education and Sex: The Medical Case against Higher Education for Women in England, 1870–1900" in *Proceedings of the American Philosophical Society* 117, no. 2 (April 1973): 79–89 discusses the arguments put forth at the time against women's access to higher education. On this subject, see also Edythe Lutzker's Ph.D. dissertation titled "Medical Education for Women in Great Britain" (New York: Columbia University, 1959). For a recent biography on Sophia Jex-Blake, see Shirley Roberts, *Sophia Jex-Blake: A Woman Pioneer in Nineteenth-Century Medical Reform* (New York: Routledge, 1993).

Chapter 10

The literature concerning the feminist debate is substantial and growing at a fast pace. Below are some suggestions to introductory reading to supplement this chapter. A good place to begin is with the journals that have focused on the recent debates concerning women and science. These include *Isis*—see in particular a collection of articles in Sally Gregory Kohlstedt, *History of Women in the Sciences: Readings from Isis* (Chicago: University of Chicago Press, 1997 and 1999)—*Hypatia: A Journal of Feminist Philosophy* (1997 and 1998), which devoted two entire issues to feminism and science, and *Osiris*. See also the 1997 edition of Sally Gregory Kohlstedt and Helen E. Longino, *Women, Gender and Science: New Directions* (Chicago: University of Chicago Press). Gil Kirkup and Laurie Smith Keller, *Inventing Women: Science, Technology, and Gender* (Cambridge, UK: Polity, 1992) explores the important and controversial debates about the gendering of science and technology. Marina Benjamin, *Sense and Sensibility: Gender and Scientific Enquiry, 1780–1945* (Oxford: Blackwell, 1991) examines women as the subject of scientific enquiry, women's role in and pursuit of scientific knowledge, and women writers on science between 1790 and 1945. Muriel Lederman and Ingrid Bartsch, *The Gender and Science Reader* (New York: Routledge, 2001) is the most recent and thorough analysis of the debates available. It is a collection of the writings of key contributors to the debate, scientists, social scientists, and humanists. The work is organized into six thematic sections dealing with the practical (such as female access to employment) to the more theoretical (how science reinforces gender and racial stereotypes) aspects of the debate. Another contribution is Maralee Mayberry, Banu Subramaniam, and Lisa H. Weasel, *Feminist Science Studies: A New Generation* (New York: Routledge, 2001), a multidisciplinary collection of essays containing recent work on feminist science studies. The final work worth mentioning in the context of contemporary debates is Angela N. H. Creager, Elizabeth Lunbeck, and Londa Schiebinger, *Feminism in Twentieth-Century Science, Technology, and Medicine* (Chicago: University of Chicago Press, 2001). The book provides the published results of a workshop "Science, Medicine, and Technology in the Twentieth Century: What Difference has Feminism Made?" held at Princeton University in 1998.

References

Abensour, Léon. 1923. *La Femme et le féminisme avant la révolution.* Paris: Leroux.

Académie des Sciences. Presentation: Historique. http://www.acad-sciences.fr/presentation/historique.htm. (Cited 4 April 2003).

Agrippa von Nettesheim, Heinrich Cornelius. 1726. *Sur la noblesse, & excellence du sexe féminin, de sa préeminence sur l'autre sexe, & du sacrament du mariage.* Leiden: T. Haak.

Albistur, Maité, and Daniel Armogathe. 1977. *Histoire du féminisme français.* 2 vols. Paris: Des Femmes.

Alcover, Madeleine. 1981. *Poullain de La Barre: Une aventure philosophique.* Paris: Papers on French Seventeenth-Century Literature.

Alic, Margaret. 1986. *Hypatia's Heritage: A History of Women in Science from Antiquity through the Nineteenth Century.* Boston: Beacon Press.

Allen, Prudence. 1997. *The Concept of Woman: The Aristotelian Revolution, 750 B.C.–A.D. 1250.* Grand Rapids: Eerdmans.

Ambrose, Saint. 1954. *Saint Ambrose Letters.* Trans. Mary Melchior Beyenka. New York: Fathers of the Church.

———. 1961. *Hexameron, Paradise and Cain and Abel.* Trans. John Savage. New York: Fathers of the Church.

Ambrose, Susan A., Kristen L. Dunkle, Indira Nair, and Deborah A. Harkus. 1997. *Journeys of Women in Science and Engineering.* Philadelphia: Temple University Press.

Anderson, Bonnie S., and Judith P. Zinsser. 2000. *A History of Their Own: Women in Europe from Prehistory to the Present.* 2 vols. Oxford and New York: Oxford University Press.

Aquinas, Thomas. 1947. *Summa Theologica.* 2 vols. Ed. and trans. Fathers of the English Dominican Province. New York: Benziger Brothers.

Aristotle. 1944. *Politics.* Trans. H. Rackham. London: Heinemann.

———. 1984. *The Complete Works of Aristotle: The Revised Oxford Translation.* 4 vols. Ed. Jonathan Barnes. Princeton: Princeton University Press.

Ascoli, G. 1906. "Les Idées féministes en France." *Revue de Synthèse Historique* 13: 25–57, 161–184.

Astell, Mary. 1730. *Some Reflections on Marriage, with Additions.* London: Printed for W. Parker.

―――――. 1986. *The First English Feminist: Reflections upon Marriage and Other Writings.* Ed. Bridget Hill. Aldershot, UK: Gower.

―――――. 1997. *A Serious Proposal to the Ladies.* Parts 1 and 2. Ed. Patricia Springhouse. London: Pickering and Chatto.

Atherton, Margaret, ed. 1993. *Women Philosophers of the Early Modern Period.* Indianapolis: Hackett.

Augustine, Saint. 1972. *City of God.* Ed. David Knowles. Harmondsworth, UK: Penguin.

―――――. 1982. *The Literal Interpretation of Genesis.* Trans. John Hammond Taylor. New York: Newman.

―――――. 1991. *On Genesis: Two Books on Genesis against the Manichees; and, On the Literal Interpretation of Genesis, an Unfinished Book.* Trans. Roland J. Teske. Washington, DC: Catholic University of America Press.

Averroes. 1956. *Commentary on Plato's Republic.* Trans. E.I.J. Rosenthal. Cambridge: Cambridge University Press.

Avicenna. 1999. *The Canon of Medicine.* Trans. Gruner O'Cameron. Chicago: Great Books of the Islamic World.

Bacon, Francis. 1901. "The New Atlantis." In *Ideal Commonwealths.* New York: P. F. Collier and Son.

―――――. 1996. *The Essayes or Covnsels Civill and Morall of Francis Bacon, First Published in 1597, Newly Written in 1625.* Corvallis: University of Oregon.

Badinter, Elisabeth. 1983. *Emilie, Emilie: L'Ambition féminine au XVIIIième siècle.* Paris: Flammarion.

Baillet, Adrien. 1972. *La Vie de Monsieur Descartes.* 2 vols. Hildesheim, Germany: G. Olms.

Barat, J. 1904. "Rapports entre l'oeuvre de Tiraqueau et le tiers livre de Rabelais." *Revue des études rabelaisiennes* 3: 138–155.

Barnard, H.C. 1971. *Madame de Maintenon and Saint-Cyr.* Wakefield, UK: S. R. Publishers.

Bateson, Mary. 1899. *Origin and Early History of Double Monasteries.* Royal Historical Transactions. New Series. London: Royal Historical Society.

Bazeley, Deborah Taylor. 1990. "An Early Challenge to the Precepts and Practice of Modern Science: The Fusion of Fact, Fiction and Feminism in the Works of Margaret Cavendish, Duchess of Newcastle (1623–1673)." Ph.D. diss., University of California, San Diego.

Behn, Aphra. 1973. *Women: From the Greeks to the French Revolution.* Stanford: Stanford University Press.

―――――. 1993. *The Works of Aphra Behn.* 4 vols. Ed. Janet Todd. London: William Pickering.

Bell, Susan Groag. 1976. "Christine de Pizan (1364–1450): Humanism and the Problem of a Studious Woman." *Feminist Studies* 3: 173–184.

Bell, Susan Groag, and Karen M. Offen, eds. 1983. *Woman, the Family and Freedom: The Debate in Documents.* Vol. 1: 1780–1880. Stanford: Stanford University Press.

Bennett, Henry. 1870. *The Lancet,* 18 June.

Benton, John, F. 1985. "Trotula, Women's Problems, and the Professionalization of Medicine in the Middle Ages." *Bulletin of the History of Medicine* 59, no. 1: 30–53.

Besterman, Theodore, ed. 1958. *Les Letters de la Marquise du Châtelet.* 2 vols. Genève: Institut et Musée Voltaire.

———. 1967. *Voltaire.* New York: Harcourt, Brace and World.

Billon, François de. 1970. *Le Fort inexpugnable de l'honneur du sexe féminin.* 1555. Ed. M. A. Screech. Wakefield, UK: S. R. Publishers.

Birch, Thomas. 1756–1757. *History of the Royal Society.* 4 vols. London: A. Millar.

Blackwell, Antoinette Louisa Brown. 1875. *The Sexes throughout Nature.* New York: G. P. Putnam's Sons.

Bleier, Ruth. 1988. "A Decade of Feminist Critique in the Natural Sciences: An Address by Ruth Bleier." *Signs* 14: 186–196.

———, ed. 1986. *Feminist Approaches to Science.* New York: Pergamon.

Boccaccio, Giovanni. 1963. *Concerning Famous Women.* 1544. Trans. Guido A. Guarino. New Brunswick, NJ: Rutgers University Press.

Boileau-Despreaux, Nicolas. 1966. *Oeuvres complètes.* 1692. Ed. Françoise Escal. Paris: Gallimard.

Bordo, Susan. 1987. *The Flight to Objectivity: Essays on Cartesianism and Culture.* Albany: SUNY Press.

———, ed. 1999. *Feminist Interpretations of Descartes.* University Park: Pennsylvania State University Press.

Borresen, Kari Elisabeth. 1981. *Subordination and Equivalence.* Washington, DC: University Press of America.

Bouchard, Amaury. 1552. *Foeminei sexus apologia adversus A. Tiraquellum,* or *An Apology for the Female Sex.* Paris: Jo Badii Ascensii.

Boyle, Robert. 1999. The *Works of Robert Boyle.* 14 vols. Ed. Michael Hunter and Edward B. Davis. London: Pickering and Chatto.

Brink, J. R., ed. 1980. *Female Scholars: A Tradition of Learned Women before 1800.* Montreal: Eden Press.

Broca, Paul. 1861. "Sur le volume et la forme du cerveau suivant les individus et suivant les races." *Bulletin Société d'Anthropologie* 2: 139–207, 301–321, 441–446.

———. 1873. "Sur les cranes de la caverne de l'Homme-Mort." *Revue d'Anthropologie* 2, no. 1: 45–60.

Brodbeck, Mary. December 1984. "French Academy of Sciences Elects Woman President." National Science Foundation Europe, Report no. 72. http://www.nsf.gov/home/int/europe/reports/72.htm. (Cited 4 April 2003).

Brooke, Elisabeth. 1995. *Women Healers.* Rochester, VT: Healing Arts Press.

Brown, Frank B. 1984. *Crisis in Secondary Education: Rebuilding America's Schools.* Englewood Cliffs, NJ: Prentice Hall.

Brunet, Gustave. 1869. *Guillaume Postel: Notice biographique et bibliographique.* Turin: J. Gay et Fils.

Bullough, Vern L. 1973. "Medieval Medical and Scientific Views of Women." *Viator* 4: 484–501.

———. 1973. *The Subordinate Sex: A History of Attitudes toward* Women. Urbana: University of Illinois Press.

Bullough, Vern L., and Jane Brundage. 1996. *Handbook of Medieval Sexuality.* New York: Garland.

Burnet, John. 1965. *Early Greek Philosophy.* Cleveland: World Publishing.

Burstyn, Joan N. 1973. "Education and Sex: The Medical Case against Higher Education for Women in England, 1870–1900." *Proceedings of the American Philosophical Society* 117, no. 2: 79–89.

Cadden, Joan. 1993. *Meanings of Sex Differences in the Middle Ages: Medicine, Science, and Culture.* Cambridge: Cambridge University Press.

Campaux, Antoine. 1865. *La Question des femmes au quinzième siècle.* Paris: Berger-Levrault.

Carroll, Berenice A., ed. 1976. *Liberating Women's History: Theoretical and Critical Essays.* Urbana: University of Illinois Press.

Carson, Anne. 1990. "Putting Her in Her Place: Woman, Dirt, and Desire." In *Before Sexuality: The Construction of Erotic Experience in the Ancient Greek World.* Ed. David M. Halperin, John J. Winkler, and Froma I. Zeitlin. Princeton: Princeton University Press.

Cattell, J. M. 1903. "A Statistical Study of Eminent Men." *Popular Science Monthly* 62: 359–377.

Cavendish, Margaret. 1688. *Observations upon Experimental Philosophy: To which is added, The Description of a New Blazing World.* 2d ed. London: A. Maxwell.

Channing, Walter. 1820. *Remarks on the Employment of Females as Practitioners in Midwifery.* Boston: Cummings and Hilliard.

Chudleigh, Mary Lee, Lady. 1701. *The Ladies Defence: or, The Bride-woman's Counsellor Answer'd: A Poem. In a Dialogue between Sir John Brute, Sir William Loveall, Melissa, and a Parson. Written by a lady.* London: Printed for J. Deeve.

Clark, Alice. 1968. *Working Life of Women in the Seventeenth Century.* 1918. London: Routledge.

Clark, Elizabeth A. 1979. *Jerome, Chrysostom, and Female Essays and Translations.* 2 vols. Studies in Women and Religion. New York: Edwin Mellen.

———. 1996. *St. Augustine on Marriage and Sexuality.* Washington, DC: Catholic University of America Press.

Clark, Gillian. 1998. "Adam's Engineering: Augustine on Gender and Creation." In *Studies in Church History* 34, *Gender and Christian Religion.* Ed. R. N. Swenson. Bury Saint Edmunds, UK: Boydell.

Clément, L. 1894. "Le Carmen de senatulo feminarum." *Revue d'histoire littéraire de la France* 1: 441–445.

Clement of Alexandria. 1996. *The Stromata, or Miscellanies.* Book 4, chapter 29, from "Fathers of the Church." New Advent Inc. http://www.newadvent.org/fathers/0210.htm. (Cited 4 April 2003).

Cleve, Felix. 1949. *The Philosophy of Anaxagoras: An Attempt at Reconstruction.* New York: King's Crown.

Cobban, Alan B. 1999. *English University Life in the Middle Ages.* London: UCL Press.

Comenius, Jan Amos. 1967. *The Great Didactic*. 1923. Ed. and trans. M. W. Keatinge. New York: Russell and Russell.

———. 1995. *Panorthosia, or Universal Reform*. Trans. A.M.O. Dobbie. Sheffield, UK: Academic Press.

Comte, Auguste. 1851. *Système de politique positive ou traité de sociologie*. 4 vols. Paris: Mathias.

Condorcet. 1847–1849. *Oeuvres*. 12 vols. Paris: Firmin Didot Frères.

———. 1976. *Selected Writings*. Ed. Keith Michael Baker. Indianapolis: Bobbs-Merrill.

Conway, Anne Finch. 1982. *The Principles of the Most Ancient and Modern Philosophy*. Ed. Peter Loptson. The Hague: Martinus Nijhoff.

Corsi, Pietro, and Paul Weindling, eds. 1983. *Information Sources in the History of Science and Medicine*. London: Butterworth Scientific.

Courtin, Antoine de. 1685. *Traité de la jalousie ou moyens d'entretenir la paix dans le mariage*. Paris: Josset.

Crenne, Hélisenne de. 1995. *Les Epistres familières et invectives de ma dame Hélisenne*. Ed. Jean-Philippe Beaulieu and Hannah Fournier. Montréal: Les Presses de l'Université de Montréal.

Crosland, Maurice. 1992. *Science under Control: The French Academy of Sciences 1795–1914*. Cambridge: Cambridge University Press.

Culpeper, Nicholas. 1671. *A Directory for Midwives: Or a Guide for Women, In their Conception, Bearing, and Suckling their Children*. London: J. Streater.

Dall'ava-Santucci, Josette. 1989 *Des sorcières aux Mandarines*. Paris: Calmann-Lévy.

D'Alverny, Marie-Thérèse. 1977. "Comment les théologiens et les philosophes voient la femme." *Cahiers de Civilisation Médiévale* 20: 105–129.

Daniélou, Jean. 1961. *The Ministry of Women in the Early Church*. Trans. Glyn Simon. New York: Morehouse-Barlow.

Darwin, Charles. 1981. *The Descent of Man, and Selection in Relation to Sex*. Ed. John Tyler Bonner and Robert M. May. Princeton: Princeton University Press.

Davies, Emily. 1971. *Thoughts on Some Questions Relating to Women*. 1910. New York: Kraus Reprint.

de Beauvoir, Simone. 1974. *The Second Sex*. New York: Modern Library.

de Gournay, Marie Le Jars. 1988. *Fragments d'un discours féminin*. Ed. Elyane Dezon Jones. Paris: Librairie José Conti.

———. 1989. *Égalité des hommes et des femmes 1622*. Preface by Milagros Palma. Paris: Côté-femmes.

Delon, Michel. 1978. "Cartésianisme(s) et Féminisme(s)." *Europe* 56: 73–86.

Descartes, René. 1953. *Oeuvres et lettres*. Ed. André Bridoux. Paris: Gallimard.

———. 1961. *Essential Works of Descartes*. Intro. Daniel J. Bronstein, trans. Lowell Bair. New York: Bantam Books.

Dewey, John. 1978. *The Middle Works*. Vol. 6: *1910–1911*. Ed. Jo Ann Boydston. Carbondale: Southern Illinois University Press.

Dickason, Anne. 1973–1974. "Anatomy and Destiny: The Role of Biology in Plato's Views of Women." *The Philosophical Forum* 5: 45–53.

Diderot, Denis. 1951. *Œuvres.* Ed. André Billy. Paris: Pléiade.

Diogenes Laertius. 1941. *Lives of Eminent Philosophers.* 2 vols. Trans. R. D. Hicks. Cambridge: Harvard University Press.

Donnison, Jean. 1979. *Midwives and Medical Men.* London: Heinemann.

D'Onofro-Flores, Pamela M., and Sheila M. Pfafflin, eds. 1982. *Scientific Technological Change and the Role of Women in Development.* Boulder, CO: Westview.

Du Bosc, Jacques. 1639. *The Compleat Woman.* London: Thomas Harper and Richard Hodgkinson.

Du Pont, Gratien. 1541. *Controverses des sexes masculin et féminin.* Paris.

Dzielska, Maria. 1995. *Hypatia of Alexandria.* Trans. F. Lyra. Cambridge: Harvard University Press, 1995.

Eckenstein, Lina. 1896. *Women under Monasticism.* Cambridge: Cambridge University Press.

Ehrman, Esther. 1986. *Mme du Châtelet, Scientist, Philosopher and Feminist of the Enlightenment.* Oxford: Berg.

Ellis, Henry Havelock. 1926. *Man and Woman: A Study of Human and Secondary Sexual Characteristics.* 6th ed. London: A and C Black.

Erasmus. 1965. *The Colloquies of Erasmus.* Trans. C. R. Thompson. Chicago: University of Chicago Press.

Evelyn, John. 1908. *The Diary of John Evelyn.* Vol. 3: *Kalendarium, 1650–1672.* London: Macmillan.

Farrington, Benjamin. 1964. *The Philosophy of Francis Bacon.* Liverpool: Liverpool University Press.

Fausto-Sterling, Anne. 1992. *Myths of Gender: Biological Theories about Men and Women.* New York: Basic Books.

Fee, Elizabeth. 1979. "Nineteenth-Century Craniology: The Study of the Female Skull." *Bulletin of the History of Medicine* 53: 415–433.

Fénelon, François Salignac de la Motte. 1948. *Oeuvres choisies.* Ed. Albert Chérel. Paris: A. Hatier.

———. 1966. *Fénelon on Education: A Translation of the "'Traité de l'éducation des filles" and Other Documents Illustrating Fénelon's Educational Theories and Practice.* Trans. Howard Clive Barnard. London: Cambridge University Press.

Feyerabend, Paul. 1993. "Interview." *Scientific American* 268, no. 5: 36.

Finkelstein, David. 1995. "A Woman Hater and Women Healers: John Blackwood, Charles Reade, and the Victorian Women's Medical Movement." *Victorian Periodicals Review* 28, no. 4: 330–352.

Flanagan, Sabina. 1998. *Hildegard of Bingen, 1098–1179.* 2d ed. New York and London: Routledge.

Fleder, Laura W. 1978. "Female Physiology in the Works of Diderot and the Medical Writers of His Day." Ph.D. diss., Columbia University.

Fleury, Abbé Claude. 1686. *Traité du choix et de la méthode des études.* Paris: Chez Jean Mariette.

Fontenelle, Bernard le Bovier de. 1955. *Entretiens sur la pluralité des mondes.* Ed. Robert Shackleton. Oxford: Clarendon Press.

———. 1990. *Conversations on the Plurality of Worlds.* Intro. Nina Rattner Gelbart, trans. H. A. Hargreaves. Berkeley: University of California Press.

Fox Keller, Evelyn. 1982. "Feminism and Science." *Signs* 7, no. 3: 589–602.

———. 1983. *A Feeling for the Organism: The Life and Work of Barbara McClintock.* San Francisco: W. H. Freeman.

———. 1985. *Reflections on Gender and Science.* New Haven and London: Yale University Press.

———. 1994. "Science and Gender: Evelyn Fox Keller." With Bill Moyers. Princeton, NJ: Films for the Humanities and Sciences, videocassette.

———. 1997. "Developmental Biology as a Feminist Cause?" *Osiris* 12: 16–28.

France, Peter, ed. 1995. *The New Oxford Companion to Literature in French.* Oxford: Clarendon Press.

Freeland, Cynthia, ed. 1998. *Feminist Interpretations of Aristotle.* University Park: Pennsylvania State University Press.

Freeman, Kathleen. 1946. *Ancilla to the Pre-Socratic Philosophers: A Complete Translation of the Fragments in Diels, Fragmente der Vorsokratiker.* Oxford: Blackwell.

French, Marilyn. 1985. *Beyond Power: On Women, Men and Morals.* New York: Summit Books.

Friedan, Betty. 1963. *The Feminine Mystique.* New York: W. W. Norton.

Galen. 1968. *On the Usefulness of the Parts of the Body (De usu partium).* 2 vols. Trans. Margaret Tallmade May. Ithaca: Cornell University Press.

Gallop, David. 1984. *Parmenides of Elba Fragments.* Toronto: University of Toronto Press.

Garrett Anderson, Elizabeth. 1874. "Sex in Mind and Education: A Reply." *Fortnightly Review* 15: 582–594.

Geddes, Patrick. 1889. *The Evolution of Sex.* London: Walter Scott.

———. "The Papers of Sir Patrick Geddes at Strathclyde University Archives." http://www.strath.ac.uk/Departments/Archives/Geddespapers. html. (Cited 4 April 2003).

Gelbart, Nina Rattner. 1998. *The King's Midwife: A History and Mystery of Madame du Coudray.* Berkeley: University of California Press.

Gélis, Jacques. 1988. *La Sage-femme ou le médecin.* Paris: Fayard.

Gershenson, Daniel, and Daniel A. Greenberg. 1964. *Anaxagoras and the Birth of Physics.* Intro. Ernest Nagel. New York: Blaisdell.

Gibson, Wendy. 1989. *Women in Seventeenth-Century France.* Basingstoke, UK: Macmillan, 1989.

Gildea, Robert. 1991. *Barricades and Borders: Europe 1800–1914.* Oxford: Oxford University Press.

Gill, Christopher. 1995. *Greek Thought.* Oxford: Oxford University Press.

Gillespie, Charles Carlston, ed. 1970–1980. *Dictionary of Scientific Biography.* 16 vols. New York: Scribner.

Gould, Stephen J. 1996. *The Mismeasure of Man.* New York: W. W. Norton.

Green, Monica H., ed. and trans. 2001. *The Trotula: A Medieval Compendium of Women's Medicine.* Philadelphia: University of Pennsylvania Press.

Gregory of Nyssa. 1954. "What We Must Answer to Those Who Raise the Question—If Procreation Is after Sin, How Would Souls Have Come into Being If the First of Mankind Had Remained Sinless?" In *On the Making of Man,* from "Early Church Fathers," Nicene and Post-Nicene Fathers, Series 2, vol. 5. Gregory of Nyssa: *Dogmatic Treatises; Select Writings and Letters.* http://www.gty.org/~phil/fathers.htm. (Cited 4 April 2003).

Grinstein, Louise S., Rose K. Rose, and Miriam H. Rafailavich, eds. 1993. *Women in Chemistry and Physics: A Biographical Sourcebook.* Westport, CT: Greenwood.

Grinstein, Louise S., and Paul J. Campbell. 1987. *Women of Mathematics: A Bibliographic Sourcebook.* New York: Greenwood Press.

Grinstein, Louise S., Carol A. Biermann, and Rose K. Rose. 1997. *Women in the Biological Sciences: A Bibliographic Sourcebook.* Westport, CT: Greenwood Press.

Halperin, David M., John J. Winkler, and Froma I. Zeitlin, eds. 1990. *Before Sexuality: The Construction of Erotic Experience in the Ancient Greek World.* Princeton: Princeton University Press.

Hanna, Ralph, III, and Traugott Lawler, eds. 1997. *Jankyn's Book of Wikked Wives.* Vol. 1: *The Primary Texts: Walter Map's Dissuasio, Theophrastus De Nuptiis, Jerome's Adversus Jovinianum.* Athens: University of Georgia Press.

Hanson, Norwood Russell. 1958. *Patterns of Discovery: An Inquiry into the Conceptual Foundations of Science.* Cambridge: Cambridge University Press.

Haraway, Donna. 1988. "The Science Question in Feminism as a Site of Discourse on the Privilege of Partial Perspective." *Feminist Studies* 14.3: 575–599

Harding, Sandra. 1986. *The Science Question in Feminism.* Milton Keynes, UK: Open University.

———. 1991. *Whose Science, Whose Knowledge? Thinking from Women's Lives.* Ithaca: Cornell University Press.

———. 1998. "Women, Science and Society." *Essays on Science and Society* 281, no. 5383: 1599–1600.

Harding, Sandra, and Merrill B. Hintikka, eds. 1983. *Discovering Reality.* Boston: D. Reidel.

Harding, Sandra, and Jean F. O'Barr, eds. 1987. *Sex and Scientific Inquiry.* Chicago: University of Chicago Press.

Harth, Erica. 1992. *Cartesian Women.* Ithaca: Cornell University Press.

Hawley, Richard, and Barbara Levick, eds. 1995. *Women in Antiquity: New Assessments.* London and New York: Routledge.

Helsinger, Elizabeth K., Robin Lauterbach Sheets, and William Veeder, eds. 1983. *The Woman Question: Defining Voices, 1837–1883.* 2 vols. New York: Garland.

Helvétius, Claude. 1969. *A Treatise on Man.* 2 vols. New York: Burt Franklin.

Hildegard of Bingen, Saint. 1990. *Scivias.* Trans. Columba Hart and Jane Bishop, ed. Barbara Newman. New York: Paulist Press.

———. 1994. *Letters of Hildegard of Bingen.* Trans. Joseph L. Baird and Radd K. Ehrman. New York: Oxford University Press.

Hoefer, M. 1852–1858. *Nouvelle biographie universelle.* 46 vols. Paris: Didot Frères.

Hoffmann, Paul. 1977. *La Femme dans la pensée des lumières.* Paris: Ophrys.

Hoolihan, C. 1985. "Thomas Young, M.D. (1726?–1783) and Obstetrical Education at Edinburgh." *Journal of the History of Medicine and Allied Sciences* 40: 327–345.

Horowitz, Maryanne Cline. 1976. "Aristotle and Women." *Journal of the History of Biology* 9, no. 2: 183–213.

———. 1979. "The Image of God in Man—Is Woman Included?" *Harvard Theological Review* 72, nos. 3–4 (July–Oct. 1979): 175–206.

Hubbard, Ruth. 1988. "Science, Facts and Feminism." *Hypatia* 3, no. 1 (spring): 4–16.

Hunter, Lynette, and Sarah Hutton, eds. 1997. *Women, Medicine and Science, 1500–1700: Mothers and Sisters of the Royal Society.* Stroud, UK: Alan Sutton.

Hurd-Mead, Kate Campbell. 1930. "Trotula." *Isis* 14: 349–367.

Hutton, Sarah. 1990. *Henry More (1614–1687): Tercentenary Studies.* Dordrecht: Kluwer Academic.

———. 1994. *Ancient Wisdom and Modern Philosophy.* Utrecht: Utrecht University Press.

Iamblichus. 1989. *Iamblichus: On the Pythagorean Life.* Trans. Gillian Clark. Liverpool: Liverpool University Press.

Iltis, Carolyn. 1977. "Madame du Châtelet's Metaphysics and Mechanics." *Studies in History and Philosophy* 8: 29–48.

Internet Encyclopedia of Philosophy. "Rene Descartes (1596–1650)." http://www.utm.edu/research/iep/d/descarte.htm. (Cited 4 April 2003).

Isidore of Seville. 1964. "Etymologias." In *Isidore of Seville: The Medical Writings.* Transactions of the American Philosophical Society NS, vol. 54, part 2. Ed. William D. Sharpe.

———. 1998. *Sententiae,* 11, 4–6. In *Corpus Christianorum,* vol. 111. Ed. Jacques Fontaine. Paris: Brepols.

Jackson, Shirley. 1993. "Feminists Find Gender Everywhere in Science." *Science,* 16 April.

Janik, Linda Gardiner. 1982. "Searching for the Metaphysics of Science: The Structure and Composition of Madame du Châtelet's *Institutions de physique, 1737–1740.*" *Studies on Voltaire and the 18th Century* 201: 85–113.

Jex-Blake, Sophia. 1870. "Medical Women." *The Lancet,* 9 July.

———. 1872. *Medical Women: Two Essays . . . 1. Medicine as a Profession for Women. 2. Medical Education of Women.* Edinburgh and London: Oliphant and Hamilton.

———. 1886. *Medical Women: A Thesis and a History.* 2d ed. Edinburgh: Oliphant, Anderson, and Ferrier.

Kaplan, Edward K. 1977. *Michelet's Poetic Vision: A Romantic Philosophy of Nature, Man and Woman.* Amherst: University of Massachusetts Press.

Kelly, Joan. 1982. "Early Feminist Theory and the Querelle des Femmes." *Signs* 8, no. 1: 4–28.

———. 1984. "Did Women Have a Renaissance?" In *Women, History and Theory: The Essays of Joan Kelly.* Chicago: University of Chicago Press.

Kennedy, James G. 1978. *Herbert Spencer.* Boston: Twayne.

Kerr, E. Anne. 2001. "Toward a Feminist Natural Science." In *The Gender and Science Reader.* Ed. Muriel Lederman and Ingrid Bartsch. London and New York: Routledge.

King, Helen. 1998. *Hippocrates' Women: Reading the Female Body in Ancient Greece.* London and New York: Routledge.

King, Karen L. 1997. *Women and Goddess Traditions: In Antiquity and Today.* Minneapolis: Fortress Press.

King, Margaret L. 1991. *Women of the Renaissance.* Chicago: University of Chicago Press.

Kirkup, Gill, and Laurie Smith Keller, eds. 1992. *Inventing Women: Science, Technology and Gender.* Cambridge, UK: Polity Press.

Kohlstedt, Sally Gregory, and Helen Longino, eds. 1997. *Women, Gender and Science: New Directions.* Chicago: University of Chicago Press.

Kristeller, Paul Oskar. 1945. "The School of Salerno: Its Development and Its Contribution to the History of Learning." *Bulletin of the History of Medicine* 17: 138–194.

La Bruyère, Jean de. 1885. *The Characters of Jean de La Bruyère.* Trans. Henri van Laun. London: John C. Nimms.

La Rochefoucauld. 1967. *Maximes.* Ed. J. Truchet. Paris: Garnier Frères.

Labalme, Patricia, ed. 1980. *Beyond Their Sex: Learned Women of the European Past.* New York: New York University Press.

Labé, Louise. 1969. *Les Poètes lyonnais, précurseurs de la Pléiade: Maurica Scève, Louise Labé, Pernette du Guillet.* Intro. Joseph Aynard. Paris: Bossard.

Lalande, Joseph Jérôme Lefrançais de. 1786. *Astronomie des dames.* Paris: Ménard et Dessenne, Fils.

———. 1786. *Bibliothèque universelle des dames: Astronomie.* Paris: Rue d'Anjou-Dauphine.

———. 1803/1970. *Bibliographie astronomique: Avec l'histoire de l'astronomie depuis 1781 jusqu'à 1802.* Amsterdam: J. C. Gieben.

Lambert, Louise de. 1761. *Œuvres de Madame la Marquise de Lambert.* 2 vols. Paris: Ganeau Bauche Fils.

Lange, Lynda, ed. 1979. *The Sexism of Social and Political Theory: Women and Reproduction from Plato to Nietzsche.* Toronto: University of Toronto Press.

Langlois, Ernest. 1919. "Le Traité de Gerson contre le *Roman de la Rose.*" *Romania* 44: 29–48.

Lawrence, C. H. 1984. *Medieval Monasticism.* London: Longman.

Le Bon, Gustave. 1879. "Recherches anatomiques et mathématiques sur les lois des variations du volume du cerveau et sur leurs relations avec l'intelligence." *Revue d'Anthropologie,* 2d series, 2: 27–104.

Le Franc, Abel. 1914. *Grands ecrivains français de la Renaissance.* Paris: H. Champion.

———. 1953. *Rabelais: Etudes sur Gargantua, Pantagruel, le Tiers Livre.* Paris: Albin Michel.

Le Franc, Martin. 1968. *Le Champion des dames.* Lausanne: Payot.

Lederman, Muriel, and Ingrid Bartsch, eds. 2001. *The Gender and Science Reader.* London and New York: Routledge.

Lee, Alice. 1902. "Data for the Problem of Evolution in Man. A Study of the Correlation of the Human in Man. A First Study of the Correlation of the Human Skull." *Philosophical Transactions of the Royal Society of London.* 196 A: 225–264.

Lefkowitz, Mary R., and Maureen B. Fant. 1992. *Women's Life in Greece and Rome: A Source Book in Translation.* London: Duckworth.

Legouvé, Ernest. 1849. *Histoire morale des femmes.* Paris: Gustave Sandré.

Lindberg, David C., ed. 1978. *Science in the Middle Ages.* Chicago and London: University of Chicago Press.

Lipinska, Melina. 1900. *Histoire des femmes médecins depuis l'antiquité jusqu'à nos jours.* Paris: Jacques and Cie.

———. 1930. *Les Femmes et le progrès des sciences médicales.* Paris: Masson.

Lloyd, Genevieve. 1984. *The Man of Reason: "Male" and "Female" in Western Philosophy.* Minneapolis: University of Minnesota Press.

Longino, Helen, and Evelyn Fox Keller, eds. 1996. *Feminism and Science.* Oxford: Oxford University Press.

Love, Rosaleen. 1979. "'Alice in Eugenics-Land': Feminism and Eugenics in the Scientific Careers of Alice Lee and Ethel Elderton." *Annals of Science* 36: 145–158.

Luchaire, Achille. 1912. *Social France at the Time of Philip Augustus.* Trans. Edward Benjamin Krehbiel. New York: H. Holt.

Lutzker, Edythe. 1959. "Medical Education for Women in Great Britain." Ph.D. diss., Columbia University.

MacDonald, Margaret Y. 1996. *Early Christian Women and Pagan Opinion: The Power of the Hysterical Woman.* Cambridge: Cambridge University Press.

———. 1999. "Rereading Paul: Early Interpreters of Paul on Women and Gender." In *Women's Christian Origins.* Ed. Ross Shepard Kraemer and Mary Rose D'Angelo. New York: Oxford University Press.

Mackenzie, Dr. 1871. Letter. *Inverness Courier,* March.

Maclean, Ian. 1977. *Woman Triumphant.* Oxford: Clarendon.

———. 1980. *The Renaissance Notion of Woman.* Cambridge: Cambridge University Press.

Malebranche, Nicolas. 1958. *Oeuvres.* 3 vols. Ed. André Robinet. Paris: J. Vrin.

———. 1997. *The Search after Truth: Elucidations on the Search after Truth.* Ed. and trans. Thomas M. Lennon and Paul J. Olscamp. Columbus: Ohio State University Press.

Marchal, Roger. 1997. *Fontenelle à l'aube des lumières.* Paris: Champion.

Martin, Thomas R. 1996. *Ancient Greece from Prehistoric to Hellenistic Times.* London and New Haven: Yale University Press, 1996.

Masson, Georgina. 1968. *Queen Christina.* New York: Farrar, Straus and Giroux.

Mattfield, Jacquelyn A., and Carol G. Van Aken. 1965. *Women and the Scientific Professions.* Cambridge: MIT.

Maudsley, Henry. 1874. "Sex in Mind and Education." *Fortnightly Review* 15: 466–483.

McAllister, Linda Lopez, ed. 1996. *Hypatia's Daughters.* Bloomington: Indiana University Press.

McDowell Richardson, Lula. 1929. *The Forerunners of Feminism in French Literature of the Renaissance from Christine of Pisan to Marie de Gournay.* Baltimore: Johns Hopkins University Press.

McGrayne, Sharon Bertsch. 1998. *Nobel Prize Women in Science*. Secaucus, NJ: Citadel.

McLemore, Ethel W. 1979. "Past Present (We)—Present Future (You)." *Association for Women in Mathematics Newsletter* 9, no. 6: 11–15.

McLeod, Enid. 1976. *The Order of the Rose*. Totowa, NJ: Rowman and Littlefield.

McMillan, James F. 2000. *France and Women: 1789–1914*. London and New York: Routledge.

Mell, Donald C., Jr., Theodore E. D. Braun, and Lucia M. Palmer, eds. 1998. *Man, God and Nature*. East Lansing: Colleagues Press.

Ménage, Gilles. 1984. *The History of Women Philosophers*. Trans. Beatrice H. Zedler. Lanham, MD: University Press of America.

Mendelson, Susan. 1987. *The Mental World of Stuart Women: Three Studies*. Brighton, UK: Harvester.

Merchant, Carolyn. 1979. "The Vitalism of Anne Conway: Its Impact on Leibniz's Concept of the Monad." *Journal of the History of Philosophy*, 17/3: 255–269.

———. 1980. *The Death of Nature: Women, Ecology and the Scientific Revolution*. New York: HarperCollins.

———. 1996. *Earthcare: Women and the Environment*. London and New York: Routledge.

Metz, René. 1985. *La Femme et l'enfant dans le droit canonique medieval*. London: Variorum Reprints.

Meurdrac, Marie de. 1680 [1999]. *La Chymie charitable et facile en faveur des dames*. Paris: CNRS.

Meyer, Gerald Dennis. 1955. *The Scientific Lady in England: 1650–1760*. Berkeley: University of California Press.

Mill, John Stuart. 1963. *Collected Works of John Stuart Mill*. Toronto: University of Toronto Press.

Millar, David. 1996. *The Cambridge Dictionary of Scientists*. Cambridge: Cambridge University Press.

Montaigne, Michel. 1876. *Essais*. Ed. Fortunat Strowski. Paris: Firmin-Didot.

Montesquieu. 1952. *The Spirit of the Laws*. Trans. Thomas Nugent. Chicago: Britannica Great Books.

———. 1973. *Persian Letters*. Trans. C. J. Betts. Harmondsworth, UK: Penguin.

Moscucci, Ornella. 1993. *The Science of Woman*. Cambridge: Cambridge University Press.

Mosedale, Susan Sleeth. 1978. "Science Corrupted: Victorian Biologists Consider 'The Woman Question.'" *Journal of the History of Biology* 11, no. 1: 1–55.

Moses, Claire Goldberg. 1982. "Saint-Simonian Men/Saint-Simonian Women." *Journal of Modern History* 54: 240–267.

Mozans, H. J. 1991. *Women in Science*. Notre Dame and London: University of Notre Dame Press.

Murphy, Daniel. 1995. *Comenius*. Dublin: Irish Academic Press.

Nadler, Steven. 2000. *The Cambridge Companion to Malebranche*. Cambridge: Cambridge University Press.

Needham, Joseph. 1959. *A History of Embryology*. 2d rev. ed. rev. New York: Abelard-Schuman.

Newman, Barbara. 1987. *Sister of Wisdom. St. Hildegard's Theology of the Feminine.* Berkeley: University of California Press.

Nihell, Elizabeth. 1760. *A Treatise on the Art of Midwifery.* London: A. Morley.

Noble, David. 1992. *A World without Women.* New York: Oxford University Press.

Nollet, Jean Antoine. 1749. *Leçons de physique expérimentale.* 2 vols. Paris: Les Frères Guérin.

O'Connor, Dorothy. 1926. *Louise Labé: Sa vie et son oeuvre.* Paris: Les Presses Françaises.

Ogilvie, Marilyn Bailey. 1986. *Women in Science: Antiquity through the Nineteenth Century.* Cambridge: MIT Press.

Ogilvie, Marilyn Bailey, and Joy Harvey, eds. 2000. *The Biographical Dictionary of Women in Science.* New York: Routledge.

Ogilvie, Marilyn Bailey, and Kerry Lynne Meek. 1996. *Women and Science: An Annotated Bibliography.* New York: Garland.

Okin, Susan Moller. 1979. *Women in Western Political Thought.* Princeton: Princeton University Press.

O'Reilly, Robert F. 1973. "Montesquieu: Anti-feminist." *Studies on Voltaire and the Eighteenth Century* 102: 143–156.

Ornstein, Martha. 1928. *The Role of Scientific Societies in the Seventeenth Century.* Chicago: University of Illinois Press.

Osborne, Martha Lee. 1975. "Plato's Unchanging View of Women: A Denial That Anatomy Spells Destiny." *Philosophical Forum* 6, nos. 2–3: 447–452.

Osen, Lynn M. 1974. *Women in Mathematics.* Cambridge: MIT Press.

Parmenides. 1996. *On Nature.* Ed. Allan F. Randall. Trans. David Gallop, Richard D. McKirahan Jr., Jonathan Barnes, and John Mansley Robinson. http://home.ican.net/~arandall/Parmenides (Cited April 2003).

Pateman, Carole, and Mary Lyndon Shanley, eds. 1991. *Feminist Interpretations and Political Theory.* University Park: Pennsylvania State University Press.

Pearson, Karl, and Alice Lee. 1897. *The Chances of Death and Other Studies in Evolution.* 2 vols. London: E. Arnold.

Pepys, Samuel. 1970–1983. *The Diary of Samuel Pepys.* 2 vols. Ed. Robert Latham and William Matthews. London: Bell and Hyman.

Peradotto, John, and J. P. Sullivan, eds. 1984. *Women in the Ancient World: The Arethusa Papers.* Albany: SUNY Press.

Perry, Marvin, Joseph R. Peden, and Theodore H. Von Laue. 1999. *Sources of the Western Tradition.* Vol. 1. 4th ed. Boston: Houghton Mifflin.

Phillips, Patricia. 1990. *The Scientific Lady: A Social History of Women's Scientific Interests, 1520–1918.* London: Weidenfeld and Nicolson.

Piaget, Arthur. 1858. *Martin Le Franc: Prévôt de Lausanne.* Lausanne: Payot.

Pickering, Mary. 1993. *Auguste Comte: An Intellectual Biography.* Vol. 1. Cambridge: Cambridge University Press.

Pizan, Christine de. 1982. *The Book of the City of Ladies.* Ed. Earl Jeffrey Richards, trans. Marina Warner. New York: Persea Books.

Plato. 1963. *The Collected Dialogues of Plato.* Ed. Edith Hamilton and Huntington Cairns. Princeton: Princeton University Press.

Plutarch. 1914–1926. *Lives.* 11 vols. Trans. Bernadotte Perrin. Cambridge, MA and London: Heinemann.

Porter, Roy, and Marilyn Bailey Ogilvie. 2000. *The Hutchinson Dictionary of Scientific Biography.* 2 vols. Oxford: Helicon.

———, eds. 2000a. *The Biographical Dictionary of Scientists.* New York: Oxford University Press.

Postel, G. de. 1553. *Les Très merveilleuses victoires des femmes du Nouveau-Monde.* Paris: Chez Jehan Ruelle.

Poulain de la Barre, François de. 1673. *De l'éducation des dames pour la conduite de l'esprit dans les sciences et dans les mœurs entretiens.* Paris: Jean du Puis.

———. 1679. *De l'excellence des hommes, contre l'égalité des sexes.* Paris: Antoine Dezallier.

———. 1988. *The Woman as Good as the Man, or, the Equality of Both Sexes.* Ed. Gerald M. Maclean. Detroit: Wayne State University Press.

———. 1990. *The Equality of the Sexes.* Trans. Desmond M. Clarke. Manchester and New York: Manchester University Press.

Power, Kim. 1996. *Veiled Desire: Augustine's Writing on Women.* New York: Continuum.

Pratt, A. Edwin. 1867. *Pioneer Women in Victoria's Reign.* London: G. Newnes.

Prévot, J. 1881. *L'Utopie éducative.* Paris: Bélin.

Prior, Mary, ed. 1985. *Women in English Society, 1500–1800.* London: Methuen.

Prost, M. Aug. 1881. *Corneille Agrippa: Sa vie et ses oeuvres.* 2 vols. Paris: Champion.

Pyenson, Lewis, and Susan Sheets-Pyenson. 1999. *Servants of Nature.* New York: W. W. Norton.

Rabelais, François. 1870–1873. *Œuvres.* Ed. Henri Burgaud des Marets and E. B. Rathéry. Paris: Firmin-Didot.

———. 1992. *The Complete Works of François Rabelais.* Trans. Donald M. Frame. Berkeley: University of California Press.

Radford Ruether, Rosemary, ed. 1974. *Religion and Sexism: Images of Women in the Jewish and Christian Traditions.* New York: Simon and Schuster.

Radford Ruether, Rosemary, and Eleanor McLaughlin, eds. 1979. *Women of Spirit: Female Leadership in the Jewish and Christian Traditions.* New York: Simon and Schuster.

Rebière, Alphonse. 1897. *Les Femmes dans la science.* Paris: Nony.

Reynier, Gustave. 1929. *La Femme au XVIIe siècle: Ses ennemis et ses défenseurs.* Paris: J. Tallandier.

Richards, Earl Jeffrey. 2000. "Christine de Pizan and Jean Gerson: An Intellectual Friendship." In *Christine de Pizan 2000: Studies on Christine de Pizan in Honour of Angus J. Kennedy.* Ed. John Campbell and Nadia Margolis. Amsterdam: Rodopi.

Richards, Samuel Alfred. 1914. *Feminist Writers of the Seventeenth Century.* London: D. Nutt.

Riché, Pierre. 1976. *Education and Culture in the Barbarian West.* Trans. John J. Contreni. Columbia: University of South Carolina Press.

Rigaud, Rose. 1973. *Les Idées féministes de Christine de Pisan.* 1911. Geneva: Slatkene Reprints.

Roberts, Shirley. 1993. *Sophia Jex-Blake: A Woman Pioneer in Nineteenth-Century Medical Reform.* London and New York: Routledge.

Robertson, J. H. 1905. *The Philosophical Works of Francis Bacon.* London: Routledge.

Rocca, Fernando della. 1959. *Manual of Canon Law.* Trans. Anselm Thatcher. Milwaukee: Bruce Publishing.

Roches, Madeleine des, and Catherine des Roches. 1993. *Les Œuvres.* Ed. Anne R. Larsen. Geneva: Droz.

Roe, Anne. 1953. *The Making of a Scientist.* New York: Dodd, Mead.

Romanes, George John. 1887. "Mental Differences between Men and Women." *Nineteenth Century* 21: 113–151.

Rose, Hilary. 1983. "Hand, Brain and Heart: A Feminist Epistemology for the Natural Sciences." *Signs* 9, no. 1: 73–90.

———. 1994. *Love, Power and Knowledge: Towards a Feminist Transformation of the Sciences.* Oxford: Blackwell.

Rossiter, Margaret. 1982. *Women Scientists in America: Struggles and Strategies to 1940.* Baltimore: Johns Hopkins University Press.

———. 1995. *Women Scientists in America: Before Affirmative Action 1940–1972.* Baltimore: Johns Hopkins University Press.

———. 1997. "Which Science, Which Women?" *Osiris* 12: 169–185.

Rosso, Jeannette Geffriaud. 1977. *Montesquieu et la féminité.* Pisa: Libreria Goliardica.

Rousseau, Jean-Jacques. 1974. *Emile.* Trans. Barbara Foxley. London: Dent.

Roussel, Pierre. 1775. *Système physique et moral de la femme.* Paris: Vincent.

Rousselot, Paul. 1881. *La Pédagogie féminine.* Paris: Delgrave.

———. 1883. *Histoire de l'éducation des femmes.* 2 vols. Paris: Didier et Cie.

Rowan, M. 1980. "Seventeenth-Century French Feminism: Two Opposing Attitudes." *International Journal of Women's Studies* 3, no. 3: 273–291.

Rudolf, Monk of Fulda. 1954. "The Life of Saint Leoba." In *The Anglo-Saxon Missionaries in Germany.* Ed. and trans. C. H. Talbot. London and New York: Sheed and Ward.

Rummel, Erika, ed. 1996. *Erasmus on Women.* Toronto: University of Toronto Press.

Salmon, Vivian. 1987. "Bathsua Makin. A Pioneer Linguist and Feminist in Seventeenth Century England." In *Neuere Forschungen zur Wortbildung Histriographie de Linguistik: Festgabe für Herbert E. Brekle.* Ed. Brigitte Asbach-Schnitker and Johannes Rogenhofer. Tubingen: Gunter Naar Verlag.

Saxonhouse, Arlene. 1991. "Aristotle: Defective Males, Hierarchy and the Limits of Politics." In *Feminist Interpretations and Political Theory.* Ed. Mary Lyndon Shanley and Carole Pateman. University Park: Pennsylvania State University Press.

Schiebinger, Londa. 1986. "Skeletons in the Closet: The First Illustrations of the Female Skeleton in Eighteenth-Century Anatomy." *Representations* 14: 42–81.

———. 1989. *The Mind Has No Sex? Women in the Origins of Modern Science.* Cambridge: Harvard University Press.

———. 1999. *Has Feminism Changed Science?* Cambridge: Harvard University Press.

Schiller, Francis. 1992. *Paul Broca: Explorer of the Brain.* New York: Cambridge University Press.

Scholz, Bernhard W. 1980. "Hildegard von Bingen on the Nature of Woman." *American Benedictine Review* 31: 361–383.

Schurman, Anna Maria van. 1646. *Qu'il est nécessaire que les filles soient savants: Discours de Mademoiselle de Schurman à Monsieur Rivet.* Paris: Rolet Le Duc.

———. 1650. *Opuscula.* Utrecht: Waesberge.

———. 1996. *Choosing the Better Part.* Ed. Mirgam de Baar et al. Dordrecht: Kluwer Academic.

———. 1998. *Whether a Christian Woman Should Be Educated and Other Writings from Her Intellectual Circle.* Ed. Joyce L. Irwin. Chicago: University of Chicago Press.

Scott, Joan Wallach. 1988. *Gender and the Politics of History.* New York: Columbia University Press.

Screech, Michael Andrew. 1953. "The Illusion of Postel's Feminism." *Journal of the Warburg and Courtauld Institutes* 16: 162–170.

———. 1958. *The Rabelaisian Marriage.* London: E. Arnold.

Scudéry, Marie Madeleine de. 1650–1654. *Artamène ou le grand Cyrus.* 10 vols. Paris: Augustin Courbé.

Seidel, Michael. 1974. "Poulain de la Barre's *The Woman as Good as the Man.*" *Journal of the History of Ideas* 35: 499–508.

Seland, Torrey. 1995. *Establishment Violence in Philo and Luke: A Study of Non-Conformity to the Torah and Jewish Vigilante Reactions.* Biblical Interpretation Series 15. Leiden: E. J. Brill.

Shaw, David. 1984. "Les Femmes Savantes and Feminism." *Journal of European Studies* 14: 24–38.

Shearer, Benjamin F., and Barbara S. Shearer, eds. 1996. *Notable Women in the Life Sciences: A Biographical Dictionary.* Westport, CT: Greenwood.

Showalter, E., Jr. 1975. "Voltaire et ses amis d'après la correspondance de Madame de Graffigny, 1738–1739." *Studies on Voltaire and the Eighteenth Century* 139: 218–220.

Singer, Charles. 1928. *From Magic to Science: Essays on Scientific Thought.* New York: Boni and Liveright.

Singer, Charles, and Henry E. Sigerist, eds. 1968. *Essays on the History of Medicine Presented to Karl Sudoff.* Freeport, NY: Books for Libraries.

Smith, Hilda. 1982. *Reason's Disciples: Seventeenth-Century English Feminists.* Urbana: University of Illinois Press.

———, ed. 1998. *Women Writers and the Early Modern British Political Tradition.* Cambridge: Cambridge University Press.

Smith, Nicholas D. 1983. "Plato and Aristotle on the Nature of Women." *Journal of the History of Philosophy* 21: 467–477.

Somerville, Mary. 1873. *Personal Recollections from Early Life to Old Age of Mary Somerville, with Selections from Her Correspondence.* Ed. Martha Somerville. London: Murray.

Soranus. 1956. *Gynecology.* Trans. Oswei Temkin. Baltimore: Johns Hopkins University Press.

Spencer, Herbert. 1892–1893. *Principles of Ethics.* 2 vols. New York: D. Appleton.

———. 1893. *Principles of Sociology.* 2 vols. New York: D. Appleton.

———. 1897. *Social Statistics.* New York: D. Appleton.

———. 1900. *The Principles of Psychology.* 2 vols. New York: D. Appleton.

Spencer, Samia I., ed. 1984. *French Women and the Age of Enlightenment.* Blooming-ton: Indiana University Press.

Sprat, Thomas. 1958. *History of the Royal Society.* London: Routledge and Kegan Paul.

Stansfeld, James. 1877. "Medical Women." *Nineteenth Century.* July.

Stanton, Donna A. 1981. "The Fiction of Préciosité and the Fear of Women." *Yale French Studies* 62: 107–134.

Stolpe, Sven. 1966. *Christina of Sweden.* Basingstoke, UK: Macmillan.

Stolte-Heiskanen, Veronica, ed. 1991. *Women in Science: Token Women or Gender Equality?* Oxford: Berg.

Stone, Sarah. 1737. *Complete Practice of Midwifery.* London: T. Cooper.

Sutton, Geoffrey V. 1995. *Science for a Polite Society: Gender, Culture, and the Demon-stration of Enlightenment.* Boulder, CO: Westview.

Teague, Frances, ed. 1998. *Bathsua Makin: Woman of Learning.* London: Associated University Presses.

Terrall, Mary. 1995. "Emilie du Châtelet and the Gendering of Science." *History of Science* 33: 283–310.

Tertullian. 1959. *Disciplinary, Moral and Ascetical Works.* Vol. 40. New York: Fathers of the Church.

Timmermans, Linda. 1995. *L'Accès de la femme à la culture.* Paris: H. Champion.

Todd, Janet, ed. 1989. *British Women Writers.* New York: Continuum.

Trotula of Salerno. 1940. *De mulierum passionibus: The Diseases of Women.* Trans. Eliz-abeth Pearl-Hohl. Los Angeles: Ward Ritchie.

Tuana, Nancy. 1988. "Feminism and Science." *Hypatia: A Journal of Feminist Philoso-phy* no. 1, 3.

———. 1989. *Feminism and Science.* Bloomington: Indiana University Press.

———, ed. 1994. *Feminist Interpretations of Plato.* University Park: Pennsylvania State University Press.

Tucker, Ruth, and Walter L. Liefeld. 1987. *Daughters of the Church: Women and Min-istry from New Testament Times to the Present.* Grand Rapids, MI: Academie Books.

Uglow, Jennifer, ed. 1999. *The Macmillan Dictionary of Women's Biography.* London: Macmillan.

Underwood, E. A. 1953. *Science, Medicine and History.* 2 vols. London: Oxford Uni-versity Press.

Van Til, William. 1978. *Secondary Education: School and Community.* Boston: Houghton Mifflin.

Vicinus, Martha, ed. 1972. *Women in the Victorian Age: Suffer and Be Still.* Blooming-ton: Indiana University Press.

Vogt, Carl. 1864. *Lectures on Man, His Place in Creation and in the History of the Earth.* London.

———. 1877–1885. *Oeuvres complètes.* 52 vols. Ed. Louis Moland. Paris: Garnier.

Voltaire, François Marie Arouet de. 1967. *The Elements of Sir Isaac Newton's Philosophy.* Trans. John Hanna. London: Frank Cass.

Wade, Ira O. 1967. *Studies on Voltaire with Some Unpublished Papers by Madame du Châtelet.* 1947. New York: Russell and Russell.

———. 1969. *Voltaire and Madame du Châtelet: An Essay on the Intellectual Activity at Cirey.* New York: Octagon Books.

Waithe, Mary Ellen, ed. 1987. *A History of Women Philosophers.* Vol. 1: *Ancient Women Philosophers, 600 B.C.–500 A.D.* Dordrecht: Kluwer Academic.

———, ed. 1991. *A History of Women Philosophers.* Vol. 3: *Modern Women Philosophers, 1600–1900.* Dordrecht: Kluwer Academic.

Walton, John, Paul B. Beeson, and Ronald Bodley Scott, eds. 1986. *The Oxford Companion to Medicine.* 2 vols. Oxford: Oxford University Press.

Wender, Dorothea. 1984. "Plato: Misogynist, Paedophile, and Feminist." In *Women in the Ancient World: The Arethusa Papers.* Ed. John Peradotto and J. P. Sullivan. Albany: State University of New York Press.

Wertheim, Margaret. 1995. *Pythagoras' Trousers: God, Physics, and the Gender Wars.* New York: W. W. Norton.

Whewell, William. 1834. "On the Connexion of the Physical Sciences." *Quarterly Review* 51: 54–68.

Whitehead, Barbara J., ed. 1999. *Women's Education in Early Modern Europe: A History, 1500–1800.* New York: Garland.

Whitmore, P. J. S. 1967. *The Order of Minims in Seventeenth Century France.* The Hague: Martinus Nijhoff.

Wiesner, Merry. 1986. *Women in the Middle Ages and the Renaissance: Literary and Historical Perspectives.* Ed. Mary Beth Rose. Syracuse, NY: Syracuse University Press.

———. 1999. *Women and Gender in Early Modern Europe.* Cambridge: Cambridge University Press.

Williams, Charles G. S., ed. 1975. *Literature in the Age of Ideas: Essays on the French Enlightenment Presented to George R. Havens.* Columbus: Ohio State University Press.

Wilson, Katharina M., and Frank J. Warnke, eds. 1989. *Women Writers of the Seventeenth Century.* Athens: University of Georgia Press.

Wood, Diane S. 2000. *Hélisenne de Crenne: At the Crossroads of Renaissance Humanism and Feminism.* London: Associated University Presses.

Archaeology, women and, 200
Aristophanes, 2, 9
Aristotle, x, 5, 30, 32, 39, 51, 119, 131, 152
    Anaxagoras and, 6
    biological theories of, 14–15
    de Gournay and, 63
    Empedocles and, 6
    female inferiority and, 2, 13
    foreshadowing of, 7
    Hypatia and, 17
    illustration of, 9
    male stage and, 122
    male/female roles and, 15
    on nature of woman, 15–16
    Plato and, 8–11, 13–16
    rejection of, 87, 100
    science/women and, 16
    on sex, 7
    on *sophrosyne,* 18
    on soul, 16
    Thomas Aquinas and, 31
    on women, ix, 3, 8, 9–10, 12, 22
Aristoxenus, 4
Artamène, ou le Grand Cyrus (Scudéry), 69–70
Artemis, 1
Article on Government (Mill), 153
Arts, women and, 145, 148, 185
Aspasia, 17, 90
Astell, Mary, xi, 71, 72
    female education and, 61, 73–75
    religious community and, 73
Astrolabe, 18
Astronomie des dames (Lalande), xiii, 117, 136
Astronomy, 35, 95, 118
    Herrad and, 37
    Hypatia and, 18
    women and, 11, 18, 72, 99, 114, 135, 136, 143
Athanasius of Alexandria, 32
Athena, 1
Atherton, Margaret, 88
Augustine, Saint, x, 24
    criticism of, 47
    Descartes and, 94
    influence of, 35
    on women, 28–29
Augustus, Emperor, 163
Averroes, 30
Avicenna, 30, 55

"Avis d'une mère à sa fille" (Lambert), 70
Axioca, 56
Axiothea, 13
Aymery, 54

Bacon, Francis, 66
    Cavendish on, 114
    Descartes and, 100
    feminist critics of, 102
    illustration of, 101
    on man/nature, 100–101
    masculinization of science and, 100–102
    method of, 85–86
    Royal Society and, 103
    science/women and, 100, 101, 103, 190
Bacon, Nicholas, 100
Baker, Ernest, 9
Balzac, Jean-Louis Guez de, 82
Barber-Surgeon's Company, midwifery and, 166
Barthez, Paul-Joseph, 121
Bartsch, Ingrid, 203
Basil, Saint, 32, 63, 91
    on women, 25, 93
Bassi, Laura Maria Caterina, 118, 137
Battle of Edinburgh, 171
Bayon, H. P., 162
Bazeley, Deborah Taylor, on Cavendish, 113
Behn, Aphra, xii
    Fontenelle and, 96–97
    illustration of, 97
    translating by, 96–97
Benedict, Saint, monasticism and, 32
Benedictines, Hildegard and, 38
Bennett, Henry, on medicine/women, 177–178
Benton, John F., on Trotula, 163
Berlin Academy, founding of, 102–103
Bernard of Clairvaux, Saint, 37, 40
Bernouilli, Jean, 131, 133
Besterman, Theodore, 131
Bibliothèque Nationale, 162
Bibliothèque universelle des dames: Astronomie (Lalande), 118
Biology, vii, 9, 14–15
    Aristotelian, 30
    male/female, 13
    women and, 72, 122, 140, 198, 200

Female inferiority, ix, x, xii, 13, 14, 22, 24, 26, 28, 31, 35, 51, 56–57, 73, 81, 86–87, 89, 93, 94, 113, 124, 132, 145, 149–159, 180, 185, 204
  acceptance of, 141
  Aristotelian view of, 8
  brain size and, 140–143
  custom and, 92
  Greek belief in, 3
  male superiority and, 147
  refuting, 74
"Female Physicians" (Davies), 171
Female superiority, 50, 53, 54–55, 148, 154, 158
Females as Physicians (Channing), 170
The Feminine Mystique (Friedan), 186
Feminism, 186
  ambivalence about, 192
  education and, 159
  Kuhn and, 183–184
  Marxism and, 197
  natural commonality of, 192
  radical critique of, 191
  science and, xvi, 184, 188, 189, 192, 200, 203, 204
Feminist critique, 199–200, 202, 204
  background to, 186–188
  criticism of, 201
  defining, 188–189
  evolution of, 189–197
"Femme" (Barthez), 121
"Femme" (Montesquieu), 127
Femmes doctes, 82
Fénelon, François de Salignac de la Mothe-, xi, 75–77, 78
  Ursulines and, 76
Feyerabend, Paul, xv, 183, 202
Finch, Sir Henry, 109
Fleury, Abbé, xi, 78–79
Foeminei sexus apologia adversus A. Tiraquellum (Tiraqueau), 54
Fontenay-le-Comte, 51
Fontenelle, Bernard Le Bovier de, xii, 81, 97
  Cavendish and, 114
  purpose of, 95–96
  science popularization and, 95–97
Forge, Jean de, 108
Fortnightly Review, 173, 175
Fox Keller, Evelyn, xvi, 102, 189, 190
  on feminists, 192

object relations theory and, 196–197
  on science/women, 191, 202
Fradonnet, André, 59
Fradonnet, Catherine, 59, 60
France, Marguerite de, duchess of Berry, 54
Franciscans, 36
Franklin, Rosalind, 194
Frederick Barbarossa, 40
Frederick V, Elector Palatine, 88
French Revolution, xiv, 125
Freud, Sigmund, phrenology and, 140
Friedan, Betty, on women's role, 186
Fronde, 83

Galen, 30, 55
Galileo, 84, 104
Gall, Franz Joseph, 140
Galton, Francis, 148
Garrett Anderson, Elizabeth, 180, 181
  Maudsley and, 175–177
  medical education for, 170
  photo of, 176
  practice of, 171
Gassendi, Pierre, 104, 110
Gaul, 25
Geddes, Patrick, xiv, 147
Gelbart, Nina Rattner, 96
Gender, 89
  assumptions about, 191
  cultural construction of, 190, 192
  equality, 71
  historian's perspective and, 198–201
  science and, xvi, 134, 204, 198, 200
Genesis, 24, 26
Geography, 37
  women and, 67, 124, 143
Geometry, women and, 62, 67, 93, 124
Gerson, Jean de, 44, 46
Gertrude, 33
Girton College, 171, 176
Glanvill, Joseph, 109
God, 110
  creations of, 48
Golden Mean, 5
Golden Rectangle, 5
Gonville College, Romanes and, 148
Gould, Stephen, craniology and, 142
Grammar, women and, 77
Gratian, John, misogynist views of, x, 34, 35
Gratian's Decree, 35

Malebranche, Nicolas de, xi, xii, 93–95
Man
  creation of, 48, 55
  nature and, 100–101
  society and, 127
*Man and Woman: A Study of Human and
  Secondary Sexual Characteristics* (Ellis),
  155
Mandeville, Bertrand, 131–132, 134
Man-woman, 10
Marcella, 27, 72
Marguerite of Austria, 55, 62
Marguerite of Navarre, 46, 52
Marinella, Lucretia, 69
Marriage, 114
  avoiding, 52
  as barrier to emancipation, 153
  career vs., 172–173
  education and, 78, 79
  nature and, 81
  as necessary evil, 32
  preparation for, 49
  women and, 27, 34, 173
Martin, Thomas, 12
Marx, Karl, debates with, 152
Marxism, feminism and, 197
Mary, x, 24, 55
  Eve and, 39
  goodness of, 39
Mary Queen of Scots, 46
Mary Stuart, 49
The Masculine Birth of Time (Bacon), 100
Masculinity, 101–102, 107
Massachusetts Institute of Technology
  (MIT), symposium at, 187–188
Mathematics
  emphasis on, 187
  universities and, 35
  women and, xii, 5, 11, 18, 60, 72, 77,
    78, 109, 124, 131, 143, 148, 194,
    199–200
Maudsley, Henry, 173, 174
  challenge to, 175–177
  on education/women, 175
  on puberty/weakness, 176
Maupertuis, Pierre Louis Moreau de, 133
  du Châtelet and, 131, 134
Maximilian of Austria, 55
Maxims (Christina of Sweden), 87
Max Planck Institute, 192
McClintock, Barbara, photo of, 191
McDowell Richardson, Lula, 50

McGrayne, Sharon Bertsch, 189, 190
McGuire, Mary Ann, 113
McNath, James, on midwives, 166
"Medical Education of Women" (Jex-
  Blake), 178–179
Medical school
  attending, 168–169
  women and, 170–171, 172, 173,
    177–181
Medical Women (Jex-Blake), 178
"Medical Women" (Stansfeld), 178
Medicine, vii, 33, 69
  midwives and, 164–170
  professionalization of, 166, 181
  universities and, 36
  women and, xii, xv, 29–32, 66, 90, 92,
    98, 121, 151, 161, 162–163, 166,
    169, 170, 173–175, 177–180, 200
"Medicine as a Profession for Women"
  (Jex-Blake), 178–179
Men, power of, 56, 151
Mendelson, Sara Heller, on Cavendish,
  113
Menstruation, xiv, 7, 15, 122, 128, 151
Mental ability, xiii, 144, 175
"Mental Differences between Men and
  Women" (Romanes), 148
Merchant, Carolyn, 95, 100, 190
Mersenne, Marin, 104, 105, 110
Metaphysics, viii, 5, 11, 139–140
Meteorology, women and, 114
Meurdrac, Marie de, xii, 98
Michelet, Jules
  female subordination and, 149–159
  male chauvinism of, 151
  on women, xiv, 151, 152, 157–158
Microbiology, 103, 143
Middle Ages, 8, 34, 39, 47, 161, 162
  Roman Catholic Church and, 21
  women and, 60
Midwives, xv
  defending, 166, 167–168, 169
  education and, 164–165
  female, 161, 164–170, 181
  Hebrew, 164
  incorporation of, 168–169
  male, 167, 169, 170
  organizing, 167–168
*The Midwives Book, or the Whole Art of
  Midwifery* (Sharp), 168
Military, women and, 13, 76
Mill, James, 153

About the Author

L eigh Ann Whaley is associate professor of European history and coordinator of the women's studies program at Acadia University in Nova Scotia, Canada. She is the author of two books on European history, *The Impact of Napoleon Bonaparte* (1997) and *Radicals: Politics and Republicanism in the French Revolution* (2000), as well as many articles. Her latest research project is on women in medicine.